Praise for C

"*Choice: Cooperation, Enterprise, and Human Action*, by Robert P. Murphy, is one of the best introductions to the foundations of modern Austrian School economics that I have ever read, especially of the work of its great founder, Ludwig von Mises. Its clarity of writing and stress on the fundamentals of Mises differentiates it from other fine economics books, such as those by Thomas Sowell and Henry Hazlitt. Murphy focuses on and translates Mises's key ideas (not just those in *Human Action*) into terms that any intelligent layperson and student can follow. In this regard he reveals Mises as a great teacher and scholar who devoted his life to exposing fallacies in the application of economic principles. We owe Murphy a great debt for *Choice*, and one can only hope that it will be a smashing success both as a textbook and a book read by the general public. I highly recommend that you get a copy and read it."
    —**Robert D. Tollison**, J. Wilson Newman Professor of Economics, Clemson University

"Austrian School economists have long emphasized thinking about actions by comparing marginal benefits and marginal costs and the importance of individual freedom to successful societies. If you seek to understand the Austrian economist's way of thinking, *Choice* is a great place to start. Robert P. Murphy does an excellent job leading the reader through the key insights in Ludwig von Mises's classic *Human Action* and then expanding upon them. He uses clear examples to show the similarities and differences between Austrian, Marxist, classical, and neoclassical approaches to economic reasoning. I strongly recommend it."
    —**Price V. Fishback**, Thomas R. Brown Professor of Economics, University of Arizona; Research Associate, National Bureau of Economic Research; Executive Director, Economic History Association

"In *Choice*, economist Robert P. Murphy has achieved the much-needed idea of rendering Ludwig von Mises's masterwork, *Human Action*, in prose that is user-friendly to twenty-first century readers of English with no prior training in economics. The result is a great read—and by preserving the core insights of Austrian economics in this way, Murphy has performed an invaluable service."
    —**Gene Epstein**, Economics and Books Editor, *Barron's*

"*Choice* is a welcome book—a well-written, penetrating presentation of Ludwig von Mises's economic analyses and insights. A most compelling read."
    —**Steve H. Hanke**, Professor of Applied Economics and Co-Director of the Institute for Applied Economics and the Study of Business Enterprise, Johns Hopkins University

"*Human Action* by Ludwig von Mises is the greatest of all economic tomes. In *Choice*, Robert P. Murphy brings this masterwork down from the summits of theory and history into the hands of today's citizens in the form of a pithy text as topical as headline news and as trenchant as the original work of the Austrian titan himself."
    —**George Gilder**, Author of *Knowledge and Power*, *Wealth and Poverty* and other books; Co-founder, Discovery Institute

"Nearly fifty years have passed since Ludwig von Mises produced the third—and his final—edition of *Human Action*. And now thanks to Robert P. Murphy in his important book *Choice*, we have the essentials of Mises's famed treatise well tailored for twenty-first century readers together with revealing comparisons of Austrian economics with the modern-day mainstream alternative."

—**Roger W. Garrison**, Professor Emeritus of Economics, Auburn University

"Ludwig von Mises's *Human Action* remains the premier presentation of Austrian economics. Its 900 pages, however, doubtlessly inhibit many people from reading this masterpiece. With his wonderful book *Choice*, Robert P. Murphy presents a convenient solution for such people: in 300 pages, he presents a very readable précis of *Human Action*, one whose fine quality will surely inspire many readers to turn to Mises himself."

—**Richard E. Wagner**, Harris Professor of Economics, George Mason University

"Robert P. Murphy's *Choice* is the perfect book for those new to the Misesian paradigm and those in need of a 'refresher course' in Austrian School economics. All those who share my belief that increasing understanding of sound economics is vital to the triumph of liberty owe Murphy a debt of gratitude."

—**Ron Paul**, former U.S. Congressman and Presidential candidate

"In the masterly book *Choice* Robert P. Murphy discusses the most serious issues of and powerful challenges to an open society. With rigor and wit he shows the importance of the role of ideas."

—**Alberto Benegas-Lynch, Jr.**, President, Economic Science Section, National Academy of Sciences, Argentina

"*Choice* does fine work in restating and updating the Austrian school's approach to understanding economics using language and concepts comprehensible to wider, non-specialist audiences. Refreshingly free of rhetorical excesses, Robert P. Murphy's text provides a clear roadmap to thinking 'like an Austrian' about the challenges facing the American and global economies."

—**Father Robert A. Sirico**, President, Acton Institute; author of the best-selling book, *Defending the Free Market*

"Robert P. Murphy is a master communicator. In *Choice* he makes the main ideas from the most important economics book of the twentieth century, *Human Action*, accessible to the average person. Once regular people read this, they'll never look at economic policies the same way again."

—**Benjamin W. Powell**, Director, Free Market Institute, Texas Tech University

"From market pricing and rational economic calculation to the folly of price controls and the wild swings of the business cycle, Robert P. Murphy's *Choice* examines the main topics of Mises's magnum opus, *Human Action*, in a way that makes the whole work much more accessible to laypeople and undergraduates alike. If you're looking for a fresh, contemporary, and clearly written presentation of core Austrian School ideas—which are as relevant today as ever—*Choice* successfully meets the demand. I recommend it highly."

—**David L. Prychitko**, Professor of Economics, Northern Michigan University

"Robert P. Murphy's *Choice* is a fresh take on perhaps the greatest work on economics of the twentieth century, Ludwig von Mises's magnum opus, *Human Action*. Written in a contemporary, approachable prose, Murphy's engaging style enlivens—for the layperson and specialist alike—the otherwise, seemingly, tedious concept of economic calculation. The reader will clearly understand that economic calculation 'underpins modern civilization and is possible only within the framework of a market economy,' as Murphy correctly points out. I can only think that Mises would have endorsed Murphy's excellent book with enthusiasm and hope for a broader understanding of economics."

—**Giancarlo Ibarguen**, Director of the Centro Henry Hazlitt and former President, Francisco Marroquin University

"With the publication of *Choice*, Robert P. Murphy joins Ludwig von Mises and Murray Rothbard in the ranks of master teachers. His complete command over the entire discipline of economics, mastered over more than a decade of study since earning his Ph.D. studies at New York University, makes him the ideal guide into the origin, nature, theorems, and applications of economics in the tradition of Carl Menger. Murphy's explanations are so succinct and lucid that *Choice* covers the same ground as Mises covered in *Human Action*, including philosophical, political, economic, and other types of objections in only one-third its length. Musicians clamor to gain admittance to classes of instruction in their instruments taught by master performers. *Choice* is a master class in economics, open and accessible to all."

—**Jeffrey M. Herbener**, Chair and Professor of Economics, Grove City College

"Robert P. Murphy's excellent and much-needed book in economics, *Choice*, is like that of a brilliant but utterly lucid professor of English guiding the reader into Milton or Shakespeare. It makes her want to turn to the text itself, and get beyond the misguided rumors we have heard of *Paradise Lost* or *All's Well That Ends Well*."

—**Deirdre N. McCloskey**, Distinguished Professor of Economics, History, English, and Communication, University of Illinois at Chicago

"In *Choice*, Robert P. Murphy's achievement is extraordinary. He not only makes *Human Action* more easily understandable, but also does what Mises could not do. He relates Mises's ideas to late twentieth and early twenty-first century developments in economics and other fields and shows how these ideas are so vitally important for both economists and the general public alike."

—**Mario J. Rizzo**, Professor of Economics and Director of the Program on the Foundations of the Market Economy, New York University

"If there is an economist out there who combines scholarly rigor with accessibility to the layman the way Robert P. Murphy does, I have not met him. If you are looking for an excellent, intermediate book between Henry Hazlitt and Ludwig von Mises, you will find it in *Choice*."

—**Thomas E. Woods, Jr.**, Senior Fellow, Ludwig von Mises Institute

"In *Choice*, Robert P. Murphy is to be congratulated for making the insights of Ludwig von Mises's great magnum opus, *Human Action*, easy to understand with logic and historical examples."
— **Mark A. Skousen**, Presidential Fellow, George L. Argyros School of Business and Economics, Chapman University; Founder and Producer, FreedomFest, Inc.

"Mises's *Human Action* has long been the most important and most challenging book to read on Austrian economics. Robert P. Murphy has substantially reduced the challenge by presenting the book's ideas in an accessible form, linked to contemporary concerns. *Choice* also provides an excellent introduction to the Austrian school in general. It deserves to be read, and read widely, and will contribute significantly to fulfilling Mises's own desire that everyone should know economics, not just experts."
— **Steven G. Horwitz**, Charles A. Dana Professor and Chair, Department of Economics, St. Lawrence University

"In *Choice*, Robert P. Murphy has provided a wonderful primer on Ludwig von Mises's masterwork, *Human Action*. Austrian School economists may find it most useful, but non-Austrians will benefit enormously from this clear explanation of the principles of Austrian insights and of where Austrian and mainstream economics both agree and differ, and why."
— **Dennis C. Coates**, Professor of Economics, University of Maryland, Baltimore; Research Professor, National Research University Higher School of Economics, Russia

"In *Choice*, Robert P. Murphy has done a great service by restating and extending for the modern era the works of Mises, Hayek, and other Austrian School economists. I expect this will be the go-to text used by the next generation of students to discover the importance of market processes for human flourishing."
— **Robert A. Lawson**, Jerome M. Fullinwider Chair in Economic Freedom, O'Neal Center for Global Markets and Freedom, Southern Methodist University

"Although it's one of the most important and influential books on economics ever written, Ludwig von Mises's *Human Action* has always had one major flaw: its inaccessibility to most readers. Robert P. Murphy's fantastic book *Choice* finally offers a condensed restatement of Mises's economics treatise in an accessible and engaging format. The most impressive contribution of this book is that it brings clarity without sacrificing rigor."
— **Daniel J. Smith**, Assistant Professor of Economics, Troy University; Book Review Editor, *The Review of Austrian Economics*

"One reason the writings of Ludwig von Mises have not penetrated college curricula and the general public may be that Robert P. Murphy had not yet written *Choice: Coordination, Enterprise, and Human Action*. I have resisted using Mises in undergraduate classes because, frankly, he is a difficult read. Murphy, on the other hand, writes clearly and concisely. His audience includes fellow economists, but is far broader than that. I can give this book as a gift to friends and family outside academia. And I can certainly use it in my university courses."
— **Randy T. Simmons**, Professor of Economics and Finance, Jon M. Huntsman School of Business, Utah State University

"Vermont Royster, a former editor of the editorial page of the *Wall Street Journal*, wrote that Ludwig von Mises's magnum opus, *Human Action*, belonged 'on the bookshelf of every thinking man.' The same can be said of Robert P. Murphy's wonderful book, **Choice: Cooperation, Enterprise, and Human Action.** Murphy has written a comprehensive study of the science of economics that is accessible to a wide audience. In tracing the implications of purposive human behavior, this important book provides crucial insights into the foundations of a free and prosperous world."

> —**Christopher J. Coyne**, F. A. Harper Professor of Economics and Associate Director, F. A. Hayek Program for Advanced Study in Philosophy, Politics, and Economics, George Mason University

"Robert P. Murphy is a very talented communicator of economic ideas. In **Choice**, he has taken an immensely complex body of theory and deeply rich intellectual history and distilled it into a manageable framework for novices and intermediate readers alike. This book will be a great way for unfamiliar readers to gain a thorough understanding of economics via an engaging and entertaining read."

> —**Daniel J. D'Amico**, William Barnett Professor of Economics, Loyola University New Orleans

"Well, this is a delight. After some 65 years of failed attempts to present Ludwig von Mises's grand treatise *Human Action* in a digestible and accessible format, Robert P. Murphy has finally succeeded. His analysis and presentation are accurate, balanced, informative, and faithful to the authentic spirit of Mises's original. **Choice** will do much good in not only spreading Mises's ideas but also in saving them from distortion and caricature. Murphy deserves our congratulations."

> —**Jeffrey A. Tucker**, Founder and Chief Liberty Officer, Liberty.me; former Editorial Vice President, Ludwig von Mises Institute

"**Choice** is a masterful, modern, witty exposition of the principles of Austrian economics: it simultaneously provides a delightful guide to Ludwig von Mises's incomparable *Human Action*, but also something more—a long-due sequel to it."

> —**Kevin Dowd**, Professor of Finance and Economics at Durham University, Partner with Cobden Partners in London, and Professor Emeritus of Financial Risk Management at the University of Nottingham in England

"Robert P. Murphy's new book **Choice: Cooperation, Enterprise and Human Action** is critical reading for students and citizens alike. It is timely, accessible, engaging and builds on the important intellectual work of Ludwig von Mises. If we are to protect freedom, secure liberty, and roll back the ever-expanding state, we must arm ourselves with the economic way of thinking. Murphy's important work is vital in our endeavor to advance a free and flourishing society."

> —**Anne Rathbone Bradley**, Ph.D., Vice President of Economic Initiatives, Institute for Faith, Work & Economics; Visiting Professor, Georgetown University; Visiting Scholar, Bernard Center for Women, Politics, and Public Policy

INDEPENDENT INSTITUTE

INDEPENDENT INSTITUTE is a non-profit, non-partisan, public-policy research and educational organization that shapes ideas into profound and lasting impact. The mission of Independent is to boldly advance peaceful, prosperous, and free societies grounded in a commitment to human worth and dignity. Applying independent thinking to issues that matter, we create transformational ideas for today's most pressing social and economic challenges. The results of this work are published as books, our quarterly journal, *The Independent Review*, and other publications and form the basis for numerous conference and media programs. By connecting these ideas with organizations and networks, we seek to inspire action that can unleash an era of unparalleled human flourishing at home and around the globe.

100 Swan Way, Oakland, California 94621-1428, U.S.A.
Telephone: 510-632-1366 • Facsimile: 510-568-6040 • Email: info@independent.org • www.independent.org

CHOICE

COOPERATION, ENTERPRISE, AND HUMAN ACTION

Robert P. Murphy

Foreword by Donald J. Boudreaux

INDEPENDENT
INSTITUTE

Oakland, California

Independent Institute
100 Swan Way, Oakland, CA 94621-1428
Telephone: 510-632-1366
Fax: 510-568-6040
Email: info@independent.org
Website: www.independent.org

Cover Design: Denise Tsui
Cover Image: © David M. Schrader / iStockphoto

Library of Congress Cataloging-in-Publication Data

Murphy, Robert P. (Robert Patrick), 1976–
    Choice / Robert P. Murphy ; foreword by Donald J. Boudreaux.
        pages cm
    ISBN 978-1-59813-217-5 (hardback) — ISBN 978-1-59813-218-2 (paperback)
1. Economics. 2. Free enterprise. I. Title.
    HB171.M975 2015
    330.12'2—dc23   2014048962

Other Books by the Author

Chaos Theory: Two Essays on Market Anarchy (2002)

Study Guide for Murray Rothbard's Man, Economy, and State (2006)

The Politically Incorrect Guide to Capitalism (2007)

The Politically Incorrect Guide to the Great Depression and the New Deal (2009)

Lessons for the Young Economist (2010)

Study Guide for Ludwig von Mises' Human Action (2010)

How Privatized Banking Really Works: Integrating Austrian Economics with the Infinite Banking Concept (2010) (with L. Carlos Lara)

Study Guide to The Theory of Money & Credit by Ludwig von Mises (2011)

Lessons for the Young Economist Teacher's Manual (2012)

Contents

Foreword

Donald J. Boudreaux

CONTRARY TO THE claims of many people who do not understand economics or science, economics is a science. Economics is a conscious and systematic search for knowledge and deeper understanding. This search is conducted to discover facts and relationships previously unknown; unlike dogma, it is not conducted to build intellectual and emotional barriers to ideas that challenge pet beliefs, superstitions, and worldviews.

Of course, because economics deals with purposeful, human decision-making, actions, and subjective preferences, it is not a physical science. As such, the appropriate method for doing economics differs from the appropriate method for doing the likes of physics, chemistry, and astronomy. Yet because lab-coated or microscope-equipped searchers for knowledge and understanding have long been, in the English-speaking world, identified as exemplars of science, scholars who search for knowledge and understanding using methods different from those used in the physical and biological sciences—and who cannot reliably make precise predictions of the sort made by physical scientists—are too often mistakenly dismissed as "unscientific."

A true scientist, though, adopts the method of inquiry best suited to his or her subject matter. This intellectual feat requires not only keen awareness of the nature of that subject matter but also cognizance of the abilities and limitations of the human mind to comprehend that subject matter.

Ludwig von Mises (1881–1973) was one of history's most successful economists at the vital task of crafting an analysis of economic reality that is both exhaustive and consistent with the human mind's capacity to make as much sense as can possibly be made of that reality. The fruit of this success is Mises's greatest scientific work, *Human Action* (1949). In this immense volume he presented his exhaustive analysis of all things economic. This treatise is not beach reading. It is deeply philosophical as well as impressively analytical (despite Mises's eschewing the language of mathematics). And yet it is accessible to any intelligent reader who can spare the time, and expend the concentrated effort, required to grasp its lessons.

Regrettably, too few people are willing to spare such time and expend such effort on reading *Human Action*. And that's too bad, because the clarity and depth of insight that would be gained is enormous.

Enter Robert Murphy and his superb *Choice*. No scholar working today rivals Murphy at combining a vast knowledge of Mises's works with a too-rare skill at writing in a style that engages as well as instructs the general public. Murphy guides the reader through each section of *Human Action*. He does so with such lucidity, skill, and completeness that, by the end, it's almost as if the reader has studied every page of *Human Action* itself. Reading Murphy's book, therefore, is the best way—short of actually reading *Human Action*—to learn economics à la Mises.

So what Murphy offers here is no mere primer. While I hope that this volume will indeed prime readers to go on to study *Human Action* (and I confidently expect this result for many readers), Murphy's book is itself a valuable treatise, short though it is. In its own right, this volume is a creative, comprehensive, and unusually accessible work of economic science.

Murphy's Work Is Also Desperately Needed

Economics has increasingly failed, over the past hundred or more years, to inform the general public. However valuable a new academic journal article that explains a refinement in some econometric technique, or a new university-press book that describes a better rule for guiding central-bank monetary policy, no such academic work is as needed today as an article or book that conveys economic understanding to large numbers of non-economists. Despite the pretenses of the typical academic economist—who often naively fantasizes that his or her new theorem or latest empirical finding will guide apolitical government officials in their selfless quest to engineer the economy into a better state—public policy in democratic societies will always reflect the economic understanding of the general public.

If the general public believes that imports hurt the domestic economy, a policy of free trade has no hope of being realized. If the general public does not understand the dangers of discretionary monetary policy, discretionary monetary policy will persist. If members of the general public do not understand that the well-being of the poor and the middle class improves as entrepreneurs and businesses are more free to innovate and compete, public policy will be a nest of obstacles to innovation and barriers to competition.

Put in the language of economics: the marginal utility today of the next new addition to academic economists' understanding of the workings of the economy is much less than is the marginal utility of an additional "unit" of greater public understanding of basic economic truths. Some new gilding on modern international-trade theory, for example, might well improve that theory, but the scholar who spent time devising this improvement would likely have contributed far more value to humanity by helping the general public understand that tariffs do not raise overall domestic employment—a truth that economists have understood for centuries but one that the general public continues to miss.

Of course, there is in economics as in other professions a division of labor. Some economists specialize in making theoretical advances and others in teaching and in reaching out to the general public. The problem today is that too few competent economists specialize in these latter tasks. The result is doubly bad, for not only are too few competent economists working to expand the public's understanding of basic economic truths, but the absence of good economists on the public stage opens it up to cranks and crackpots who win applause (and sometimes even riches) by reinforcing, rather than by correcting, the public's wrongheaded notions about the economy.

Another division within economics warrants mention—namely, that between what my colleague Peter Boettke (in his wonderful Independent Institute book *Living Economics*) calls "mainline economics" and "mainstream economics." The former is reflected in the legacy of the wisdom of the Late Spanish Scholastics of the fifteenth and sixteenth centuries and such Classical School economists as Adam Smith, Jean-Baptiste Say, and Frederic Bastiat, and it includes all insights and investigative methods that are helpful for better understanding the human economy. The latter is the much more narrow "formal" economics that today dominates the profession. While practitioners of mainline economics measure their success by how well their investigations improve their understanding of reality, practitioners of mainstream economics too frequently measure their success by how closely their methods resemble those of the physical sciences.

Murphy's *Choice*, happily, rests squarely within mainline economics. And as such it is simultaneously accessible to the nonprofessional economist and deeply scholarly. This combination is difficult to pull off, but Murphy does it well. With it, Murphy stakes out for himself a prominent place on the public stage, where he can help to expose the fallacies propounded by economic charlatans.

Mises himself sometimes wrote, and wrote beautifully, for the general public. For example, his 1952 collection, *Planning for Freedom*, features excellent essays accessible to any intelligent non-economist. What Robert Murphy offers here, though, is something quite unique: a genuine treatise on economics that instructs and entertains even non-economists. The prominence of Murphy's place on the public stage is therefore enhanced by his volume's depth and breadth. The lay reader of *Choice* will learn not only important basic truths about the economy, but also a great deal about the science of economics itself.

> —**Donald J. Boudreaux** is Professor of Economics at George Mason University, the Martha and Nelson Getchell Chair for the Study of Free Market Capitalism at George Mason's Mercatus Center, and Associate Editor of *The Independent Review: A Journal of Political Economy*. He blogs at cafehayek.com.

Acknowledgments

MY BIGGEST DEBT of gratitude for this project belongs to David Theroux and his colleagues at the Independent Institute for conceiving this book, working with me on its development, and organizing its publication. William Lowndes provided the initial vision for the book as well as the requisite financial support through his Lowndes Foundation. I share all of their enthusiasm for the project and recognize the importance of bringing Ludwig von Mises's essential insights to a new generation of students and readers.

I am also grateful to the Ludwig von Mises Institute for graciously providing access to their library as I researched the book. Many people provided feedback on specific sections of early drafts, but I owe special thanks to David Gordon and Silas Barta.

Finally, the anonymous scholarly reviewers arranged by the Independent Institute were quite helpful, and in particular their comments improved the treatment of monetary calculation.

Introduction

THE MID-1980S THROUGH mid-2000s were known as the "Great Moderation," a period when it seemed that the leaders of the world's largest central banks had finally figured out how to ensure smooth economic growth and modest rates of price inflation. However, this tranquility was shattered by the collapse of the housing bubble and ensuing financial panic in the fall of 2008. The public and politicians alike wanted economists to explain what caused the crash, and they wanted recommendations to prevent a similar crisis in the future.

Yet according to one school of thought—so-called Austrian economics—the policy solutions recommended by most professional economists are actually the problem. Government intervention in the institutions of money and banking sowed the seeds of the worldwide asset bubble in the early and mid-2000s, which could only result in a giant crash according to this line of thought. Once the crash had occurred, the recession was prolonged by yet more government intervention in the form of massive deficits, expansion of unemployment payments, and ever more regulations on businesses in the private sector. Only by returning to a genuinely free market, based on the classical liberal notions of private property, civil liberties, and peace among nations, can we return to the prosperity and steady improvement of living conditions that we had come to take for granted.

Those who endorse the Austrian analysis believe it is crucial to spread this message, not just to academics, but to the intelligent layperson as well. That is the primary function of the present volume. It provides an introduction and *an invitation* to the most important work of arguably the most important Austrian economist. Specifically, the present volume represents a modern restatement of the essential elements of Ludwig von Mises's 1949 masterpiece, *Human Action*.

Historical Context: The Classical Economists

In 1776, Adam Smith published his famous *The Wealth of Nations*. Although Smith was not (as is sometimes claimed) the father of economics,[1] his famous book was certainly the pivotal work in classical British political economy. Other pioneers in this tradition were David Ricardo (1772–1823), James Mill (1773–1836), and his more famous son, John Stuart Mill (1806–1873). Together with the great French tradition embodied in such writers as Jacques Turgot (1727–1781), J. B. Say (1767–1832), and Frédéric Bastiat (1801–1850), the body of economic knowledge produced in the late eighteenth and early nineteenth centuries is known as classical economics. It focused on the accumulation of wealth and the distribution of income among classes of economic agents, and its policy prescriptions were generally laissez-faire, meaning that the government should let the market handle economic affairs.

Although the classical economists contributed many insights still in use today—especially by the economists who still embrace laissez-faire policy conclusions—their major shortcoming was in their understanding of value and prices. Although each writer had his own nuances, the classical economists generally explained the price of a good by reference to its cost of production, which ultimately could be traced to the amount of labor necessary for creating the good. Ironically, it was the generally pro-capitalism classical economists who bequeathed the labor theory of value that would prove so important in the writings of Karl Marx. (Indeed, by some definitions, Marx himself was an important classical economist.)

---

1. For example, many historians of economic thought consider Richard Cantillon's 1755 *Essai sur la Nature du Commerce en Général* (which has been translated as *An Essay on Economic Theory*) to be the first true economic treatise.

The Subjectivist, Marginal Revolution
and the Austrian Contribution

In standard histories of economic thought, three writers are credited with ushering in what is called the *marginal revolution* in economics. They are jointly acknowledged because their works appeared at roughly the same time (two in 1871 and the third in 1874), and they all independently discovered the new analytical approach that would lay the foundation for modern (i.e., post-classical) value and price theory. These economists were William Stanley Jevons (1835–1882), Léon Walras (1834–1910), and Carl Menger (1840–1921).

What these pioneers shared in common was the replacement of the classical cost or labor theory of value with a marginal subjective theory of value. Rather than trying to explain the price of a bottle of wine by reference to the labor effort involved in growing the grapes, the subjectivist explanation flipped the causality around: People valued a bottle of wine—and would therefore pay money for it—because it gave them happiness or "utility," and because of this, it made sense for producers to grow grapes for wine production.

In addition to flipping the causality of price determination from final prices to input prices, rather than vice versa, the revolution in economic theory also refined the precise way in which subjective desires affected market prices. Specifically, the term *marginal* meant that individuals made decisions "on the edge" (think of a margin on a sheet of paper). Despite their cost or labor theory of value, the classical economists obviously understood that market prices were intimately related to the usefulness of goods. Yet here they ran into a conundrum: Why was it that something essential to life, such as water, had a much lower market price than something that was of merely ornamental value, such as diamonds? The marginal approach to value and price theory easily solved this so-called water-diamond paradox.[2] Nobody in the marketplace is

---

2. Adam Smith discussed the water-diamond paradox in this fashion in *The Wealth of Nations*: "The things which have the greatest value in use have frequently little or no value in exchange; on the contrary, those which have the greatest value in exchange have frequently little or no value in use. Nothing is more useful than water: but it will purchase scarce anything; scarce anything can be had in exchange for it. A diamond, on the contrary, has scarce any use-value; but a very great quantity of other goods may frequently be had in exchange for it." (Adam Smith, *The Wealth of Nations*. In Two Volumes: Volume One. London: J.M. Dent

ever actually in a position to choose between water and diamonds, considered as entire classes of goods. Rather, a person in a given transaction is choosing between a specific quantity of water, such as an 8-ounce bottle, and a specific quantity of diamonds, such as the rock on a particular engagement ring. That specific engagement ring can typically shower much more happiness or utility than that specific bottle of water, and so there is no mystery why people are prepared to pay so much more money for the diamond than for the water.

For the present book, Menger's role in the overturning of classical economics is crucial because his contribution—his 1871 *Grundsätze* (translated as *Principles of Economics*)—is the founding work of the Austrian School of economics. The term *Austrian economics* was first coined during arguments over economic method between Menger and members of the German Historical School. Ironically, it was created by Menger's enemies, as a pejorative description of the origin of the unorthodox Mengerian views because Austria was considered a backwater compared to Germany. The term stuck, such that nowadays economists from around the world—many located in the United States—refer to themselves as Austrian because of their theoretical affinity for the Mengerian tradition and not because of their geographical origins.

The Importance of the Austrian School

Although Menger, Jevons, and Walras are all recognized as marking the turning point away from the classical labor theory of value and replacing it with the new marginal utility theory, Menger's work differed from the approach of his peers in significant ways. For one thing, Menger eschewed the mathematical formulation that characterized the others and that would eventually dominate mainstream economics. To this day, one of the notable differences between Austrian economists versus other economists is that the Austrians focus on logical deduction and verbal exposition, rather than mathematical

---

and Sons, Ltd. Aldine House, first published in this edition 1910, last reprinted 1957, chapter IV, p. 25). The claim in the text above is not that the great classical economists were helpless in the face of this so-called paradox. Rather, the claim is that their commonsense observations could not easily be reconciled with their formal theoretical apparatus for explaining market prices. In contrast, the new marginal utility theory could quite easily handle the empirical fact that water had a much lower market price than diamonds.

model building and econometric testing. Indeed, the present writer once saw an economist flip through a scholarly article written by an Austrian and joke, "Where are the equations?"

Beyond the mere differences in style and mode of exposition, there are substantive differences in the Austrian approach as well. Although virtually all economists since the revolution in thought of the 1870s would endorse some version of subjectivism in economic theory, the Austrians pride themselves on having the most consistent and thorough application of this innovation, with their approach sometimes being described as *radical subjectivism.*[3] Since the marginal revolution, it is commonplace among economists of all major schools—Austrian and non-Austrian alike—to attribute market prices at least in part to the subjective tastes (*preferences*, in more formal language) of consumers. Yet the Austrians go further than this, exploring the implications of individuals having subjective expectations about the future. This stands in contrast to standard mainstream models, where individual agents may have idiosyncratic preferences but share the same correct understanding of "how the economy works" in the simplified world of the model.

Another defining attribute of the Austrian School is to focus on the market process rather than following the mainstream attention to describing the market equilibrium position. As we will see through the course of the present book, the Austrians have a particular explanation of what causes the phenomenon of interest in a market economy; they try to explain why it is that capitalists can typically earn a positive return on their financial investments, singling out the phenomenon of *interest* for particular attention. In contrast, most mainstream economists look at an economy as a set of simultaneous conditions that must all be satisfied in order for the system to be in equilibrium. For example, in graduate school, the author encountered an exam problem that described the physical nature of the capital goods on a tropical island and then asked what the equilibrium real interest rate "had to be" for the lone man stranded on the

---

3. In this vein Nobel laureate and Austrian economist Friedrich Hayek's statement is apropos: "It is probably no exaggeration to say that every important advance in economic theory during the last hundred years was a further step in the consistent application of subjectivism." F. A. Hayek, *The Counter-Revolution of Science* (Glencoe, 1952), 31. A standard reference in Austrian radical subjectivism is Gerald O'Driscoll and Mario Rizzo, *The Economics of Time and Ignorance* (New York: Basil Blackwell, 1985).

island. It would be hard to overstate the gulf between this approach and that of the Austrians, when it comes to explaining the market rate of interest.

These reflections lead to yet another defining characteristic of the Austrian School, and the one making them most important for study in our troubled economic times: Far more than any other school, the Austrians have a rich conception of the capital structure in an economy. Mainstream models of the economy formally include capital, but they often aggregate it into a lump sum quantity, with a simple K denoting how much capital exists in the economy at any moment. If the people in the model save a higher fraction of their income, then K grows faster and boosts future output. With such a crude approach, the only downside to saving and investing "too much" is that too much present consumption would be traded off in exchange for a greater amount of future consumption, according to the subjective preferences of the consumers and their desire for consumption levels through time. This standard mainstream approach can't handle the possibility of firms investing in the *wrong* things.

In contrast, the Austrians view the capital in the economy not as a simple "stock" that could be summed up by a number. Rather, they see it as a complex, interlocking structure of heterogeneous capital goods, including tractors, cargo planes, oil tankers, drill presses, assembly lines, hammers, nails, irrigation ditches, laboratories, universities, various groups of farm animals, and semi-finished goods stored in warehouses at different locations across the country. With this richer conception, the Austrians can analyze the effects not just of how much is invested, but in which particular capital goods the investment takes place. It would hardly make the country richer, for example, to invest in a massive expansion of the number of screwdrivers, with no production of additional screws.

As we will see in the course of this book, the unique Austrian perspective on capital and interest theory gives rise to their theory of the business cycle. To repeat the claims made at the start of this Introduction, the Austrian analysis suggests that the typical "medicine" offered by governments and central banks to heal a broken economy are actually poison. For this reason, studying the Austrian School is important not just for historical curiosity or academic novelty, but because its advocates may have the knowledge necessary to end our recurring economic malaise.

The Historical Importance of Ludwig von Mises and *Human Action*

Following Menger, several literal Austrians (in the sense of national origin) and then members of the Austrian School (in the sense of their school of thought) carried on his tradition, continuing to the present. Some notable members of the Austrian School and their major achievements were Eugen von Böhm-Bawerk (1851–1914), with his seminal contributions to capital and interest theory, as well as his critiques of Marxist political economy; Friedrich von Wieser (1851–1926), with his elaboration of marginal utility theory and the concept of opportunity cost; Friedrich A. Hayek (1899–1992), who explained market prices as a form of communication and who won the Nobel Prize in 1974 for his work on the business cycle; Murray Rothbard (1926–1995), a lucid writer who united Austrian economics with libertarian political philosophy, but also developed technical innovations in monopoly and welfare analysis; and Israel Kirzner (1930–), known primarily for his extensive work on entrepreneurship.

Yet arguably the most important Austrian—second only to Menger himself, the founder of the School—was Ludwig von Mises (1881–1973). Chronologically, Mises fell in the middle of the Austrian thinkers listed above, and also served as an intellectual bridge. He synthesized and extended the tradition he inherited from Menger, Böhm-Bawerk, and Wieser, presenting a powerful framework that was then further amplified by his own followers, Hayek, Rothbard, and Kirzner among others.

According to his own recollections of being a young Austrian going to university, Mises discovered Menger's *Principles* in 1903 and became an economist.[4] Mises would soon rise to prominence himself. His 1912 book, translated into English as *The Theory of Money and Credit*, used subjective marginal utility theory to explain the market value of units of money, something that had eluded earlier theorists following the intellectual revolution of the 1870s. In this way, Mises bridged the gap between what we now call *micro-* and *macroeconomics*, providing a unified explanation for the market exchange rate between

---

4. Ludwig von Mises, *Memoirs* (Auburn, AL: Ludwig von Mises Institute, [1978] 2009).

all commodities, including the commodity that happened to serve as money.[5] In addition, in this crucial book, Mises drew on Böhm-Bawerkian capital theory, the interest theory of Swedish economist Knut Wicksell (1851–1926), and the earlier work of the British Currency School on the role of banks in economic crises, in order to advance what Mises called the *circulation credit theory of the trade cycle*. This is nowadays known as *Austrian business cycle theory*, the teaching of which is a major objective of the present book.

Mises's contributions in *The Theory of Money and Credit* would have earned him a seat at the table of important twentieth-century economists, but he went much further. In a seminal 1920 academic paper, followed up by a 1922 book-length treatment,[6] Mises went beyond the standard arguments over incentives and the danger of corruption to offer a fundamentally more decisive critique of socialism: Without market prices for the "factors of production"—labor, natural resources, and capital goods—the central planners in a socialist state would have no method of determining whether their "economic plan" embodied a rational use of society's scarce resources.

This problem doesn't exist in a market economy with private property, Mises argued, because the availability of actual prices allowed accountants to compute profit and loss statements. These calculations gave critical feedback to the entrepreneurs, letting them know if the consumers implicitly endorsed or rejected their business decisions. Yet since, even in principle, there could be no such feedback in a socialist system, Mises argued that it was a faulty substitute for capitalism. Even if they had full technical advice from the best

---

5. Earlier theorists had adopted a bifurcated approach, using the new marginal utility theory to explain the relative prices between goods, but using aggregate concepts such as "the total quantity of money" to explain absolute prices. For example, the earlier theorists could use marginal utility theory to explain why, in equilibrium, one apple would trade for two bananas. But to explain why one apple would have a price of $1, while a banana would have a price of 50 cents, the theorists would invoke the total quantity of dollars compared to the total quantity of fruit and the "velocity of circulation" of money. Mises's approach treated dollar bills no differently from apples or bananas; it showed how the same principles of marginal utility could explain all market exchange ratios, even those involving the good serving as money.

6. Mises's original article appeared in German in 1920. An English translation, "Economic Calculation in the Socialist Commonwealth," appeared in Hayek's ([1935] 1990) collection, *Collectivist Economic Planning* (Clifton, NJ: Augustus M. Kelley. The book-length treatment was Mises's *Socialism* (Indianapolis, IN: Liberty Classics, [1922] 1981).

physicists, chemists, engineers, and other experts, and even if they had nothing but the best of intentions, the central planners would lack critical information in assigning uses to scarce resources because the socialist planners wouldn't know the *economic cost* of these resources. Would it make sense to use a certain amount of steel, factory time, and labor hours to produce a certain number of automobiles? Mises argued that the central planners would truly have no idea: Even if they could estimate the benefits of new cars for the motorists who received them, they wouldn't be able to calculate the *costs* of making the cars, since they would lack market prices for steel, factory time, and labor hours. Far from being more "rational" than capitalism—as the socialist writers claimed—an economy organized by central planners would be "groping in the dark."

During his time in Vienna, Mises's scholarly publications included not only technical economic analysis but also an exposition and defense of classical liberalism.[7] In addition, Mises cultivated a following of some of the brightest minds of the time in his famous *"Privatseminar"* (private seminar) held every Friday in his office at the Chamber of Commerce. According to one participant, a typical night would involve three hours of discussion at Mises's office, then dinner, and finally "lighter" topics at a café until 1 a.m.[8] The list of attendees at Mises's seminar included economists, sociologists, and philosophers who would achieve fame of their own. This aspect of Mises's influence is typical, showing that he was not only a great thinker but also an inspiration to others with his important ideas.

Due to his Jewish ethnicity and classically liberal views, Mises would not have fared well under Nazi rule. Seeing the storm clouds brewing, Mises wisely left Austria for Switzerland, where he landed a position at the Graduate Institute of International Studies in Geneva. In 1940, he and his wife Margit emigrated from Switzerland to the United States. Mises taught at New York University from 1945 until 1969, when he formally retired.

During his time in Switzerland, Mises wrote the German-language *Nationalökonomie*, published in 1940. This full-blown treatise contained a grand

7. Ludwig von Mises, *Liberalism: In the Classical Tradition*, trans. Ralph Raico (Irvington
-on-Hudson, NY: Foundation for Economic Education, [1927] 1985).

8. Gottfried Haberler, "Mises's Private Seminar," *The Mont Pelerin Quarterly*, 3, no. 3 (October 1961): 20f.

synthesis of Mises's technical treatment of important areas in economic theory, as well as his methodological views on the proper foundation of economic science itself. Yet the treatise also contained Mises's views on political philosophy and history, in the sense that Mises related his understanding of how government policies affect the economy and through that the unfolding events of the real world. By doing so, Mises showed the tremendous importance of educating the public on sound economic theory; his task was not merely academic.

To the admirers of Mises, his grand treatise could hardly be overrated. In the description written by several self-identified Misesians:

> Thus, *Nationalökonomie* marked the culmination of the Austrian theoretical approach, and, in a real sense, the rebirth of the Austrian School of economics. It was designed to play a decisive role in reconstructing the whole of economic science in its moment of crisis, including reformulating and unifying price theory, monetary theory, and business cycle theory, and at the same time establishing the correct methodological foundations of the social sciences. Using this mighty architectonic of economic theory, Mises formulated a radical and impermeable defense of laissez-faire policy conclusions that were distinctly unfashionable when the book first appeared.[9]

After moving to New York, Mises began writing an English-language version of his great work. This would become *Human Action*, first published in 1949. We again quote from the Introduction to the Scholar's Edition of the book:

> *Human Action*, building on and expanding its German predecessor [i.e., *Nationalökonomie*], transformed Austrian economics, as it is understood today, into a predominantly American phenomenon with a distinctly Misesian imprint, and made possible the continuation of the Austrian School after the mid-twentieth century . . . . A high place must be reserved in the history of economic thought, indeed, in the history of ideas, for Mises's masterwork. Even today, *Human Action*

---

9. Jeff Herbener et al., "Introduction," in Ludwig von Mises, *Human Action*, Scholar's Edition (Auburn, AL: Ludwig von Mises Institute, [1949] 1998).

points the way to a brighter future for the science of economics and the practice of human liberty.[10]

To understand why Mises proved to be such an inspiration to generations of scholars, both inside and outside formal economics, we need only quote from his stirring final paragraph of *Human Action*:

> The body of economic knowledge is an essential element in the structure of human civilization . . . . It rests with men whether they will make the proper use of the rich treasure with which this knowledge provides them or whether they will leave it unused. But if they fail to take the best advantage of it and disregard its teachings and warnings, they will not annul economics; they will stamp out society and the human race.[11]

Lest the average reader think only professional economists were on the hook for communicating this important knowledge, just a few pages before Mises emphasized:

> Whether we like it or not, it is a fact that economics cannot remain an esoteric branch of knowledge accessible only to small groups of scholars and specialists. Economics deals with society's fundamental problems; it concerns everyone and belongs to all. *[Economics] is the main and proper study of every citizen.* (italics added)[12]

Thus we see that Mises was not merely a great technical economist, but a champion of evangelizing to the masses—a task in which he himself was a leader. It was because of his passionate defense of individual liberty, grounded in his command of economic science, that Mises became such an icon and indeed a hero in certain circles.[13] As the man whom Nobel laureate Friedrich A. Hayek called "the master of us all,"[14] Ludwig von Mises will forever retain

---

10. Herbener et al., "Introduction," xxiv.

11. Mises, *Human Action*, 881.

12. Mises, *Human Action*, 875.

13. For example, his ardent follower Murray Rothbard would eventually write a long essay, *Ludwig von Mises: Scholar, Creator, Hero* (Auburn, AL: Ludwig von Mises Institute, 1988).

14. See Hayek's essay, "Can We Still Avoid Inflation?" in *The Austrian Theory of the Trade Cycle and Other Essays*, ed. Richard Ebeling (Auburn, AL: Ludwig von Mises Institute, [1978] 1996).

a position of great importance for anyone wishing to learn of the Austrian tradition in economic science.

The Purpose of, and Need for, the Present Book

The purpose of the present book is to provide a modern, condensed treatment of the issues Mises covers in his magnum opus, *Human Action*. As we explained in the preceding section, Mises is the single best representative of the Austrian School of economic thought, and *Human Action* is the single best example of Mises's tremendous output. It is therefore entirely appropriate for us to devote a new book to the task of communicating the essentials of *Human Action* to a new generation of readers, including economics students but also the intelligent layperson.

After stressing the historical importance of the great work, one might wonder: Why not just tell people that they must obtain and read *Human Action* itself? Why the need to write a new book based on Mises's treatise?

The answer is that, despite its shining qualities, *Human Action* poses three major roadblocks that discourage potential new readers. First, it is frankly very long, clocking in at more than 900 pages. Second, Mises wrote in a formal style and employed an extensive vocabulary, for example, declaring early on that "the term 'rational action' is therefore pleonastic and must be rejected as such." Finally, Mises assumes a broad knowledge on the part of his readers, commenting casually on historical controversies from the fields of physics, philosophy, and of course economics.

For the above reasons, *Human Action* intimidates many potential readers, who would otherwise be quite receptive to its essential elements. The present book is necessary, then, to relay the main insights from *Human Action* in a style that will resonate with the modern reader. The present book will assume no prior knowledge in economics or other fields. When necessary, it will give the historical and scholarly context necessary to explain the contribution Mises makes on a particular issue.

To faithfully reproduce the material in *Human Action*, the present book mirrors its basic structure; it copies the same Parts One through Seven. However, to condense the presentation to a more manageable size, it does not always follow Mises's chapter breakdown.

It is hoped that the present work provides new readers with an enjoyable and educational introduction to the life's work of one of history's most important economists. Some readers may be stirred to read the other books referenced in this text, including the original *Human Action* itself.

As Mises stressed, a widespread knowledge of economics is necessary for the maintenance of civilization. Every citizen shares the burden of learning at least the basics of this science in order to preserve our heritage and pass it on to our descendants. The present book offers an accessible yet comprehensive introduction to the nature and power of economics.

Relationship between Contents of *Choice* (Murphy) and *Human Action* (Mises)

ALTHOUGH THE TEXT closely follows the progression laid out in *Human Action*, the correspondence is not identical. The following table takes each chapter from the present text, summarizes it, and then "maps" it to the relevant chapter(s) in Mises's work from which it primarily draws. To help avoid confusion and to be faithful to the Scholar's Edition layout of *Human Action*, the Roman numerals for its chapters have been retained.

Murphy	Mises
PART I Human Action	
Chapter 1 The Science of Human Action *Explains the boundaries of economics relative to other fields, and as a subset of "praxeology."*	Introduction, Chapter I
Chapter 2 The Definition and Components of *Action* *Defines "action" in the Misesian sense and lists its major constituents.*	Chapters I, IV, and VI
Chapter 3 Economic Theory versus Historical Understanding *Clarifies the role of economic history (including economic statistics) in the Misesian approach.*	Chapter II
Chapter 4 Further Economic Concepts and Principles Flowing from Action *Defines major economic concepts and relays foundational "laws."*	Chapters IV, V, VI, and VII

Murphy	Mises
PART II Action within the Framework of Society	
Chapter 5 Human Society and the Division of Labor	Chapter VIII
Explains human cooperation by its higher productivity.	
Chapter 6 The Role of Ideas and the Importance of Reason	Chapters III and IX
Describes Mises as rationalist and outlines major challenges to his project.	
PART III Economic Calculation	
Chapter 7 Even the Economists Missed the Importance of Monetary Calculation	Chapters XI, XII, and XIII
Underscores the unique emphasis Mises places on calculation, and explains barter pricing.	
Chapter 8 What Economic Calculation Can and Can't Do	Chapter XII
Acknowledges the limits to calculation.	
PART IV Catallactics: Economics of the Market Society	
Chapter 9 Defining and Studying the Market Economy	Chapters XIV and XV
Catallactics defined as exchanges under private property and money, studied with thought experiments.	
Chapter 10 How Prices Are Formed on the Market	Chapters XVI, XXI, and XXII
Explains principles by which money prices are formed for consumer and producer goods.	
Chapter 11 Indirect Exchange and Money	Chapter XVII
Explains the origin of money, the difficulties in applying the "new" marginal utility approach to money and how Mises solved them, and the importance of gold.	

Murphy	Mises
Chapter 12 The Misesian Approach to Money & Banking *Defines technical terms necessary to understand Mises's theory of the business cycle, and explains how "free banking" would work.*	Chapter XVII
Chapter 13 Capital, Time Preference, and the Theory of Interest *Summarizes the development of interest rate theory within the Austrian tradition, and stresses the distinction between financial capital and physical capital goods.*	Chapters XVIII, XIX, and XXII
Chapter 14 Austrian Business Cycle Theory *Draws on strands from three prior chapters to explain Mises's theory of unsustainable credit-induced booms sowing seeds for subsequent busts.*	Chapter XX

PART V Social Cooperation without a Market

Chapter 15 The Impossibility of Economic Calculation under Socialism *Defines the nature of socialism and why central planners can't rationally allocate resources, even in principle.*	Chapters XXV and XXVI

PART VI The Hampered Market Economy

Chapter 16 Government Intervention in the Market Economy *Defines "interventionism" as a misguided attempt to avoid the extremes of pure capitalism and pure socialism, which fails to achieve objectives of the interventions.*	Chapters XXVII, XXVIII, XXIX, XXX, XXXI, XXXII, XXXIII, XXXIV, XXXV, and XXXVI

PART VII The Place of Economics in Society

Chapter 17 Economics and Public Opinion *Explains why error persists in economics, but nonetheless it is still the duty of all citizens to study the subject in order to preserve society.*	Chapters XXXVII, XXXVIII, and XXXIX

PART I

Human Action

1

The Science of Economics
and Human Action

What Do Economists Study?

ALTHOUGH VIRTUALLY EVERYONE recognizes the importance of economic issues, most people have little understanding of the scope of economic science and its relation to other disciplines. Topics such as money, inflation, and unemployment are clearly ones that economists study, whereas gravity, electricity, and magnetism are studied by physicists. But drawing a precise boundary line around the subject matter of economics can be difficult; not even professional economists agree on the solution. Even so, it's important for a general introduction to economics to take a stand because defining the boundaries of economic science will clarify for the reader what economics *is* and, at the same time, will shed light on the proper *method* for "doing economics."

Before offering a working definition of the scope of economics, we should first emphasize that it truly is a separate field of scientific inquiry. As the great Austrian economist Ludwig von Mises wrote:

> Economics is the youngest of all sciences . . . [E]conomics opened to human science a domain previously inaccessible and never thought of. The discovery of a regularity in the sequence and interdependence of market phenomena went beyond the limits of the traditional system of learning. It conveyed knowledge which could be regarded neither as logic, mathematics, psychology, physics, nor biology.[1]

---

1. Mises, *Human Action*, 1.

Granted that economists have something to offer humanity, what exactly is it? To quote Nobel laureate James Buchanan, what should economists do?[2]

As we already have explained, the awkward fact is that not even economists can agree on this question. For one thing, some of the most prestigious textbooks don't even bother to precisely define the topic of inquiry. For example, Hal Varian's popular graduate-level text on microeconomics[3] jumps right into a firm's "production function" in the very first sentence. A little better is David Romer's popular graduate-level text in macroeconomics, which declares in the opening sentence, "Macroeconomics is the study of the economy as a whole."[4] Yet this explanation sheds little light, since we want to know what does it mean to "study the economy"? If we ask whether the charging of interest is in accordance with Islamic law, does that question fall under economics, theology, or both? Sending a rocket into space involves fuel and usually government spending, so does that mean rocket science is a branch of economics?

It may be that graduate-level textbooks don't rigorously define economics because the authors assume their readers are already familiar with the nature of the science. Turning to an undergraduate macroeconomics text, we find authors Tyler Cowen and Alex Tabarrok informing their readers, "Economics is the study of how to get the most out of life."[5] This is promising, yet still somewhat vague. Best-selling undergraduate textbook author Greg Mankiw writes, "Economics is the study of how society manages its scarce resources."[6] This is more informative but is hardly a crisp definition.

Perhaps our problem is looking at textbooks, which presuppose an academic environment and are understandably eager to "jump into the details." If we turn instead to popular economics books written for a general audience, maybe we will get a better sense of how economists view the nature of their discipline. For example, economist Steven Levitt, one of the authors of the bestselling *Freakonomics*, claims:

---

2. Buchanan famously asked this question in a 1964 article, "What Should Economists Do?" *Southern Economic Journal*. 30, no. 3 (January).

3. Hal Varian, *Microeconomic Analysis*, 3rd ed. (New York: W. W. Norton [1978] 1992), 1.

4. David Romer, *Advanced Macroeconomics* (USA: McGraw-Hill, 1996), 1.

5. Tyler Cowen and Alex Tabarrok, *Modern Principles: Macroeconomics* (USA: Worth, 2010). The quotation comes from the copyright page of the book, serving as a dedication.

6. Greg Mankiw, *Principles of Microeconomics*, 5th ed. (USA: South-Western Cengage Learning, [2007] 2009), 4.

Economics is above all a science of measurement. It comprises an extraordinarily powerful and flexible set of tools that can reliably assess a thicket of information to determine the effect of any one factor, or even the whole effect. That's what "the economy" is, after all: a thicket of information about jobs and real estate and banking and investment.[7]

Although Levitt's description no doubt characterizes the activities of many of today's professional economists, his explanation would apply to *any* scientist relying on techniques such as regression analysis, including not just sociologists and criminologists, but also meteorologists, a field that obviously is quite distinct from economics. We're still left wondering: What exactly is it about *economics* that sets it apart from other disciplines?

Popular economics authors Steven Landsburg and David Friedman, in their respective books for the general public, finally offer the clear statements we have been seeking. After describing his younger misconceptions, Landsburg explains:

Here is what I *now* think economics is about. First, it is about observing the world with genuine curiosity and admitting that it is full of mysteries. Second, *[economics] is about trying to solve those mysteries in ways that are consistent with the general proposition that human behavior is usually designed to serve a purpose.* (italics added)[8]

In his own description of the nature of economic science, David Friedman elaborates on this notion of purpose: "Economics is that way of understanding behavior that starts from the assumption that individuals have objectives and tend to choose the correct way to achieve them."[9]

Landsburg and Friedman's characterizations cast economics as a science that studies purposeful human behavior, which of course includes conventional economic topics such as starting a business, looking for a job, and investing for retirement. Yet the scope of purposeful human behavior is obviously much broader than narrowly economic matters. After all, offering a marriage proposal, kicking a field goal, and committing an act of terrorism are examples

---

7. Steven Levitt and Stephen Dubner, *Freakonomics* (USA: William Morrow, 2005), 13.
8. Steven E. Landsburg, *The Armchair Economist* (USA: The Free Press, [1993] 1995), vii.
9. David Friedman, *Hidden Order* (USA: HaperCollins, 1996), 3.

of purposeful human behavior, too—are these topics acceptable fodder for an economist to study?

Ludwig von Mises on Economics and the Broader Study of "Human Action"

Ludwig von Mises, and many of the Austrian economists who followed him, resolved these thorny problems in the following way. He first recognized that the classical economists—giants such as Adam Smith and David Ricardo—made immortal contributions to the field by explaining certain patterns in the movement of prices and other events in the marketplace. These pioneers showed that there were indeed laws of economics that were just as real as laws of physics or chemistry and which government officials had to acknowledge if they wished to be successful in their own actions.

However, the great deficiency of the classical economists was that they tried to explain the market price of a good by its cost of production and, ultimately, by the human labor embodied in its construction. During the marginal revolution of the 1870s, economists abandoned the labor theory of value and instead embraced the modern subjective theory of value. Rather than explaining the price of a good by reference to its costs, now economists started with the fact that the buyer derives satisfaction or utility from obtaining one more unit of the good; that is the bedrock principle to understand why a buyer willingly pays for it.[10]

This new way of thinking ushered in a transformation of the scope of economics itself. As Mises describes it:

> [T]he transition from the classical theory of value to the subjective theory of value was much more than the substitution of a more satisfactory theory of market exchange for a less satisfactory one. The general theory of choice and preference goes far beyond the horizon which encompassed the scope of economic problems as circumscribed by the [classical] economists . . . . It is much more than merely a theory of

---

10. In the text above, we are discussing the marginal revolution in respect to Mises's definition of the boundaries of economic science. Earlier in the Introduction, and later on in this book, we discuss the subjective theory of value in greater detail.

the "economic side" of human endeavors . . . It is the science of every kind of human action. Choosing determines all human decisions . . . . The modern theory of value widens the scientific horizon and enlarges the field of economic studies. Out of the political economy of the classical school emerges the general theory of human action, *praxeology.* The economic or catallactic [i.e., events involving an exchange] problems are embedded in a more general science, and can no longer be severed from this connection. No treatment of economic problems proper can avoid starting from acts of choice; economics becomes a part, although the best [developed] part, of a more universal science, praxeology. (italics in original.)[11]

We now understand why Mises chose to give his grand treatise on economics the initially odd title *Human Action.* It is because Mises views the conventional topics of economic inquiry—prices, money, the business cycle—as falling under the umbrella of a more general subject matter, namely human action itself. Rather than looking at "economic man" the way that the classical economists did—as a fictitious being motivated by the desire to accumulate material wealth—the new approach looked at acting man or woman as such. In other words, Mises argued that it was no longer necessary to assume, as the classical economists did, that people, at least in their roles in the marketplace, were motivated by selfish, pecuniary desires. All the economist had to assume was that people were motivated by desires, period. The same analytical tools that best explained greedy hedge fund managers were also appropriate for explaining the actions of Mother Teresa.

In the present book, we will follow the example of Mises in his approach to this subject matter. In Part One, we explore the general implications of the fact that humans *act*, meaning that they make conscious decisions in an attempt to achieve desired goals. Once we have outlined the scope of a scientific study of human action in general—what Mises dubbed *praxeology*—we will narrow the focus to human action within the context of society and the institution of private property. In this realm of the study of market exchanges—what Mises dubbed *catallactics*—we will find the traditional subject matter of economics textbooks.

---

11. Mises, *Human Action*, 3.

To many professional economists, the attention we give here to the boundaries and nature of economic science may seem excessive. After all, natural scientists such as physicists don't spend a lot of time pontificating about what physics is, but instead roll up their sleeves and start doing it. Yet Mises and many of his followers thought that it was crucial to study the foundations of economic science in order to develop it properly. Very few people dispute the current understanding of what physics *is* and how it can help humanity, but there is far less consensus—even among economists themselves—on the proper scope, use, and method of economic science. As we will see throughout the course of this book, *how* economists view the nature of their field ends up having a strong impact on the *way* they do their economics and can affect the policy conclusions they may give to government officials. Therefore, although our discussion so far may appear as irrelevant philosophy to some economists, for those following in the tradition of Ludwig von Mises, these matters are as critical as laying a proper foundation before building a house.

2

The Definition and Components of Action

"Action" Defined

MODERN ECONOMISTS VIEW the conventional study of prices, money, and recessions as part of a broader study of intentional human choices that are guided by underlying desires or preferences. For this reason, economists feel justified in commenting on apparently noneconomic areas, such as marriage decisions and the impact of seatbelt legislation. In the terminology of Mises, modern economics is just one important part of the broader scientific study of action.

To avoid confusion, and to be sure the reader understands exactly what economists have in mind with such language, we should provide some further clarification. First, when we say that economists study action, we mean purposeful behavior, which does not include all human behavior. If a patient lifts his leg in response to the doctor tapping his knee with a small hammer, that isn't action in the way we are using the term; it is merely a reflex. However, if the doctor insults the patient, who then kicks him in retaliation, that *is* action.[1]

Also keep in mind that action need not involve observable bodily movements. If one student in class is listening intently to the lecture while another is on the verge of dozing off, the professor might not be able to distinguish between the two merely from looking at their faces. Yet the former student is engaging in action—she is choosing to pay attention—whereas the latter student might be falling asleep without even realizing it.

---

1. As our discussion makes clear, Mises's approach differs drastically from the behaviorism of B. F. Skinner and his followers.

In a related vein, sometimes the significance of an action consists in the failure of a person to behave in a particular way. For example, if everyone in a neighborhood ignores the cries for help emanating from someone on the street, outsiders will be outraged when they learn of the episode. In our terminology, these neighborhood residents still acted because they consciously chose to stay indoors, rather than rendering assistance.

Having defined the concept of action as purposeful behavior, several results logically follow, simply by thinking through the definition and what it entails. We'll explore some of these results in the remaining sections of this chapter.

If There's Action, There Must Be an Actor

The most obvious implication of invoking the notion of action is that we are admitting the existence of another mind at work. We do this so effortlessly in our everyday lives that we take it for granted, but it is quite an extraordinary hypothesis. When the physicist looks at a falling rock, for example, it would be considered quite unscientific to explain the phenomenon by suggesting that the rock "wants to get closer to the center of the earth." Yet in economics, it is perfectly acceptable to explain high beachfront real estate prices by suggesting that homeowners "want to get closer to the ocean."

The reason for the different approach in the case of the rock versus the homeowners is that each of us knows what it "feels like" to be a thinking being—or so the author of the present book hypothesizes!—and it sure seems as if other human beings are quite similar to ourselves. Thus, it is quite reasonable to assume that there's "something going on inside their minds," just as our own bodily movements seem to be motivated by conscious intentions. We perceive an "ego" or "will" that is somehow anchored in the physical bodies of other human beings. Philosophers and cognitive scientists have much to say on these weighty matters,[2] but for our purposes, we need only to point out that this is what we're doing, every time we interpret an event as an example of *action*, as opposed to the mindless movement of matter according to the laws of physics.

---

2. A philosophical term relevant to this discussion is *teleology*, which involves the use of ends or purposes or goals as an explanation of a phenomenon.

When we interpret events as being at least partially due to one or more actions, it forces us to specify who the actors are. For example, we might say, "In 1941 Japan bombed the United States." Yet if we think through the statement more carefully, we realize that it's just shorthand, since a nation per se isn't really an actor with an independent mind and desires. A more accurate statement would be, "In 1941 various Japanese pilots chose to obey orders to drop bombs on an American naval base."

Purposeful Behavior Implies an Underlying Purpose (Preferences)

Another obvious implication of invoking the concept of action is that the acting individuals must have underlying goals or desires, what economists more formally call *preferences*. After all, if the observing economist is going to explain an event by saying a conscious mind is behaving purposefully, then it only makes sense to attribute an actual *purpose* to that conscious mind.

This may sound deep and mysterious, but it's quite straightforward. When rain falls from the sky, the meteorologist need not invoke purposes; the event can be scientifically attributed to mechanical operations of nature. Yet when a boy's arm moves toward a glass, his fingers close around it, his arm brings the glass up to his lips, and finally his hand dumps the water into his open mouth, then it is normal and scientific to attribute the event to the boy's intentional behavior. Without further information, the observing economist can't be quite sure what the exact purpose is; the boy might be thirsty, he might be swallowing a pill, or he may be following his parents' instructions to drink more water. Yet it is obvious that there is *some* purpose behind the boy's bodily movements.

Preferences Are a Subjective Ranking, Not an Objective Measurement

If we develop the idea of preferences that flows from the concept of action, we realize that preferences are a ranking because an action is always a *choice* between various alternatives. If a girl chooses chocolate versus vanilla ice cream, the economist can conclude only that she preferred the former to the latter; the economist can't say *how much* she preferred chocolate. Moreover, it would be equally nonsensical to try to compare the girl's preferences for ice cream to someone else's, for example, by saying, "Marcia enjoys chocolate 13 percent more than Jim does." There is no way to tie such a statement to action since Marcia and Jim possess independent minds. Each person has his or her own subjective preferences, which are individual and idiosyncratic rankings of various possibilities from best to worst.

It is important to stress this point because the conventional textbook treatment misleads many students, and even some professional economists. Historically, economists in the nineteenth century believed that people were motivated by a measurable psychic substance called *utility*. They thought a person chose one action versus another because the preferred course provided more units of utility than the other.

However, by the early twentieth century, most economists had abandoned the idea of a measurable (or *cardinal*) unit of utility. Instead, they explained the actions of consumers and producers by reference to a ranking of desired outcomes (called *ordinal* preferences).[3] These terms are easy to remember because the cardinal numbers, like 3.2 and 500, facilitate arithmetical operations. In contrast, it would be nonsensical to apply addition or division to the ordinal numbers—first, fourteenth, thirty-seventh, and so on.

To understand the modern view of utility, an analogy will help: People make use of the concept of friendship all the time. It makes sense for Tina to say, "Alice is my best friend, while John is my second-best friend." Such a statement implies that Alice is a better friend than John and that Tina has more friendship with Alice than with John. However, it is nonsensical to ask, "What is the percentage by which Alice's friendship is higher than John's?" This is because friendship is an ordinal, not a cardinal concept. In the same way, economists use utility as a concept to rank the outcomes that acting individuals desire. The higher an outcome is on a preference ranking, the more utility it renders to the individual.

To avoid confusion, before leaving this section we should note that today, professional economists typically rely on formal models that involve math-

---

3. A classic exposition of the switch from cardinal to ordinal utility in consumer theory is in John Hicks, *Value and Capital: An Inquiry into Some Fundamental Principles of Economic Theory* (Oxford: Oxford University Press, [1939] 1961).

ematical utility functions, where an agent inside the model derives a numerical amount of *utils* based on, for example, how many units of various goods he or she consumes. Yet even here, the underlying logic of ordinal preference rankings still holds. Any good textbook will explain that there is nothing magical about the specific numbers assigned by a utility function; it is simply a convenient way to represent the underlying preferences, which are an ordinal ranking of the various options from better to worse.[4]

An Acting Individual Thinks
He or She Can Influence the Future

We have already explained that the concept of action implies that a mind is at work with subjective goals or preferences. In this section, we discuss one final implication: An acting individual must have some underlying theory of cause and effect, where the individual's behavior can be the trigger to activate the effect. For a simple example, return to our scenario of a boy's arm and hand movements that involved a glass of water. To interpret these events as purposeful behavior, we must say that the boy has some theory or expectation about the result of pouring water down his throat. If the boy is swallowing a pill, then he picked up the glass because he believed that pouring the water into his mouth would make it easier to swallow the pill. If he didn't believe that, then it wouldn't really make sense for outside observers to "explain" the boy's arm movements by saying, "Oh, the boy had to take a pill."

Sometimes economists describe this aspect of intentional behavior by saying that individuals are rational. As with utility, this term can also be confusing. Ludwig von Mises and his followers used the term very loosely; "rational action" was a redundant phrase, they thought, because all action was based on reason. In this view, someone doing a rain dance is acting rationally because he is using his mind to reason about his situation—a lack of water—and to come up with a proposed solution. It's true that the man chose

---

4. See, for example, Varian, *Microeconomic Analysis*, 94–98. Note that even von Neumann-Morgenstern utility functions take ordinal preference rankings as the starting point of the analysis; John von Neumann and Oskar Morgenstern showed that certain properties of the ordinal preferences are sufficient for pinning down the type of cardinal utility functions that could represent them.

a poor means to achieve the desired end, but that doesn't render his behavior irrational, according to Mises. No, the fact that we are interpreting the man's bodily movements as a rain dance means that we are attributing a plan to the man, and hence we think he is a rational being. To see this distinction, consider that we don't say a falling boulder acts irrationally; rather, we say that a falling boulder doesn't act, period. Thus, for Mises (and his followers), the important boundary line is between action and nonaction, not between successful action and unsuccessful action.

However, many other economists adopt a stronger notion of rationality. They would argue that economic science isn't useful or interesting as a tool for interpreting the world unless economists make the default assumption that people have a *correct* understanding of how the world works and have generally correct expectations about the future. These economists understand, of course, that people in the real world make boneheaded mistakes all the time, but they think a theory allowing for systematic error would be too open-ended to be useful. Therefore, these economists push their models to the limits by assuming rational (in their sense) agents, to see what outcomes pop out and then to compare them with the real world.

Students must be careful, then, to understand exactly what different economists mean by the term *rational* because, for Mises and his followers, it separates action from nonaction and is completely applicable to every human; so long as someone is consciously trying to achieve a goal, he is engaging in action, and this is necessarily rational. In contrast, for other economists, the term *rational* is an assumption that is satisfied by real humans only to varying degrees; a man buying an electric car might not correctly calculate the financial benefit of avoided gasoline purchases and thus would not be behaving totally rationally, according to these other economists. The danger in this latter approach is that it allows the critic of economic science to dismiss the entire enterprise as based on "unrealistic assumptions" about the people acting in an economy. Mises's approach shields him from such an attack. So long as one agrees that people have minds and act to achieve their subjective goals, Mises's results fully apply.

Even though it's important to be aware of the contrast in usage of the term *rational* by different economists, in practice the two approaches to economics can look quite similar. This is because a market based on private property has built-in mechanisms that tend to weed out important decisions based on improper calculations or false expectations about the future.

Summary

Most economists view their field broadly as the study of purposeful behavior, which Ludwig von Mises defined as *action*. When the economist as social scientist invokes the concept of action to interpret her observations of human behavior, this commits her to several things. First, she must believe that other minds are at work. Second, she must think that these minds have unique goals or preferences. Third, these underlying preferences are ordinal, meaning that they are a ranking from better to worse. Economists often use the term *utility* instead of preferences, but it makes no sense to compare one person's utility to another's, let alone to try to add them up for "total" or "social" utility.

Finally, the concept of action implies that the acting individual possesses reason and has a theory about how his action can influence the future. Economists differ in how accurate they assume an acting individual's expectations are, but they all agree on the importance of expectations in modern economics.

3

Economic Theory versus Historical Understanding

Introduction

PROBABLY THE SINGLE biggest objection mainstream economists have with Mises's paradigm is his insistence that economics is an a priori science. This Latin phrase comes from philosophical discussions of how humans come to possess knowledge. If people can know a particular truth a priori, it means that they can grasp it merely by thinking about it;[1] they don't need to look out their window or use their sensory experiences in any way to learn this fact.

Many economists, seeing the success and prestige of physicists and other natural scientists, thought that importing the methods used in physics would make economics more rigorous and scientific. Yet Mises and many of his followers rejected this "scientism," claiming that the social sciences required their own method. Physics, chemistry, and the other natural sciences are not a priori disciplines; scientists in these fields must observe the physical world to discover the "laws" of nature. In contrast, Mises and his followers adopted a completely different approach when it came to discovering the laws or principles of economics because they believed it was an a priori discipline.

The Laws of Economics Are within You

Here is Mises describing the proper procedure of economic science:

---

1. A useful mnemonic device is to say that an a priori truth can be grasped prior to sensory observation.

The scope of praxeology is the explication of the category of human action. All that is needed for the deduction of all praxeological theorems is knowledge of the essence of human action. It is a knowledge that is our own because we are men; no being of human descent that pathological conditions have not reduced to a merely vegetative existence lacks it. No special experience is needed in order to comprehend these theorems, and no experience, however rich, could disclose them to a being who did not know a priori what human action is. The only way to a cognition of these theorems is logical analysis of our inherent knowledge of the category of action. We must bethink ourselves and reflect upon the structure of human action. *Like logic and mathematics, praxeological knowledge is in us; it does not come from without.* (italics added)[2]

Mises believed that the economist should build economic theory upon logical deductions from the starting point of human action. In the preceding chapter, we saw that this concept yielded several implications, such as the existence of ordinal preferences and subjective expectations. Notice the procedure that we followed: It's not that the economist goes into the world and observes, say, a shopper's preferences at the grocery store. Rather, if the economist decides to interpret the bodily movements of the shopper as action, then the fact of the shopper having preferences suddenly becomes a logical implication of the economist's decision. The existence of the shopper's preferences is not the "best hypothesis" that the economist can come up with to explain his observations; rather, the existence of the shopper's preferences is a logical necessity flowing from the decision to classify the observations as exhibiting human action, in Mises's sense of the term.

Mises thought that the entire body of economics was of the same nature as our brief treatment of preferences, expectations, and so forth. Mises argued that economists proceed step by step using logical deduction, not empirical induction, from the initial given fact of human action in order to arrive at the various principles or "laws" of economics. It is, of course, possible that economists could conclude something false using this method, but the way to demonstrate the error would be to go through their chain of reasoning and point out the step in which they made an invalid deduction. Notice that this

2. Mises, *Human Action*, 64.

is utterly different from the typical description of how, say, physicists work, in which they make a conjecture about the laws of nature and then conduct an experiment to see how well the results match the theoretical prediction.

An Analogy with Geometry

As Mises mentions in the block quotation above, mathematics is an example of an a priori subject. To understand what Mises has in mind for the development of economics, an analogy with mathematics will be helpful. More specifically, we will consider geometry and the famous Pythagorean theorem of standard Euclidean geometry. This theorem states that in a right triangle, the square of the hypotenuse is equal to the sum of the squares of the other two sides of the triangle.[3]

In the first place, note the word *theorem* as opposed to *theory*. Mathematicians might describe their work as proving theorems, whereas most physicists wouldn't say that they have ever proven results in their field. No matter how rigorously the results have been tested, and no matter how confident people are that nature will behave in the same way in the future, strictly speaking all knowledge in physics, chemistry, astronomy, and other physical sciences is only tentative; everything in these fields is "just" a theory. In principle, it's *possible* that we will wake up tomorrow and discover that the laws of physics no longer operate as they seemed to have done up until today. For example, astronomers could spot a comet that was apparently moving at three times the speed of light. Such an outcome is impossible according to Einstein's theory of relativity—which is why the astronomers would check their measurements over and over in our fictitious scenario—but maybe Einstein was simply wrong.

In contrast, it's not even clear what it would *mean* to wake up tomorrow and discover that the Pythagorean theorem is false. There's nothing we could observe that would lead us to this view. Obviously, we might find what looks like a triangle violating the theorem, but upon closer inspection, we would realize that the object in front of our eyes was not a right triangle that satisfied the properties of Euclidean geometry. To illustrate the contrast in different

---

3. For example, if the two short sides of a right triangle have lengths 3 and 4, then the length of the side opposite the right angle, called the *hypotenuse*, must be 5, because $3^2 + 4^2 = 5^2$.

words, we can easily imagine a world in which Einstein's theory of relativity is false, but the very structure of our minds makes it impossible to imagine a world in which the Pythagorean theorem is false.

Many critics of Mises's approach are puzzled by the analogy with geometry, so let's be careful to avoid misunderstanding. Mathematicians have developed frameworks of non-Euclidean geometry in which the Pythagorean "theorem" is false. It's also true that scientists currently believe that the physical universe does not conform to Euclidean assumptions: Space is curved, for example, not flat like the *x-y* coordinate plane that students learn as children. Yet none of this changes the fact that the Pythagorean theorem is true; it is a theorem, not a theory. Perhaps one day, teachers will not bother showing it to their students and will instead just focus on theorems proven within non-Euclidean geometry. But that would just mean that Pythagoras' result was no longer useful; it would not have been falsified in the same way that Isaac Newton's work is no longer considered an accurate description of how nature operates.

We have emphasized the difference between results in geometry versus results in physics because once we grasp what type of result the experts in geometry versus physics are proclaiming, we can immediately understand the different methods they use to achieve those results. When a geometry teacher sets out to prove the Pythagorean theorem to her students, she starts with the definitions and other assumptions of Euclidean geometry and then proceeds through logical deduction to reach the statement of the theorem. If a student has grasped the argument, the result is now his forever; no observation could show it to be false. The only thing that would make him change his mind is to demonstrate that actually the teacher had made an invalid move in one or more steps of the proof.

In contrast, if physics professors try to justify the material to their students, they ultimately will appeal to empirical observation, often conducted during a carefully controlled experiment. Indeed, the field of quantum physics contains principles and concepts that defy common sense, but they are considered valid because of precise conformity with experimental observations.

Turning back to economics, Mises's viewpoint—which nowadays is definitely in the minority among professional economists—is that economists operate more like mathematicians than physicists, in the sense that they deduce theorems from the starting point of human action. All the student of economics needs to grasp such demonstrations is an understanding of the concept of action and the patience to follow chains of logical deduction. The economist cannot "prove" economic laws by pointing to historical outcomes or even statistics concerning prices, unemployment, and other items. For Mises, this would be as nonsensical as a geometry teacher telling her class to go out and measure hundreds of right triangles to establish the truth of the Pythagorean theorem. At best, such an activity would illustrate Pythagoras' result, but under no circumstances could a student come back with measurements that would prove the teacher either right or wrong.

Some readers may believe that Mises and his followers[4] spend too much time dwelling on what is philosophy rather than economics, but in Mises's view, it was crucial for economists to understand the proper foundation of their discipline. He did not think he was recommending a *new* approach, but rather he thought he was merely codifying what good economists had been doing for centuries since the birth of their discipline.[5] However, Mises recognized that—especially in the twentieth century—more and more economists were dazzled by the methods of the natural scientists and wanted to take economics in a different direction, thinking they would thereby provide it with a more solid foundation. Mises resisted this trend, fearing that it would obscure and dilute the genuine success of economic science, just as surely as most mathematicians would recoil from attempts to base their discipline on empirical observations of the physical world. Among many of his objections, Mises stressed that there are no constants in the social sciences as there are in the natural sciences; there is nothing in the action of humans analogous to the charge on an electron or the speed of light. Furthermore, there can be no truly controlled experiments in the social sciences, which is yet another problem with trying to use the method of physics in economics.

The analogy with geometry clarifies what it means for a discipline to be a priori. To say that one can learn such knowledge "without experience" doesn't mean, of course, that a human being locked in a closet his whole life

---

4. For a strong statement of the Misesian view in straightforward language, see Murray Rothbard, "In Defense of Extreme Apriorism," *Southern Economic Journal*, 23, no. 3 (1957).

5. On this point, see Hans Hoppe's *Economic Science and the Austrian Method* (Auburn, AL: Ludwig von Mises Institute, 1995), as well as Peter Boettke, *Living Economics: Yesterday, Today, and Tomorrow* (Oakland, CA: The Independent Institute), 210.

would likely stumble upon the Pythagorean theorem on his own. People presumably need the experience of seeing shapes in the world and of hearing a lecturer guide them through various chains of reasoning in order to learn standard results in geometry. By the same token, someone growing up in an isolated tribe that did not use money, would most likely fail to develop explanations of hyperinflation and the business cycle. Only people who have experienced, either directly or indirectly through the testimony of others, the collapse of a currency and the alternation of booms and busts in modern economies would even attempt to explain such phenomena.[6]

Even so, Mises's insight is that the experts in both fields—the mathematician deriving results about triangles and the economist deriving results about money and the business cycle—would not need empirical observations in the course of their explanation. The intelligent observer could either endorse or reject their demonstrations purely by thinking them through; there would be nothing to go out and "test."

Economic Theory versus Economic History

Today's mainstream economists who are tempted to recoil from Mises's insistence on the a priori nature of economics should take pause. If these economists were to write out what it means to "think like an economist," they would probably list insights such as "There's no such thing as a free lunch," "People make decisions on the margin," and "Trade is a positive-sum game." These are standard elements in the economist's toolbox, and it is crucial for economists to transmit such knowledge to the general public, particularly if government officials are proposing new legislation based on fallacies that ignore these insights. Yet notice that these insights are *not* ones that we can establish through empirical observation; they are logical implications of "thinking like an economist." Thus, whether they realize it or not, even today's mainstream economists rely on a body of knowledge that is derived a priori by thinking through the implications of certain concepts. It's true that these insights might be motivated or illustrated through the use of statistics or poignant case stud-

---

6. For a very readable yet scholarly treatment of the a priori and its use in Austrian economics, see David Gordon, "The Philosophical Origins of Austrian Economics," monograph (Auburn, AL: Ludwig von Mises Institute, 1996).

ies, but strictly speaking, much of what even mainstream economists believe, they learned through introspection and "thought experiments," rather than study of empirical data.

Sometimes those unfamiliar with Mises's body of work, take him to be rejecting empirical studies altogether. They castigate him as an antiquated, unscientific doctrinaire, unwilling to let "the real world" interfere with his writings.

Such criticisms miss the mark. In the first place, Mises acknowledges that even the development of pure economic theory must be guided by what is *relevant* to actual human beings. In his words:

> [T]he end of science is to know reality. It is not mental gymnastics or logical pastime. Therefore praxeology restricts its inquiries to the study of acting under those conditions and presuppositions which are given in reality…
>
> However, this reference to experience does not impair the aprioristic character of praxeology and economics. *Experience merely directs our curiosity toward certain problems and diverts it from other problems.* It tells us what we should explore, but it does not tell us how we could proceed in our search for knowledge. (italics added)[7]

For a specific illustration of how experience can guide a priori reasoning, Mises gives the example of what economists call the *disutility of labor*:

> The disutility of labor is not of a categorial and aprioristic character. We can without contradiction think of a world in which labor does not cause uneasiness, and we can depict the state of affairs prevailing in such a world. But the real world is conditioned by the disutility of labor. Only theorems based on the assumption that labor is a source of uneasiness are applicable for the comprehension of what is going on in this world.[8]

In Mises's view, therefore, economists should be guided by empirical observation when deciding on the topics to pursue in their research, but their

---

7. Mises, *Human Action*, 65.
8. Mises, *Human Action*, 65.

work itself would consist of logical deductions, starting not just from the concept of action, but also supplemented with auxiliary assumptions such as the disutility of labor, the existence of money, and so on. Clearly, Mises was not arguing that economists must lock themselves in a closet, and spin out treatises on economics without ever looking out the window.

It is particularly ironic that some critics accuse Mises of ignoring historical experience, since he and his most famous disciple, Nobel laureate Fredrich Hayek, founded the Austrian Institute for Business Cycle Research in 1927.[9] It should be clear, then, that neither Mises nor his followers rejected historical research or empirical investigation as such; indeed Murray Rothbard, a staunch defender of a priori economics, devoted his doctoral dissertation to the Panic of 1819 and later wrote a book on the Great Depression.[10]

Today's economists might be more sympathetic to Mises's seemingly quaint position if they understood the historical origins of the Austrian School. When Carl Menger engaged in his famous "dispute over method" (*Methodenstreit*) with members of the German Historical School, they were ultimately arguing over whether there could be such a thing as economic law at all. The members of the German Historical School argued that the rules or principles applicable to the German economy of the 1800s might be inapplicable, say, to the economy of Rome under Caesar Augustus. But if the economist had to act as an historian before knowing what principles would work for a particular time and culture, this would be tantamount to denying the existence of a science of economics.[11]

Mises wrote an entire book[12] on the complex relationship between the field of the economic theorist and that of the historian, but the following quotation from *Human Action* provides an excellent summary of his perspective:

---

9. See Murray Rothbard, *Making Economic Sense* (Auburn, AL: Ludwig von Mises Institute, 1995), Chapter 108.

10. See Murray Rothbard, *The Panic of 1819: Reactions and Policies* (New York: Columbia University Press, 1962) and *America's Great Depression*, 5th ed. (Auburn, AL: Ludwig von Mises Institute, 2000).

11. The text above summarizes Mises's commentary on the *Methodenstreit* in his *The Historical Setting of the Austrian School of Economics* (Auburn, AL: Ludwig von Mises Institute, [1969] 2003).

12. See Ludwig von Mises, *Theory and History* (Auburn, AL: Ludwig von Mises Institute, [1957] 2000).

The domain of historical understanding is exclusively the elucidation of those problems which cannot be entirely elucidated by the nonhistorical sciences. [The historian's understanding] must never contradict the theories developed by the nonhistorical sciences. [Historical understanding] can never do anything but . . . establish the fact that people were motivated by certain ideas, aimed at certain ends, and applied certain means for the attainment of these ends, and . . . assign to the various historical factors their relevance . . . . Understanding does not entitle the modern historian to assert that exorcism ever was an appropriate means to cure sick cows. Neither does it permit him to maintain that an economic law was not valid in ancient Rome or in the empire of the Incas.[13]

As this quotation suggests, Mises was carrying the torch of Menger in defending the legitimacy of economics as a valid science, with its own laws that were valid in all places and at all times, against certain critics who said that the free-market principles that seemed to operate in modern democratic societies might be completely inapplicable in a different social and cultural setting. Seen in the context of such critics, Mises's insistence on the a priori foundation of economic science is more understandable.

"Subjective Value Theory" Is an Objective Theorem in Misesian Economics

As our discussion has shown, Ludwig von Mises was very concerned with building a seat for economics at the table of scientific inquiry. Economics was its own discipline, with its own laws or principles, and economists had discovered a type of knowledge that lay outside the scope of older sciences, he argued. If government officials tried to enact policies in defiance of economic law, they would fail just as surely as if NASA engineers tried to design a rocket that ignored the laws of physics.

The knowledge produced by economic science is therefore *objectively* true, in the same way that the discoveries in physics and chemistry do not depend on the subjective whims of the particular physicists and chemists involved. There

---

13. Mises, *Human Action*, 68.

is just one body of physical law; Russian, American, and Brazilian physicists all work in the same field. By the same token, there is just one body of economic law, regardless of the identities of the economists who add to it.

These remarks may seem obvious to some readers, but it is important to avoid confusion since one of the major achievements of modern economics is termed *subjective value theory*. Yet the word *subjective* in this description refers to the fact that economists now explain market prices not on the objective features of a commodity, such as how many hours were used in building it, but rather on the subjective perspective with which consumers in the market perceive the commodity. Thus, subjective value theory is not itself subjective; it is an objective, scientific result in modern economics.

As a final clarification, the word *theory* in subjective value theory can also be misleading because in Mises's framework, the subjectivist approach to market prices is a theorem. People use the term subjective value theory partly to distinguish the modern approach from the classical labor or cost theory of value,[14] but the reader should not think that there is anything tentative or falsifiable in the modern subjective value theory. It is simply a more logically coherent framework with which to explain the emergence of prices from the purposeful behavior of individuals in the market—and this explanation will unfold during the course of this book. Yet as with other parts of economics, there is no experiment or observation that would ever refute subjective value theory; at the most, economists in the future may abandon it in favor of a more useful framework.

---

14. For a readable discussion of the problems with the labor (or cost) theory of value, and the superiority of the modern subjectivist theory, see Robert P. Murphy, "The Labor Theory of Value: A Critique of Carson's *Studies in Mutualist Political Economy*," *Journal of Libertarian Studies*, 20, no. 1 (Winter 2006): 17–33.

4

Further Economic Concepts and Principles Flowing from Action

Introduction

MISES ORGANIZES HIS grand treatise, *Human Action*, so that Part One covers the economic concepts and principles that are applicable in all situations, wherever action—in Mises's sense of "purposeful behavior"—is present. As the book progresses, Mises narrows the focus of his study, deriving results that are applicable only in certain settings.

Following Mises's plan, this chapter describes some of the most important concepts and principles that are applicable to action as such rather than to narrower fields such as "action occurring in a society using private property and money." The results discussed in this chapter apply to any person, in any social setting, so long as he or she uses reason to adopt means to achieve a desired purpose.

Classifying Goods

Following the revolution of the 1870s, economic concepts are defined with respect to the subjective framework of the individual actor and the goals he or she is trying to achieve. Keep this in mind as we walk through Mises's definitions of key concepts:

> Economic goods which in themselves are fitted to satisfy human wants directly and whose serviceableness does not depend on the cooperation of other economic goods, are called consumers' goods or goods of the first order. Means which can satisfy wants only indirectly when

complemented by cooperation of other goods are called producers' goods or factors of production or goods of a remoter or higher order. The services rendered by a producers' good consist in bringing about, by the cooperation of complementary producers' goods, a product. This product may be a consumers' good; it may be a producers' good which when combined with other producers' goods will finally bring about a consumers' good. It is possible to think of the producers' goods as arranged in orders according to their proximity to the consumers' good for whose production they can be used. Those producers' goods which are nearest to the production of a consumers' good are ranged in the second order, and accordingly those which are used for the production of goods of the second order in the third order and so on.

• • •

An economic good does not necessarily have to be embodied in a tangible thing. Nonmaterial economic goods are called services.[1]

We can illustrate Mises's definitions in a Robinson Crusoe framework.[2] When Crusoe finds himself on what he believes to be a deserted island, he realizes that he will soon be hungry. He spots some coconuts hanging from various trees. Given Crusoe's understanding of the material world and his expectation that coconuts will alleviate hunger, Crusoe classifies the coconuts as consumer goods, or first-order goods. Crusoe might use his raw labor power to climb trees and begin acquiring these consumer goods.

He might, however, devise an even better plan. Crusoe could use his raw labor power to break off a long and sturdy branch from a tree and then use it as a tool to knock down coconuts. In this case, the branch would not directly provide satisfaction to Crusoe; he can't eat the wood to satisfy his hunger. Yet the branch is still an economic good; Crusoe finds it valuable. This is because once he has acquired it, Crusoe can use the branch as a means to

---

1. Mises, *Human Action*, 93–94.

2. Much of the discussion in the rest of this chapter is based on the treatment of "'Robinson Crusoe' Economics" in Chapter 4 of Robert P. Murphy's *Lessons for the Young Economist* (Auburn, AL: Ludwig von Mises Institute, 2010). Crusoe, of course, is the character in Daniel Defoe's novel, though modern readers may be more familiar with Tom Hanks's character facing a similar plight in the film, *Cast Away*.

obtain the consumer good: a coconut. Thus the branch in this example would be a producer good, or a factor of production, and would be classified as a second-order good.

Pushing the story one step further, suppose Crusoe realizes that he is not strong enough to break off the kind of sturdy branch that would be best suited for knocking down coconuts. He sees a heavy rock with a sharp point; it will fit into the palm of his hand. Crusoe now attributes subjective value to the rock as well, classifying it as a good in his mind because he expects to use the rock to chip away at a sturdy branch and remove it from its tree. Thus the rock in this example is a third-order good since it aids Crusoe's raw labor power in yielding a second-order good, a sturdy branch, which in turn will augment his raw labor power in obtaining a first-order good, a coconut.

Notice that the explanation flows from the subjective desire—to alleviate hunger—to the consumer good that will directly achieve the goal, then back to the producer good that will help achieve the consumer good, and so forth. Through it all, the relevant criterion for classification is how the individual mentally incorporates the physical items in his or her subjective framework. Nothing intrinsic to branches makes them second-order goods. If someone else came along who wanted to use a branch to scratch an itch on her back, then the same physical branch would be a first-order or consumer good in her mind.

Within the class of producer goods, also called factors or means of production, economists make further distinctions. Producer goods that are the direct gifts of nature were historically called *land*, but a more accurate term is *natural resources*. In Crusoe's world, his natural resources would include somewhat permanent items such as a flowing stream or a tree that will yield an indefinite flow of coconuts, but the category would also include depletable resources such as a small deposit of tin that Crusoe can use to make cooking pans and fish hooks.

The single most important and versatile producer good is labor, which is the flow of productive services the individual performs with his or her body. In terms of the logic of economic principles, it would be perfectly sensible to group labor along with other natural resources that provide a durable flow of services with adequate maintenance. However, economists have historically accorded labor special treatment because labor is the one factor of production that every individual possesses and also because labor is the one producer good that is required for every production process. When Crusoe devotes his physical efforts toward the indirect satisfaction of goals, he is engaged in labor. On the other hand, if he achieves direct satisfaction of goals through use of his body, then economists call this *leisure*. Crusoe will allocate his body power among labor and leisure activities according to what he sees as most important. Historically, economists have referred to the *disutility of labor* to underscore the fact that individuals directly enjoy leisure and will only devote some of their scarce time to labor if it allows the indirect achievement of more important ends than the leisure being sacrificed.

We should note that leisure doesn't necessarily imply lounging around on the beach, and labor (or work) doesn't necessarily imply physical exertion. Crusoe might love swimming in the ocean, which provides a good workout and can even leave his muscles sore the next day. But before he can enjoy himself in this activity, he first engages in the extremely boring—but physically undemanding—task of gathering small twigs for the night's fire.

Finally, capital goods are those factors of production that are created by people, as opposed to being direct gifts from nature. Every capital good is produced from the combination of labor and at least one natural resource. Most capital goods are also produced with the help of pre-existing capital goods. For Crusoe on his island, examples of capital goods would be a fishing net that he constructs out of vines and his labor and a shelter that he creates out of rocks, branches, mud, leaves, and his labor.

Action as an Exchange

We usually think of an exchange as something that occurs between at least two people, but in the widest sense of the term, it refers to all action, as Mises explains:

> Action is an attempt to substitute a more satisfactory state of affairs for a less satisfactory one. We call such a willfully induced alteration an exchange. A less desirable condition is bartered for a more desirable. What gratifies less is abandoned in order to attain something that pleases more. *That which is abandoned is called the price paid* for

the attainment of the end sought. *The value of the price paid is called costs.* Costs are equal to the value attached to the satisfaction which one must forego in order to attain the end aimed at.

The difference between the value of the price paid (the costs incurred) and that of the goal attained is called gain or profit or net yield. Profit in this primary sense is purely subjective, it is an increase in the acting man's happiness, it is a psychical phenomenon that can be neither measured nor weighed. (italics added)[3]

Once again, we can illustrate these new concepts with our imaginary Crusoe. Suppose he decides to devote one hour of his time to obtain a particularly long and sturdy branch with the use of his sharp rock. If no such rock were available, Crusoe would have spent his hour collecting twigs for a fire he planned on making later that evening. Therefore, the end that Crusoe achieved was the sturdy branch.[4] The price paid for this end was the collection of twigs that he could have had, but now doesn't, because he decided to use his time to obtain the branch. The cost of his decision is not something tangible; it is instead the subjective or psychic value that Crusoe would have attributed to the collection of twigs, had he obtained them. Notice that cost exists even for Crusoe, alone on his island without any semblance of money, and further notice that the cost of his action was not something that is subtracted from Crusoe in an absolute sense. Rather, the cost of his decision refers to the value he places on the next best alternative. To stress this aspect of the situation—that true costs are not merely the amount of money involved with a decision—economists often use the term *opportunity cost*.

The gain or profit from Crusoe's choice—to use his time obtaining the branch rather than collecting twigs—is itself subjective because it's the higher value Crusoe attributes to the sturdy branch than to the twigs. As with cost, profit is subjective in the context of action; only when we introduce further assumptions of a market economy with money does the accountant's notion of these terms have any meaning. In addition, Mises argues that such concepts as

---

3. Mises, *Human Action*, 97.

4. Although Mises doesn't use the term in the quotation above, we can define the subjective value of the end achieved as the benefits of the choice, to serve as a foil to the costs.

income and *savings* or *investment* serve as guides to action only in the context
of a market economy with money.[5]

Time and Uncertainty

Later in the book, we will see that Mises places great importance on what is
called *time preference* in his explanation of interest rates in a market economy.
At this stage, however, he merely stresses that the very concept of action implies a structure of time—with the boundaries of past, present, and future—as
well as the notion of cause and effect. In his words:

> The notion of change implies the notion of temporal sequence. A rigid,
> eternally immutable universe would be out of time, but it would be
> dead. The concepts of change and of time are inseparably linked to-
> gether. Action aims at change and is therefore in the temporal order.
> Human reason is even incapable of conceiving the ideas of timeless
> existence and of timeless action.

• • •

> It is acting that provides man with the notion of time and makes him
> aware of the flux of time. The idea of time is a praxeological category.
>
> Action is always directed toward the future; it is essentially and
> necessarily always a planning and acting for a better future. Its aim is
> always to render future conditions more satisfactory than they would
> be without the interference of action. The uneasiness that impels a man
> to act is caused by a dissatisfaction with expected future conditions as
> they would probably develop if nothing were done to alter them. In
> any case action can influence only the future, never the present ... [6]

In a similar way, Mises argues that the "uncertainty of the future is already
implied in the very notion of action."[7] After all, if "man knew the future,
he would not have to choose and would not act." The argument resembles a
philosophical riddle or paradox: If someone knew the future with certainty,

---

5. Mises, *Human Action*, 211–12.

6. Mises, *Human Action*, 99–100.

7. Mises, *Human Action*, 105.

then it would be impossible to take action that would avert this outcome. What we mean by action is thus only comprehensible in a framework in which the individual actor has expectations about what the future might hold unless the individual takes measures to yield a different future.

As Mises makes clear in his discussion, he is fully aware that results in physics challenge the everyday notions of causality and time and that many philosophers deny the existence of free will. Mises is not threatened by such claims because they have no bearing on his own position with regard to economics. Suppose two astronauts moving in different inertial frames may not agree on the chronological order of events happening outside of their ships. If we as economists are going to interpret a given astronaut's behavior as action, however, we must attribute a mental framework of present versus future to the astronaut. Further, even if we believe that the astronaut's bodily movements can be explained by the mechanistic movement of atoms in his nervous system, according to the blind laws of physics, nonetheless if we perceive action then we necessarily perceive a will, a set of desires or goals, motivating the astronaut. To repudiate Misesian economics, experts in other disciplines would need to deny the existence of human action itself. Seeing how much is at stake, the reader can now appreciate why Mises chose this phrase as the title of his grand work and why he spends so much time on apparently philosophical issues rather than jumping right into the more conventional economic topics.

The Law of (Diminishing) Marginal Utility

Mises defines *utility* as "causal relevance for the removal of felt uneasiness," and says the term is "tantamount to importance attached to a thing on account of the belief that it can remove uneasiness."[8] The key insight of the marginal revolution of the 1870s was that individuals act not merely on the basis of utility, but according to marginal utility.

To say that an individual values goods and services on the margin means that he or she makes decisions based on the particular units involved, rather than the entire supplies of the goods. This approach allows the economist to explain everyday consumer behavior. For example, suppose a man has $20 in

---

8. Mises, *Human Action*, 120.

his wallet and sees bottles of water priced at $1 each. Further suppose the man places three bottles into his shopping cart. Using the law of marginal utility, we can easily explain these observations: The man valued the *first* bottle of water more than the twentieth dollar, he valued the *second* bottle more than the nineteenth dollar, and he valued the *third* bottle of water more than the eighteenth dollar. Yet he didn't value the *fourth* bottle of water more than the seventeenth dollar, and that's why he pushed his cart away.

As simple as this explanation is, notice that it depends on the concept of marginal utility. If we merely relied on generic statements such as, "The man liked bottled water more than money," or, "The man thought $1 was a reasonable price for a bottle of water," we would not be able to explain why he stopped putting water bottles into his shopping cart—after all, if he thought it made sense to spend $1 on a bottle of water, why wouldn't he spend every last penny buying as many bottles as he could afford?

Historically, the marginal revolution of the 1870s solved what was called the *water-diamond paradox.*[9] Classical economists such as Adam Smith understood that there was a connection between the value placed on goods and their ability to satisfy human desires, but there was a stumbling block in the explanation: Certain goods had a higher value than other goods, even though they weren't nearly as important for human welfare. After all, without water people will die, but we can certainly get along without diamonds.

The focus on marginal utility solved this conundrum. Nobody is ever in the position of choosing between all of the diamonds versus all of the water; if someone were, he or she would presumably value the water more highly than the diamonds. In practice, people are always choosing between a particular amount of diamonds versus a particular amount of water, given the amounts of both that they already possess, and whether the goals that can be achieved with the additional diamonds are more important than the goals that can be achieved with the additional water. This is why people usually value comparable amounts of diamonds more than water and why the market price of diamonds is far higher than for water.

When discussing marginal utility, we need a clear idea of what it means for there to be successive units of "the same" good—what Mises calls *homo-*

---

9. We discuss this historical issue in greater detail in the Introduction to this book.

geneous units of a good. Here, too, the individual's subjective framework is decisive. Various physical objects count as units of "the same" good if they are interchangeable from the individual's point of view, in light of the various goals or preferences the individual has in mind for the objects. For example, a chemist could weigh two different bottles of water and conclude that one had 8.01 ounces of liquid, whereas the other had 7.99 ounces. Yet the thirsty consumer might view the two physical objects as interchangeable; there would thus be "two units of bottled water" even though they weren't literally "the same thing." In contrast, a bottle of 8.01 ounces of soda would probably not constitute part of the supply of bottled water, since water can satisfy certain preferences or goals that soda cannot, and vice versa.

Yet even though consumers might view the 8.01 oz. and the 7.99 oz. bottles of water as interchangeable—meaning both are "units of bottled water"—they do not attach the same importance to successive bottles. In other words, even though subjective preferences define what it means for physical objects to be considered as successive units of a good, nonetheless, consumers subjectively value successive units of a good differently. Specifically, they consider the goal that a unit of the good will satisfy when there are n units available, but which will not be satisfied if there are only $n-1$ units. This is the marginal goal, or *marginal employment*, in Mises's terminology. The utility of the least urgent use to which the good is being deployed is the marginal utility. Because consumers will always use the available quantity of a good to satisfy the most important goals or preferences, the importance of the goals satisfied with successive units of a good will necessarily decrease. This phenomenon is called the *law of diminishing marginal utility*.

A simple example will illustrate. Suppose Fred is on a camping trip, and he has three sport bottles that he filled with tap water before leaving his house. The bottles happen to be in different colors—red, orange, and yellow. However, for Fred's purposes, the bottles are interchangeable, as each contains roughly the same quantity of tap water; on this trip, Fred doesn't care about the color.

Fred plans on drinking the red bottle right away, keeping the orange bottle in case he gets thirsty at night, and giving the yellow bottle to his dog. He empties it into the dog bowl on the ground.

Unfortunately, just as Fred is about to take a swig from the red bottle, his dog bounds over and accidentally overturns the bowl, spilling the water onto the forest floor. His dog looks up with pleading eyes. Now that his available supply of water has been reduced to two bottles, Fred must reevaluate his plans. The fact that it was the yellow bottle that was lost is irrelevant; the question is, how should Fred deploy his two bottles? Fred decides that of the three original uses, having water to drink in the night is the least important. Therefore, Fred takes the orange bottle out from his backpack, moves the bowl to a patch of the ground that is more level, and refills the dog bowl—this time making sure his dog doesn't knock it over.

In this story, the marginal utility of the third bottle of water was the importance that Fred attached to the least important use—namely, having water available at night to alleviate his thirst. Since the bottles of water were interchangeable in Fred's mind, the yellow bottle was no more important or valuable than the orange bottle. When the contents of the yellow bottle were lost, Fred simply redeployed the orange bottle from its original task. Therefore, the marginal utility of the third bottle of water was the importance that Fred attributed to quenching his thirst in the night.

We can take the camping story in the other direction, as well. Suppose that Fred suddenly recalls that he had packed two more water bottles—which happened to have the colors green and blue—in another bag. Now, assuming Fred hasn't changed his opinion about the usefulness of water, we know that he will devote one of the new bottles to the task of relieving his thirst at night. Then he will have a fourth bottle of water to devote to some other use. Perhaps he will give an extra drink to his dog, perhaps he will save it for the next morning, or perhaps he will drink it on the spot. Yet whatever Fred does with it, we know that the task will be less important in Fred's mind than the original three uses. For example, if Fred decides to rinse his face and hands with the water, it can't be the case that Fred considers this more important than, say, giving his dog a drink. That's because he originally had the option of using one bottle of water to rinse himself and yet chose to give his dog a drink instead.[10]

---

10. Strictly speaking, the law of diminishing marginal utility is only applicable at one moment of action. In our story, Fred is making separate decisions at separate points in time, when his circumstances have actually changed. Indeed, if Fred's hands got dirty while picking up the dog bowl and moving it, it might be perfectly sensible for him to consider rinsing them with water to be more important than he originally thought. Such complications aside,

Even though we have illustrated the law of diminishing marginal utility with a contrived story, the reader can appreciate its general validity. Note that this economic law is based not on empirical observation but on the logical consequences of action in a setting of multiple units equally suitable for a wide range of purposes. Thus the law itself is derived through a priori reasoning, but it is nonetheless useful in interpreting events that we perceive with our senses.

As a final point, Mises notes that there are scenarios in which a minimum amount of a good is necessary to achieve a specific goal. For example, if someone has one, two, or three car tires, perhaps he or she will use them to make tire swings for three children in the back yard. Yet acquiring a fourth tire raises the possibility of using the tires to make a car operational. In cases like this, an analyst might argue that the marginal utility of the fourth tire is higher than that of the first through third tires—apparently violating the law of diminishing marginal utility.

Mises, however, says that such examples are confused because they construe marginal utility as being "about things." In reality, such examples pose no problem for "the rightly formulated law of marginal utility according to which value depends on the utility of the services expected."[11]

Murray Rothbard, one of Mises's most prolific disciples, elaborated on this resolution of the (apparent) problem. Rothbard posited the case of a man who needed four eggs to bake a cake, another situation in which the marginal utility of a good might appear to increase as the quantity increased from three to four units. But Rothbard explained that even though the four eggs might appear physically to be homogeneous units of the same good, in economic terms, they were not because the fourth egg allowed for the satisfaction of ends that were not attainable with the first three eggs. Therefore, Rothbard argued, the proper way to handle the situation was to count the relevant unit of choice as four eggs, to which the law of diminishing marginal utility applied straightforwardly.[12] In other words, the man would devote the first unit of eggs to making a cake, while perhaps the second unit would be devoted to

---

the purpose of the camping story is to imperfectly illustrate the rule that as the available supply of a good increases, the marginal utility of the good decreases.

11. Mises, *Human Action*, 125.

12. Murray Rothbard, *Man, Economy, and State* (Auburn, AL: Ludwig von Mises Institute, [1962] 2009), 73–74.

making an omelet, and yet a third unit of eggs might be devoted to making a second cake. Here, successive units of four eggs would clearly be devoted to goals of diminishing importance.

The Law of (Diminishing) Returns

When an individual combines varying amounts of two different factors of production—call them *a* units of factor *A* and *b* units of factor *B*—the quantity of output that they produce will also vary—call them *g* units of the consumer good *G*. The *law of diminishing returns* says that if we hold the amount of *A* fixed, then by varying the amount of factor *B* there is a maximum value of *g/b*, in other words, there is an upper limit to how much of the output good we can produce per unit of factor *B*. Consequently, if we hold the amount of *A* fixed and keep adding more units of *B*, eventually we will reach the point of diminishing returns, where output may still increase with additional units of *B*, but not in proportion. According to Mises, the law of diminishing returns is not an empirical regularity but rather a fact that flows from our classification of *A* and *B* as scarce economic goods.[13] It takes empirical observation to determine where diminishing returns applies for a particular production process, but Mises argues that the existence of such a point is something we can deduce logically.

A simple numerical example will illustrate the law of diminishing returns. Consider Table 4.1 (on the facing page) which depicts the number of dishes that can be washed per hour at a cafeteria with one industrial strength dishwashing machine and a variable number of workers.

As Table 4.1 indicates, the maximum number of dishes washed per worker occurs when three workers are using the machine; with any other number of workers, the ratio of dishes washed (per hour) per worker is lower than 210. In

---

13. In terms of our symbols, Mises is arguing that if the ratio of output goods to an input *B* could be made arbitrarily high—so that *g/b* could rise to infinity—then *B* must not be a scarce economic good. Mises gives an example of a formula; once we know the formula, we can make as much of a new substance as we want, without the formula running out. Yet this is why we don't classify a formula itself as a scarce economic good, the way we would classify gasoline or labor hours.

Table 4.1. Dishes Washed (Per Hour) at Cafeteria with Industrial Strength Dishwashing Machine and Variable Number of Workers

Number of Workers	Dishes Washed per Hour	Dishes per Worker
0	0	N/A
1	100	100
2	300	150
3	630	210
4	820	205
5	1,000	200
6	1,110	185
7	1,190	170
8	1,240	155
9	1,260	140
10	1,200	120

somewhat misleading language, the manufacturer might say that the machine "runs optimally" with three workers.

However, with this information alone, we can't be sure that the manager of the cafeteria will employ three workers to operate the machine. For example, on slow shifts when the cafeteria isn't very busy, perhaps the customers of the cafeteria won't use more than 200 dishes per hour. In this case, it would be wasteful to hire more than two workers for the shift.

On the other hand, for particularly busy shifts, the manager might schedule up to nine workers for dish duty, even though this has far surpassed the point of diminishing returns. Notice that even though the dishes per worker drops after the third worker, the total number of dishes washed per hour still rises with each worker—up through the ninth worker. If it's important for the dish room to keep up with the customers in order to ensure clean plates for people entering the cafeteria, then it might be perfectly sensible for the manager to schedule up to nine workers. We can be sure, however, that the manager will not schedule a tenth worker, because his presence would actually reduce the number of dishes washed per hour.

Before leaving this discussion, we should make one final point. Even in the case where the manager frequently wants the crew to clean 1,260 dishes per hour, we can't be sure that he or she will settle for the combination of one dishwashing machine and nine workers. If space in the cafeteria permits, the owner might perform some calculations and decide that it makes sense to install a second machine, operating side-by-side with the first one. If the output per worker is the same for *each* machine as indicated in Table 4.1, then the new operation could wash 1,260 dishes per hour using only six workers total—three for each machine. By adding a second machine, the owner allows the manager to use the machines more efficiently in the sense of increasing the output per worker and thereby reducing the number of workers necessary to achieve the same physical output. In a sense, the owner has replaced three workers with an additional machine, without sacrificing physical output.

Whether this decision makes economic sense for the owner is a complex issue that would depend on obvious factors such as the level of workers' wages compared to the price of the machine, the higher electricity bill and maintenance expenses on the machine, and the lifespan of the machine; it would also depend on how much interest the bank charged, how often the machines broke down, and how long it took to get them up and running when they did. The important point for our purposes is not to determine the exact conditions under which the owner would install a second machine but merely to illustrate that such conditions exist. Even though it might make sense to employ additional units of an input after the point of its diminishing returns, there is still a natural tendency to alter the quantity of other inputs and move back to the point of maximized physical output per unit of input.

PART II

Action within the Framework of Society

5

Human Society and the Division of Labor

Introduction

IN PART ONE of his treatise, Mises lays out the scope of the scientific study of human action—*praxeology* as he calls it—and deduces some of the key implications flowing from action as such. Then, in Part Two, Mises turns his attention to the relations among many individuals who are engaged in action.

In Mises's view, human society is ultimately founded on two key facts: the higher productivity of the division of labor and humans' ability to perceive this situation with their reason. Without either of those conditions, Mises argues that there would be no basis for social cooperation, meaning society as we know it would crumble. The reader should therefore understand the attention Mises bestows upon these two key conditions, a treatment that we follow here.

Human Society

Human society is widespread cooperation. Within society, individuals still act according to all of the principles that hold for Robinson Crusoe, alone on his island. Yet when many acting individuals come together in cooperation, there is a new dimension: Rather than treating the external world as a mindless environment that blindly obeys mechanistic laws—the way that Robinson Crusoe can make exchanges with nature—people form social bonds when they treat each other as rational beings with their own subjective goals. In short, individuals form a society when they recognize that others act.

The recognition of other, acting individuals opens up a whole new dimension of exchange—now used in the everyday sense of the word—in which one person does something distasteful that another person enjoys in the expectation that a reciprocal action will justify the first one. For example, Bill may help his neighbor Jonas build a barn in the expectation that next month Jonas will help Bill with his barn. When an individual exchanges with another, willful being, it is different from a mere exchange with nature because the willful being might renege on the implied promise. Moreover, to foster social bonds, institutional requirements and patterns of behavior must be obeyed. This is why human society carries with it the complex but essential issues of law, justice, property rights, and morality, whereas none of these topics would matter for Robinson Crusoe. Of course, even Robinson Crusoe has to obey laws of a certain kind in order to achieve his goals; perhaps he must cook his fish, for example, to avoid becoming sick. Yet there is a much greater restriction on the actions of a man living in society, who must pay for the fish he takes from the grocery store to avoid disrupting the incredible bounty of fish and other food that social cooperation makes possible.

There is a sense in which society comes before the individual; each individual is born into a pre-existing society, and everything we know, we have learned as we grew up in a world that was largely created independently from our existence. However, it would be a mistake to conclude that society is somehow more fundamental than the individual. Society is "nothing but the combination of individuals for cooperative effort," according to Mises, and it "exists nowhere else than in the actions of individual men."[1]

We can sometimes use shorthand and speak of society acting in a certain way—"Our society is sick! Have you turned on a TV lately?"—but this is merely a metaphor, and one that can easily be abused. In reality, only individuals act. It is true that individuals may act differently when they are in a crowd, but even if we say, "An angry mob executed a man in an act of vigilante justice," what we mean is that certain individuals consciously chose to grab a man and kill him, while other individuals nearby consciously chose to applaud their choices.

---

1. Mises, *Human Action*, 143.

Mises was quite explicit when stating his understanding of the foundation of social cooperation, and hence of human society itself. It is not an innate, biological sense of camaraderie; on the contrary, Mises thought it was something far more pragmatic:

> Within the frame of social cooperation there can emerge between members of society feelings of sympathy and friendship and a sense of belonging together. These feelings are the source of man's most delightful and most sublime experiences. They are the most precious adornment of life; they lift the animal species man to the heights of a really human existence. However, they are not, as some have asserted, the agents that have brought about social relationships. They are fruits of social cooperation, they thrive only within its frame; they did not precede the establishment of social relations and are not the seed from which they spring.
>
> *The fundamental facts that brought about cooperation, society, and civilization and transformed the animal man into a human being are the facts that work performed under the division of labor is more productive than isolated work and that man's reason is capable of recognizing this truth.* But for these facts men would have forever remained deadly foes of one another, irreconcilable rivals in their endeavors to secure a portion of the scarce supply of means of sustenance provided by nature. Each man would have been forced to view all other men as his enemies; his craving for the satisfaction of his own appetites would have brought him into an implacable conflict with all his neighbors. No sympathy could possibly develop under such a state of affairs. (italics added)[2]

The above quotation from Mises is instructive for two reasons. First, it demonstrates that Mises is fully aware of the power of friendship and other feelings of sympathy that humans feel for each other; indeed Mises describes them as "the most precious adornment of life." So Mises is clearly not some heartless robot, oblivious to the motivations of everyday people.

---

2. Mises, *Human Action*, 144.

Yet even though he recognizes and cherishes this dimension of human existence, he asserts that it cannot provide the basis for society. The widespread reading of Charles Dickens's stories would not be enough. Instead, Mises argues that society was originally founded upon the two conditions that (a) humans are more physically productive when they act in concert with each other, and that (b) they were able to perceive and understand this crucial fact.

Many people recoil from these types of statements, thinking that Mises's perspective somehow jeopardizes genuine sympathy and altruism. "After all," such critics might say, "if social bonds are really based on self-interest, then ultimately you are endorsing people's selfish actions. You're not giving them any higher reason to treat others with respect and dignity, except claims of mere expediency." Yet Mises could turn such an objection on its head. If it weren't the case that social cooperation led—at least in the long run and in most cases—to benefits for virtually all participants, then what hope could there be to uphold society? If the danger is that people have a natural temptation for selfish action that harms others, what better device could we use to restrain them than to point out that the advantages of conforming to the rules of life within society outweigh the disadvantages?

We can illustrate one dimension of Mises's viewpoint with an evolutionary argument. Humans seem to have innate feelings of sympathy for their fellow man and woman. These are very healthy and evolutionarily fit traits to possess, in the context of human society resting on the superior productivity of the division of labor. If one culture respected and fostered these feelings among its members while another culture ridiculed them and praised ruthlessness, the former culture would be more successful, other things being equal. This may be what Mises had in mind when he said that feelings of sympathy are the fruit of social cooperation, not its seed. On the other hand, if it were not the case that humans acting in cooperation were more productive than humans acting in isolation, these feelings of sympathy would be detrimental. A culture that praised cooperation and selfless heroism would be at a disadvantage to a culture that encouraged the exploitation of the weak.

We have walked through this evolutionary argument—even though it is not one that Mises himself directly makes in *Human Action*—to show the baselessness of what is called *social Darwinism*. This view took the results of biology and applied them in a perverse fashion to human social relationships, claiming that the strong must dominate the weak for the good of the species. Those preaching social Darwinism thought that they had the courage to reject conventional morality in light of the teachings of science, yet Mises pointed out that they were ignoring the lessons of economic science:

> The theory of evolution as expounded by Darwin, says a school of social Darwinism, has clearly demonstrated that in nature there are no such things as peace and respect for the lives and welfare of others. In nature there is always struggle and merciless annihilation of the weak who do not succeed in defending themselves. [The classical liberal's] plans for eternal peace—both in domestic and in foreign relations—are the outcome of an illusory rationalism contrary to the natural order.
>
> However, the notion of the struggle for existence as Darwin borrowed it from Malthus and applied it in his theory, is to be understood in a metaphorical sense. Its meaning is that a living being actively resists the forces detrimental to its own life. This resistance, if it is to succeed, must be appropriate to the environmental conditions in which the being concerned has to hold its own. It need not always be a war of extermination such as in the relations between men and morbific microbes. *Reason has demonstrated that, for man, the most adequate means of improving his condition is social cooperation and division of labor. They are man's foremost tool in his struggle for survival.* But they can work only where there is peace. Wars, civil wars, and revolutions are detrimental to man's success in the struggle for existence because they disintegrate the apparatus of social cooperation. (italics added)[3]

Thus Mises turns the tables on those who argue that social bonds are somehow unnatural and at odds with the evolution of the species. On the contrary, it is only through the achievements made possible by social life that humans have subordinated other animals that are physically stronger and faster and have virtually eliminated the threat posed by many bacteria and viruses.

Notice, too, the constant emphasis Mises puts on reason and the importance attached to human recognition of the higher productivity available with the division of labor. Even though an evolutionary argument might explain

---

3. Mises, *Human Action*, 175.

why feelings of sympathy come innately to humans, such a mechanism is inadequate to explain the emergence and maintenance of society. Mises argues that society is composed of countless actions on the part of its individuals, and underlying each act of social cooperation is the implicit recognition that such cooperation is more advantageous than antisocial action. Mises is claiming not that individuals consciously aim to "create society,"[4] but that the billions of individual actions upholding society are done consciously—that's what makes them actions.

The Relationship between Economic Science, Classical Liberalism, and Religion

Most of Ludwig von Mises's fans admire him not simply because of his achievements in pure economic science but also for his passionate defense of political liberty. Indeed, Mises has been dubbed the "last knight of liberalism,"[5] in a reference to classical liberalism. A classical liberal in the tradition of Mises is not the same as a liberal in modern American politics.[6] On the contrary, Mises was a liberal in the sense that he championed the individual against the state and, for that reason, favored strict limits on government power, not only to protect obvious liberties such as a free press and the freedom of speech, but also to protect economic freedoms from government meddling. In the modern American political scene, what Mises meant by *liberal* would nowadays be *libertarian*.

Because so many people are Austrians in their economics and libertarians in their politics, critics often dismiss the former as a mere apology for the latter. In other words, critics often claim that the Austrian School is not really

---

4. See Mises's discussion on page 188 of *Human Action*. Mises's follower, Friedrich Hayek, was fond of quoting Adam Ferguson's description of social phenomena that were the products of human action but not of human design.

5. Jörg Guido Hülsmann, *Mises: Last Knight of Liberalism* (Auburn, AL: Ludwig von Mises Institute, 2007).

6. For example, Nobel laureate and Keynesian economist Paul Krugman—who famously delivers arguments for greater government intervention in the economy from his perch at the *New York Times*—titles his blog, "Conscience of a Liberal." Although appropriate in the context of modern American politics, Krugman's use of the term *liberal* is not at all the way Mises uses the term in *Human Action* and elsewhere in his writings.

an objective economic science, but merely a thinly veiled attempt to justify the political conclusions, such as opposition to regulations on business, that a foe of big government already brings to the analysis.

In light of these typical criticisms, it is useful to quote Mises's explanation of the relationship between "value-free" Austrian economics, on the one hand, and classical liberalism—what today we would call libertarianism—on the other:

> Liberalism is a political doctrine. It is not a theory, but an application of the theories developed by praxeology and especially by economics to definite problems of human action within society.
>
> As a political doctrine liberalism is not neutral with regard to values and the ultimate ends sought by action. It assumes that all men or at least the majority of people are intent upon attaining certain goals. It gives them information about the means suitable to the realization of their plans. The champions of liberal doctrines are fully aware of the fact that their teachings are valid only for people who are committed to these valuational principles.
>
> While praxeology, and therefore economics too, uses the terms happiness and removal of uneasiness in a purely formal sense, liberalism attaches to them a concrete meaning. It presupposes that people prefer life to death, health to sickness, nourishment to starvation, abundance to poverty. It teaches man how to act in accordance with these valuations.[7]

As Mises makes clear in the above quotation, there is a connection between economic science and political libertarianism, but not in the crass way that the critics allege. Economic science per se does not smuggle in value judgments, and it does not know in advance what the policy conclusions "have to be." Rather, economic science is entirely objective, merely showing the cause-and-effect relationships flowing from different institutional arrangements and government policies.

To make matters concrete, economics as an objective science merely says: If you want to lift people out of poverty and if you want to avoid the business

---

7. Mises, *Human Action*, 153–54.

cycle, then you must have private property rights and a sound currency.[8] Yet the classical liberal, armed with these objective conclusions from economic science, goes further and says because I think it better to eradicate poverty and avoid the business cycle, therefore I oppose socialism as well as inflationary monetary policy.

This explanation of the classical liberal position opens up Mises to another line of attack, in which his critics charge him with a crude materialism. Mises first responds that it is an undeniable fact that the vast majority of people endorse the materialistic goals of rising physical output, reduced sickness and mortality, and increased lifespans. Yet beyond that, Mises argues with great eloquence that this alleged tradeoff between material prosperity and nobler pursuits is a false dichotomy:

> The nineteenth century was not only a century of unprecedented improvement in technical methods of production and in the material well-being of the masses. It did much more than extend the average length of human life. Its scientific and artistic accomplishments are imperishable. It was an age of immortal musicians, writers, poets, painters, and sculptors; it revolutionized philosophy, economics, mathematics, physics, chemistry, and biology. And, for the first time in history, it made the great works and the great thoughts accessible to the common man.[9]

Finally, we should address the concerns of religious readers, who may recoil from Mises's agnostic perspective. Even though Mises himself embraced a utilitarian ethics—in which the goodness or badness of an institution, policy, or even personal action was to be judged ultimately according to its effect on human welfare—this did not mean that his worldview was anti-religious. As he explained, "It would . . . be a serious mistake to conclude that the sciences of human action and the policy derived from their teachings, liberalism, are antitheistic and hostile to religion."[10]

---

8. These specific conclusions from economics will become clearer as we proceed through the book.

9. Mises, *Human Action*, 155.

10. Mises, *Human Action*, 155.

It's true, Mises admitted that classical liberalism was "radically opposed to all systems of theocracy." Yet even here, it was not the theocrat's theism that was the issue; rather, it was the theocrat's desire to enact government policies that, according to economic science, would be disruptive of social cooperation and would thereby harm human welfare. In this framework, one of the characteristic marks of a free society—the so-called separation of church and state—is a natural outgrowth, for with this separation classical liberalism "establishes peace between the various religious factions and gives to each of them the opportunity to preach its gospel unmolested."[11]

The Division of Labor[12]

As we have seen, Mises believed that the higher productivity available under the division of labor was the foundation of civilization itself. In this section we'll spell out what we mean by the term and start to explore why it's associated with higher productivity.

At its simplest, the division of labor means that people "divide up" the work to be done: Rather than each person growing his own food, making his own clothes, building his own shelter, and performing his own dental work, under the division of labor these tasks are divided and allocated to individuals. Only some people specialize in growing food: we call them farmers. Only some people make clothes: historically, they were called tailors. And so on.

To grasp just how important the division of labor is, imagine a world without it. If each person or each household tried to fill all of its own needs, then most of the world's current population would die within a month or two, and the small band of survivors would live a primitive existence, especially as the tools they used wore out, machines broke down, and gasoline supplies ran out.

Why would modern civilization collapse without the division of labor? The quick answer is that the productivity of labor would plummet. In other words, the total amount of food grown, the total number of shirts and pants

---

11. Mises, *Human Action*, 157.

12. The discussion of the division of labor and comparative advantage draws heavily from the treatment in Chapter 8 of Robert P. Murphy's *Lessons for the Young Economist*.

produced, the total number of houses built, and so on, would greatly fall if each person or household tried to be economically self-sufficient.

For various reasons, the productivity of labor is magnified greatly when it is divided. Simply put, people can produce more total output when they specialize in their tasks, rather than trying to produce a small portion of each item for themselves alone. When some individuals devote themselves exclusively to farming, and others exclusively to dentistry, more total food is produced and more cavities are filled. With more total output to go around, everyone can eat more, wear more clothes, and so forth under the division of labor.

These claims should be intuitive: Most people would agree that if they had to grow their own food, make their own clothes, and so on, they would soon be plunged into abject poverty. Yet even though the conclusion is sensible, it's useful to spell out some of the specific reasons that specialization makes labor so much more productive:[13]

Less Time Wasted Switching between Tasks.

Picture something as simple as three children cleaning up the table after dinner. Most likely, the children can get the job done more quickly if they divide up the tasks and specialize, for the simple reason of cutting down on unnecessary walking. For example, one child can scrape the plates off into the garbage and carry the dishes to the sink. The second child can wash, and the third can dry. This system is much more efficient—they will all be done much sooner—than if each child grabbed a dish, scraped it into the garbage, then carried it over to the sink and washed it, then stepped to the right to dry the same dish and finally put it away. The same principle applies to other productive operations.

Promotes Automation

By taking a complicated task and breaking it down into its components, the division of labor promotes the use of automation. If people grew their own food

---

13. Note that our framework to explain why the division of labor leads to higher productivity does not correspond to Mises's framework on page 157 of *Human Action*. The two treatments are compatible, but the reasons are organized differently.

in the backyard, it wouldn't make sense for anyone to develop tractors. Even if we focus on one particular factory, its output will be higher if the workers specialize in their jobs because it's then easier to incorporate machinery and tools to help them.

Economies of Scale

This is a generalization of the first two principles. For many operations, there are economies of scale at least up to a certain level of output. This principle means a doubling of inputs more than doubles the output. For example, if a chef switches from making enough pasta to feed one person to feeding fifty people, the time spent on preparation of the sauce, boiling the water, and so on certainly doesn't increase fifty times. This principle alone explains why it makes sense for roommates to alternate preparing meals, rather than each roommate cooking a whole meal for him- or herself every night. Another everyday illustration of economies of scale involves making a cup of coffee: Whether you want to make one cup or four, the prep work is largely the same, which is why people often ask, "I'm making coffee, anyone else want some?"

Certain Tasks Require a Minimum Threshold of Workers

Closely related to the general concept of economies of scale is the particular feature that some tasks can be done only with a minimum number of workers. For example, if neighbors would like to remove large tree stumps from their yards, it might prove physically impossible for each neighbor to complete this task alone. Only if several people concentrate their efforts on a single stump, can it be removed. This fact also helps explain why it is more productive for people to cooperate with each other, rather than work in isolation only on tasks that provide direct benefit to the individual.

Natural Aptitude

So far our principles have shown that even if the whole world were filled with identical people, there would still be advantages from specialization. In the real world, of course, people are not identical. Some people are simply born to be better farmers than others—and this natural advantage can include geographical factors. For example, a strong boy in Idaho would probably be able to grow more potatoes per year than a sickly, bed-ridden boy in Idaho, but at the same time, a strong boy in Florida can grow more oranges per year than even a strong boy in Idaho. And the bed-ridden boy in Idaho might be born with a wonderful knack for language and thus make a much better copy editor or novelist than either of the healthy boys, who are much better equipped to be farmers.

Acquired Aptitude

The true advantages of the division of labor occur when people develop their natural aptitudes through training and practice. Someone who's always had a knack for numbers in school would do a better job working at an accounting firm after graduating high school, compared to another high school graduate who always struggled with math. But if the student with good math skills then goes to college and majors in accounting, her superiority would be even more pronounced. Finally, if we followed that same person and checked in at age 50, after she had spent twenty-eight years working as an accountant, then obviously she would be far more proficient at the accounting job—meaning her labor would be very much more productive—than any other human who did not have such a background.

The above list is not necessarily exhaustive, but it lays out some of the main reasons that specialization makes labor so much more productive. In the next section, we explain one of the key insights of classical economics.

The Ricardian Law of Association
(a.k.a. the Principle of Comparative Advantage)

The benefits of specialization can be reaped only when people are able to trade with each other. If some people focus on growing food while others focus on building houses, then this arrangement works only if the farmers are allowed to trade their surplus food in exchange for some of the builders' surplus houses. Otherwise, the farmers will freeze and the builders will starve.

Without the ability to move goods around the economy, the huge leap in total output would be a hollow victory.

It's easy enough to see the mutual benefits of specialization and trade when two people have different areas of expertise. For example, if Joe excels at planting and harvesting wheat, whereas Bill is an expert at sewing pants, then it's obvious that the two will both enjoy a higher standard of living if Joe concentrates on producing wheat while Bill concentrates on producing pants.

However, economists have discovered that the principle applies even in cases where one person is more productive in every possible way. In the jargon of economics, we can say that even if one person has an absolute advantage in every line of production, he or she still benefits by specializing in his or her comparative advantage, which is the field where the superiority is relatively greatest.

Historically, economists have credited David Ricardo with the principle of comparative advantage. Others before him—notably Adam Smith—had explained the benefits of trade between nations, but the argument had typically been couched in terms of absolute advantage. For example, if the workers in England could make more sweaters per hour than workers in France could, yet at the same time workers in France could make more bottles of wine per hour, then obviously it made sense for the English to focus on sweaters and the French to focus on wine. Through international trade, the English and the French could both enjoy more sweaters and more wine per capita than would be possible if the countries didn't allow trade.

Yet Ricardo went further, showing that even if a country had the absolute advantage in both industries—sweaters and wine in our example—it would still benefit by specializing in the sector where its advantage was more pronounced. Ricardo's demonstration explodes the arguments of American protectionists, for example, who want to shield an advanced U.S. economy from the less developed Mexican economy. According to these protectionists, unfettered trade with Mexico can only hurt the United States, bringing it down to toward the Mexican level, whereas it would help the Mexican economy. Yet Ricardo showed that this reasoning is incorrect; free trade benefits even a country such as the United States, where workers may be more productive in virtually every sector compared those in a trading partner with lower living standards.

Ricardo's demonstration of the principle of comparative advantage is typically associated with international trade; however, Mises's law of association is a more general principle, applicable to social interactions even between two individuals in the same community. That is why we will illustrate the principle here with an example of two people operating in a monetary economy, rather than looking at barter trade of goods between countries. Consider Table 5.1 below:

Table 5.1. Illustration of Comparative Advantage

	Time It Takes to Perform Tasks in Clothing Store	
	Tidy Up Store at Day's End	Convince Customer to Buy
John (hired help)	60 minutes	120 minutes
Marcia (owner)	30 minutes	15 minutes

In Table 5.1, we see the hypothetical performance times at a clothing store in the mall for John, who is hired help, and Marcia, the store's owner. As the numbers indicate, Marcia is better at both making sales *and* tidying up the store at the day's end, in preparation for opening the next morning.

Because Marcia has the absolute advantage in both making sales and tidying up, you might at first think that it is most efficient for her to spread her workday among the two tasks, rather than bringing John into the picture. But that's not correct. By hiring John and having him focus on taking out the trash, mopping the floors, and so on, at the end of each day, Marcia can concentrate on her comparative advantage, which is making sales. In other words, Marcia can allow customers to stay in the store and browse for longer, thus making more sales, since she is delegating the necessary tidying up to John.

If Marcia is running her business in a monetary economy, it is quite simple for her to figure out whether it makes sense to hire outside help or to close the store early so that she can tidy up herself. For example, suppose that the typical customer purchase yields Marcia net earnings of $20.[14] That means for every 15 minutes that Marcia devotes to helping customers on the floor, on

---

14. For example, Marcia might sell $50 of clothes at the retail price, but she in turn had to spend $30 for those clothes in terms of the original wholesale price, as well as the overhead expenses of renting the store space, paying the electric bill, and so on.

average she brings in an extra $20 that she can pay herself. If Marcia has to kick the customers out early, so that she can spend the last 30 minutes of each day tidying up, on average she thereby loses out on $40 in potential income from her business.

Does it make sense for Marcia to hire John, who runs a cleaning service catering to stores in the mall? It depends on what John charges for his services. So long as he is willing to charge less than $40 to come in and clean up Marcia's store at the end of each day, it makes sense for Marcia to delegate these simple tasks to John. Since John is just a young man with no significant skills, he is happy to charge just $15 for his hour of work. As these hypothetical numbers illustrate, large gains result from the trade between Marcia and John. Both Marcia and John would consider the arrangement quite attractive.

Just to round out the discussion, notice that it would not make sense for Marcia to hire John to help her with making sales or for John to quit the cleaning business and go into clothing retail. Because John is a worse salesman than Marcia, he would make a sale only once every two hours. That means if John tried to replicate Marcia's business and devoted himself to selling clothes, his net earnings would work out to an average of $20 every two hours, or a mere $10 per hour. John can make much more than that cleaning.

Our example has illustrated the principle of comparative advantage: Even though Marcia is more productive at both tidying up her store and in making sales, she still benefits from associating with John. Marcia has the absolute advantage in both tasks but the comparative advantage only in making sales. John has the absolute advantage in neither task, but he does have the comparative advantage in cleaning.

Recall that in Mises's view, the mere fact of the superior physical productivity of the division of labor was not enough to secure the foundation of society. It was furthermore necessary for people to recognize this fact. The chief tool with which they would grasp this fact—and all others—was reason.

Two Kinds of Social Cooperation: Contracts versus Commands

The preceding discussion has shown the tremendous advantages of social cooperation under the division of labor: In order for humans to enjoy modern living standards, it's necessary for people to specialize in just a few tasks, producing far more than they need for their own use so they can contribute the vast bulk of what they produce to others. Viewed from afar, to see people behave in this manner would show the onlooker that they were cooperating in a common purpose. In a broad sense, this is what society ultimately is.

There are two basic patterns for society, or two basic approaches to organizing widespread human cooperation: The first pattern is cooperation based on voluntary contracts, in which each participant has a symmetrical relationship to the others. The second pattern for society is cooperation based on subordination or hegemony, in which one ruler or a group of rulers exercises power over everyone else.

Even in a country where people suffer under a totalitarian dictatorship, with complete isolation from the rest of the world, they still form a society. They would still specialize in certain tasks, with some growing food, others working in factories, and still others marching in the army. Even though the behavior of the people living in such a system may be heavily influenced by threats, strictly speaking they are still choosing to follow the orders of the ruler, and in that sense they are acting.

Nonetheless, a market economy based on the institution of private property and money can operate only in a voluntary, contractual society. Even though the hegemonic society enjoys the advantages of the division of labor, its material output is but a pittance compared to the tremendous productivity unleashed by a truly free people. This is a constant theme in the work of Mises: Our intuitive notion of what is ethical and just corresponds to what is also preferable from a pragmatic perspective.

6

The Role of Ideas and
the Importance of Reason

Introduction

FAR FROM BEING a naïvely pragmatic thinker who cared only
about the nuts and bolts of economic issues, Ludwig von Mises was above
all a rationalist who championed the crucial role of ideas in the progress of
civilization. In Mises's view, even totalitarian governments ultimately rested
on public opinion.[1] For this reason, Mises took the time—as few other economists did, before or since—to methodically critique what he perceived as the
faulty ideas of his intellectual opponents, and to provide a thoroughgoing
defense of his own approach.

To a modern reader, certain passages of *Human Action* may seem unneces-
sarily lengthy because Mises spends what may seem to be an inordinate amount
of space dismantling a viewpoint that is no longer in vogue. Yet during his early
career—particularly when he held his *Privatseminar* in Vienna—Mises encountered doctrines that he realized would undercut the teachings of economic
science. Because Mises believed that the fate of civilization itself ultimately
depended on the public coming to recognize these economic insights, Mises
made sure to provide the strongest case possible. Furthermore, today we see
variants of the numerous objections Mises encountered in his own time, so it
is definitely worthwhile to study Mises's responses.

---

1. Mises, *Human Action*, 189–90. If such a statement seems implausible, consider that
totalitarian governments exercise far greater control over the educational system, media,
and Internet than do more limited governments. It is clear that even the totalitarian dictator
understands the importance of molding public opinion; he doesn't merely resort to threats
of violence against dissidents.

In this chapter, we will explain Mises's views on the role of ideas in history and the importance of reason; finally, we will provide quotations from some of Mises's key intellectual opponents to help the modern reader understand exactly whom Mises was fighting.

The Role of Ideas in History

Mises was a firm believer in the power of ideas to influence individual action and, hence, the course of world events. In this respect, he agreed with one of his arch rivals, John Maynard Keynes, who wrote, "The ideas of economists and political philosophers, both when they are right and when they are wrong, are more powerful than is commonly understood. Indeed the world is ruled by little else." Keynes then drove home the point with a famous line: "Practical men, who believe themselves to be quite exempt from any intellectual influence, are usually the slaves of some defunct economist."[2]

Mises recognized that people were motivated by vastly different ideas, many of which seemed fanciful and clearly erroneous to educated onlookers. What's worse, Mises acknowledged that a specific person will often hold ideas that are mutually incompatible; in other words, many people have a system of beliefs that contains contradictions. Furthermore, Mises was aware that people held religious and otherwise metaphysical views that could not be subject to empirical refinement, even in principle.

In light of the above facts, one might suppose that Mises was pessimistic about the role of reason in human affairs. However, Mises made an important observation in the face of the apparent diversity of worldviews that different people held:

> With regard to things beyond there can be no agreement. Religious wars are the most terrible wars because they are waged without any prospect of conciliation.
>
> But where earthly things are involved, the natural affinity of all men and the identity of the biological conditions for the preservation of their

---

2. John Maynard Keynes, *The General Theory of Employment, Interest, and Money* (New York: Harcourt, Brace and Company [1936] 1965), 384.

lives come into play. The higher productivity of cooperation under division of labor makes society the foremost means of every individual for the attainment of his own ends whatever they may be. The maintenance and further intensification of social cooperation become a concern of everybody. Every world view and every ideology which is not entirely and unconditionally committed to the practice of asceticism and to a life in anchoritic reclusion must pay heed to the fact that society is the great means for the attainment of earthly ends. But then a common ground is won to clear the way for an agreement concerning minor social problems and the details of society's organization. However various ideologies may conflict with one another, they harmonize in one point, the acknowledgement of life in society.[3]

We see now the connection between Mises's conception of classical liberalism and his understanding of the moral duty of civilized men and women to educate their fellows on economic principles. Most people are in broad agreement with the value judgments that poverty, sickness, and business depressions are bad and should be minimized, while wealth, health, and stable economic growth are good things that policymakers should promote. Because of this fact, and because of the teachings of objective economic science, the classical liberals are now in a position to use rational arguments to persuade their neighbors to embrace their recommendations. This is fertile ground on which to deploy reason since the disputes are not over ultimate objectives, but merely the proper means to achieve them. In other words, Mises believes that the majority of modern disputes over government policy stem from ignorance of the objective cause-and-effect relationships that are the domain of the economist. As Mises put it:

> The main objective of praxeology and economics is to substitute consistent correct ideologies for the contradictory tenets of popular eclecticism. There is no other means of preventing social disintegration and of safeguarding the steady improvement of human conditions than those provided by reason. Men must try to think through all the problems

---

3. Mises, *Human Action*, 179–80.

involved up to the point beyond which a human mind cannot proceed farther . . . . They must fight error by unmasking spurious doctrines and by expounding truth.[4]

The reader must understand that Mises was not engaging in a rhetorical flourish when he said that social disintegration was kept at bay by the use of reason. Indeed, Mises even saw the Nazi leaders—who hated Mises both for his Jewish ethnicity and his hostility to state power—as acting in a rational manner, once we take into account their faulty views on how the world works. Mises argues:

> Now, whoever accepts the ideology of nationalism and socialism as true and as the standard of his own nation's policy, is not in a position to refute the conclusions drawn from them by the Nazis. The only way for a refutation of Nazism left for foreign nations which have espoused these two principles is to defeat the Nazis in war. And as long as the ideology of socialism and nationalism is supreme in the world's public opinion, the Germans or other peoples will try again to succeed by aggression and conquest, should the opportunity ever be offered to them. There is no hope of eradicating the aggression mentality if one does not explode entirely the ideological fallacies from which it stems. This is not a task for psychiatrists, but for economists.[5]

So we see, Mises literally thought that world peace rested on the capacity of people to use their reason in order to grasp the advantages of social co-operation. This aspect of his thought helps to shed light on the passion with which Mises describes the workings of a market economy based on private property and monetary calculation. For Mises, sharing the logical deductions of economic science with the masses was a moral duty because the fate of civilization itself rested on teaching enough people the truth.

Some of Mises's Chief Intellectual Opponents

As we explained in the beginning of this chapter, modern readers may have difficulty understanding the significance of some of Mises's discussions. In

---

4. Mises, *Human Action*, 185.
5. Mises, *Human Action*, 187.

this section, by presenting quotations from the leading proponents of views against which Mises battled, we hope to make his own strategy in *Human Action* (and elsewhere) more understandable.

The Marxist View of Historical Development

First we will draw on the writings of Karl Marx, who had a much different conception of the interaction between ideas and history. Remember that Mises thought human ideas ultimately shaped historical evolution. For example, in Mises's view, the development of political freedom in Western Europe created the institutional prerequisites of modern democratic capitalism, which in turn fostered the Industrial Revolution. Yet in Karl Marx's view, the causality was the exact opposite. The following comes from Marx's introduction to his 1859 *A Contribution to the Critique of Political Economy*:

> In the social production of their subsistence men enter into determined and necessary relations with each other which are independent of their wills—production-relations which correspond to a definite stage of development of their material productive forces . . . . It is not the consciousness of men which determines their existence, but on the contrary it is their social existence which determines their consciousness. At a certain stage of their development the material productive forces of society come into contradiction with the existing production-relations . . . . Then comes an epoch of social revolution. With the change in the economic foundation the whole immense superstructure is slowly or rapidly transformed.[6]

In the above passage, Marx argues that social revolutions occur only when the productive material forces of society have evolved to the fullest of the current stage. The revolutionaries themselves may believe that their ideas are the cause of the overthrow, but their very ideas have been molded by the system into which they were born and grew up.

---

6. Karl Marx, Introduction to *A Contribution to the Critique of Political Economy* (1859), quoted in Max Eastman, ed., *Capital, The Communist Manifesto, and Other Writings By Karl Marx* (New York: The Modern Library, Inc., 1932), 10–11.

We see the same understanding of history in somewhat plainer language in the 1848 *Communist Manifesto*:

The means of production and of exchange on whose foundation the bourgeoisie built itself up, were generated in feudal society. At a certain stage in [their] development . . . the conditions under which feudal society produced and exchanged . . . became no longer compatible with the already developed productive forces; they became so many fetters. They had to burst asunder; they were burst asunder.

Into their places stepped free competition, accompanied by social and political constitution adapted to it, and by economical and political sway of the bourgeois class. (italics added)[7]

As the italicized statement above indicates, Marx held the opposite of Mises's interpretation of the historical rise of capitalism. Mises thought that the political struggles in medieval Europe, which gave rise to the distinctly Western notion of limited government and individual rights—codified by constitutional checks on government power—fostered the growth of modern industry and all of the wonders we associate with capitalism. For Marx and his colleague, Friedrich Engels, the causality was the reverse: The feudal mode of economic organization had developed to its full potential, necessarily giving way to the capitalistic (bourgeois) mode of organization. The moral, legal, constitutional, and even intellectual superstructure needed to justify and implement the bourgeois era came afterward.

Besides casting the transition into socialism as a scientific inevitability, Marx's position allowed him to deride the teachings of the economists as mere appendages to the bourgeois social order. Marxists went so far as to claim that there were multiple logics and that what appeared to be a correct argument against socialism to a bourgeois economist was in fact wrong when analyzed by a thinker from the proletariat ranks. Precisely because of this popular Marxist rhetorical move, Mises devoted several sections in his Chapter III of *Human Action* to refuting *polylogism*, the doctrine of multiple logics. One of Mises's

---

7. Karl Marx and Friedrich Engels, the *Communist Manifesto* (1848), quoted in Max Eastman, ed., *Capital, The Communist Manifesto, and Other Writings By Karl Marx*, 326.

strongest arguments here was to point out that the Marxists never showed exactly how the doctrines of the classical economists were valid in bourgeois logic but invalid in proletariat logic; they never made the attempt because doing so would show that in fact the Marxists couldn't respond to the demonstrations of the economists.

The German Historical School's Denial of Economic Law

In some respects, the Austrian School of economics was born in the *Methodenstreit*—battle over method—between Carl Menger and some of his disciples against Gustav Schmoller and other members of the German Historical School. As we have already explained,[8] Mises thought that Schmoller's position would invalidate the very notion of economic law. Instead of deriving true laws that the economist would trust over, say, the personal account in the diary of a senator in Imperial Rome, Schmoller's approach would make the economist an institutional historian with no concrete framework of principles that would be valid for all economies.

To appreciate the gulf between Schmoller and Menger, and hence Mises, consider the following quotation:

> The idea that economic life has ever been a process mainly dependent upon individual action—an idea based on the impression that it is mainly concerned with satisfying individual needs—is mistaken with regard to all stages of human civilisation, and in some respects is more mistaken the further we go back.[9]

As the above quotation reveals, not only did Schmoller think that the proper way to explain economic life must depend on the era under scrutiny, but he also rejected *methodological individualism*, which is the principle that the economist must explain complex social phenomena as the outcome of individual human actions. It would be difficult to disagree more strongly with Mises's project.

---

8. See page 36.

9. Gustav von Schmoller, *The Mercantile System and Its Historical Significance* (London: Macmillan, 1902), 3–4.

The Logical Positivist Claim That
Only Verifiable Statements Are Meaningful

Among Mises's chief targets of criticism are the logical positivists, a group of influential thinkers who formed the so-called Vienna Circle in the interwar period. Their ideas were imported into the English-speaking world through A. J. Ayer in his 1936 book, *Language, Truth, and Logic*. The following excerpts from Ayer's book will help shed light on Mises's own discussion in *Human Action* and why he saw a threat to his conception of economic science in the writings of the logical positivists:

> The criterion which we use to test the genuineness of apparent statements of fact is the criterion of verifiability. We say that a sentence is factually significant to any given person, if, and only if, he knows how to verify the proposition which it purports to express—that is, if he knows what observations would lead him, under certain conditions, to accept the proposition as being true, or reject it as being false. If, on the other hand, the putative proposition is of such a character that the assumption of its truth, or falsehood, is consistent with any assumption whatsoever concerning the nature of his future experience, then, as far as he is concerned, it is, if not a tautology, a mere pseudo-proposition. The sentence expressing it may be emotionally significant to him; but it is not literally significant.[10]

In contrast with Mises's understanding of economics, logical positivists assert that to state something meaningful, the economist would need to produce propositions that we could evaluate only after our future experiences; these propositions might turn out to be true, but they might also be wrong. The only other option was to produce a sentence that was a tautology (meaning conclusions that are necessarily true because of the definitions and premises with which we start the analysis). However, according to the logical positivists, though tautologies are meaningful, they don't convey any new information about reality; they simply walk through the implications of our social conventions on the definitions of various terms. For example, if someone proclaims, "A bachelor does not have a wife," then this is a true, meaningful statement,

---

10. A. J. Ayer, *Language, Truth, and Logic* (Great Britain: Penguin Books, [1936] 1971), 16.

and we don't have to go out and empirically test it by sampling thousands of bachelors. Yet this type of a priori statement doesn't really teach us anything about the world except that English speakers define the word *bachelor* in a certain way. Here's how Ayer describes the situation: "In saying that if all Bretons are Frenchmen, and all Frenchmen Europeans, then all Bretons are Europeans, I am not describing any matter of fact . . . I am . . . indicating the convention which governs our usage of the words 'if' and 'all'."[11]

Because Mises thought we could demonstrate the truth of economic laws without relying on empirical evidence, he agreed with the logical positivists that they were tautologies. However, where Mises parted ways with Ayer's circle was their claim that tautologies were *mere* tautologies that gave us no new information about reality. Mises rejected this claim, as the following passages from *Human Action* make clear:

> All geometrical theorems are already implied in the axioms. The concept of a rectangular triangle already implies the theorem of Pythagoras. This theorem is a tautology, its deduction results in an analytic judgment. Nonetheless nobody would contend that geometry in general and the theorem of Pythagoras in particular do not enlarge our knowledge. Cognition from purely deductive reasoning is also creative and opens for our mind access to previously barred spheres. The significant task of aprioristic reasoning is on the one hand to bring into relief all that is implied in the categories, concepts, and premises and, on the other hand, to show what they do not imply. It is its vocation to render manifest and obvious what was hidden and unknown before.
>
> In the concept of money all the theorems of monetary theory are already implied. The quantity theory does not add to our knowledge anything which is not virtually contained in the concept of money. It transforms, develops, and unfolds; it only analyzes and is therefore tautological like the theorem of Pythagoras in relation to the concept of the rectangular triangle. However, nobody would deny the cognitive value of the quantity theory. To a mind not enlightened by economic reasoning it remains unknown. A long line of abortive attempts to

11. Ayer, *Language, Truth, and Logic*, 74.

· solve the problems concerned shows that it was certainly not easy to attain the present state of knowledge.[12]

In the above quotation, Mises shows that economic laws are not obvious and that they do indeed enlarge our body of knowledge, even though economic laws do not need to be verified with empirical observation. Unlike the statement, "A bachelor doesn't have a wife," the propositions in economics, just like the Pythagorean theorem in geometry, teach us something new about reality.

Although Mises himself doesn't invoke the following thought experiment, it may help the reader to understand the philosophical issues involved in the dispute. Suppose that intelligent aliens showed up in Earth's orbit next week and began to communicate with humanity. The physics professors on Earth would expect the aliens to have discovered the empirical fact that, say, nothing can move faster than light because this is an objective fact about the physical universe; it's not something that humans superimposed on their own subjective observations. In stark contrast, the English professors would have not the slightest expectation that the aliens would have discovered that a bachelor doesn't have a wife since that type of statement doesn't refer to anything about external reality, independent of human linguistic convention. Yet, in the way Mises understands the various disciplines of scholarly thought, so long as the aliens seemed to have minds with the same logical structure, then Earth's mathematicians should expect that the aliens would have discovered some form of Euclidean geometry. Furthermore, if the aliens lived in social groups and engaged in specialization and trade, then Earth's economists should not be surprised if the aliens had developed a version of marginal utility theory.

Finally, consider that even if the aliens were lacking the type of education that humans refer to as Euclidean geometry and economic principles, they would be grateful to learn them and would take them back to their home planet as a genuine form of new knowledge that would be useful in their own lives. In contrast, if they learned the fact that "a bachelor has no wife," then they would remember it only as a bit of trivia about the intelligent life forms they had discovered on a blue planet third from its star. That type of knowledge would not be useful to them, whereas, say, a new framework for

12. Mises, *Human Action*, 38.

understanding the purchasing power of money might be extremely valuable to them if their own analog of economists had not yet discovered something comparable.

The Empiricist Claim That to Be Scientific, Economics Must Make Testable Predictions

Our extensive discussion of Mises's methodological views—in particular, how he thought that economic science must be logically deduced from human action, meaning that its laws would be valid a priori—will make more sense if we showcase the perspective of Milton Friedman. The following quotations come from Friedman's justly famous essay, "The Methodology of Positive Economics," first published in 1953. Friedman's essay is an excellent illustration of the widespread view that to be scientific, economists must follow what is often taught as the scientific method to children in school. As we will shortly see, Friedman differs radically from Mises on the question of how economists come to discover economic laws.

Friedman opens his essay by contrasting positive economics with normative economics. Positive economics explains how the world is, whereas normative economics prescribes how the world should be. In Friedman's terminology, then, positive economics accords with Mises's view that economics is a value-free, objective science, which merely tells us cause-and-effect relationships, irrespective of the economist's value judgments.

Friedman also agrees with Mises that most political battles stem not from disagreement over fundamental value judgments, but rather from different views about positive economic relationships. For example, the reason some people support minimum wage legislation, while others vehemently oppose it, is not that one group wants to help poor workers, whereas another group wants to hurt them. Rather, Friedman claims, the political battle stems from the fact that both groups want to help poor workers, but they disagree over the proper means of doing so. So far, so good; this, too, is broadly consistent with Mises's views on the classical liberal program and why the economist must strive to educate the public about the teachings of economics.

However, at this point, Friedman parts company with Mises. While they both agree on the importance of teaching the public and policymakers the essential findings of objective, positive economic science, Friedman and Mises disagree over how to discover such findings. We have already extensively documented Mises's views on the subject. Now we will see what Milton Friedman had to say:

> The ultimate goal of a positive science is the development of a "theory" or "hypothesis" that yields valid and meaningful (i.e., not truistic) predictions about phenomena not yet observed . . .
>
> Viewed as a body of substantive hypotheses, theory is to be judged by its predictive power for the class of phenomena which it is intended to "explain." Only factual evidence can show whether it is "right" or "wrong" or, better, tentatively "accepted" as valid or "rejected" . . . . The only relevant test of the validity of a hypothesis is comparison of its predictions with experience.[13]

Later on, Friedman explicitly tackles the approach of constructing economics on the basis of tautologies:

> One effect of the difficulty of testing substantive economic hypotheses has been to foster a retreat into purely formal or tautological analysis . . . . Tautologies have an extremely important place in economics and other sciences as a specialized language or "analytical filing system." Beyond this, formal logic and mathematics, which are both tautologies, are essential aids in checking the correctness of reasoning . . .
>
> But economic theory must be more than a structure of tautologies if it is to be able to predict and not merely describe the consequences of action; if it is to be something different from disguised mathematics.[14]

Although Friedman's remarks sound superficially reasonable, they are actually mere assertions. He hasn't demonstrated why economic theory must "be able to predict" in a way that is different from merely describing "the consequences of action." For example, suppose that the economist can deduce from introspection that monetary inflation will cause prices to be higher than they otherwise would be. It's true, such introspection alone cannot let the

13. Milton Friedman, *Essays in Positive Economics* (Chicago: The University of Chicago Press, 1953), 7–9.

14. Friedman, *Essays in Positive Economics*, 11–12.

economist predict the absolute level of various prices in the future. Yet why should economists focus on the latter question as the ultimate criterion of scientific validity? Friedman hasn't really explained his position, he has merely asserted it at the outset.

As we have already explained in detail, Mises believed that economics provided something new that was not part of the natural sciences, mathematics, or history. From the starting point that humans act, the economist could logically deduce—thereby forming a tautology, it's true—that individuals have subjective preferences with ordinal rankings, that choices come with opportunity costs, and that the value of second-order capital goods is dependent on the value of the first-order consumer goods that the individual believes they have the technological power to produce. Say what one will about these types of statements, they are clearly within the realm of economics and are not merely "disguised mathematics." Although they have not been derived by reference to empirical observation, thinking through these tautologies definitely aids acting individuals as they navigate the real world. Logical, deductive economics as championed by Ludwig von Mises is not mere word games.

PART III

Economic Calculation

7

Even the Economists Missed the Importance of Monetary Calculation

Introduction

IN PART ONE, we explored the nature and implications of human action—purposeful behavior—as such; all of our results applied to any action, even the action of an isolated person making exchanges with nature. In Part Two, we refined the analysis, restricting attention to action in society. We learned that human labor is far more productive when people engage in large-scale teamwork, rather than each person or household attempting to produce everything internally. In Mises's opinion, the higher productivity available through division of labor formed the basis of society itself. However, unlike Marx, Mises didn't believe that the material forces of production would directly translate into the proper social structure; society was constructed from individual actions, meaning that all social institutions had to be implemented by individuals and the ideas that motivated them. This was why Mises devoted so much space in *Human Action* to seemingly philosophical problems; he wanted to secure the footing of economics as a genuine science in order to teach its essential findings to the masses. Only if people understand the underpinnings of modern civilization will they support the customs, institutions, and government policies that make life in society possible.

In Part Three, we are making a transition. Part Four contains the study of human action embedded in a specific set of circumstances: a society with private property and the use of money, commonly known as the market economy or simply capitalism. Before we can begin the more traditional economic analysis—covering issues like entrepreneurship, interest rates, and the business cycle—we must first examine *economic calculation*. As we proceed, it will become clearer what Mises means by this term, but we can provisionally define economic calculation as the evaluation of a course of action where at least some of the benefits and costs can be quantified in terms of their money prices. Thus, we might call it *monetary calculation*.

Although just about every economist would agree that in the real world economic calculation is important, Mises thought that his colleagues—let alone the general public and government officials—did not fully appreciate just how significant it is, and moreover that it is utterly dependent on the institutional setting of private property and money prices. In his words:

> Every action can make use of ordinal numbers. For the application of cardinal numbers and for the arithmetical computation based on them special conditions are required. These conditions emerged in the historical evolution of the contractual society. Thus the way was opened for computation and calculation in the planning of future action and in establishing the effects achieved by past action . . .
>
> It was cognition of what is going on within a world in which action is computable and calculable that led men to elaboration of the sciences of praxeology and economics. Economics is essentially a theory of that scope of action in which calculation is applied or can be applied if certain conditions are realized. No other distinction is of greater significance, both for human life and for the study of human action, than that between calculable action and noncalculable action. *Modern civilization is above all characterized by the fact that it has elaborated a method which makes the use of arithmetic possible in a broad field of activities.* This is what people have in mind when attributing to it the—not very expedient and often misleading—epithet of rationality.
>
> The mental grasp and analysis of the problems present in a calculating market system were the starting point of economic thinking which finally led to general praxeological cognition . . . . Economic calculation is the fundamental issue in the comprehension of all problems commonly called economic. (italics added)[1]

---

1. Mises, *Human Action*, 200.

In the above quotation, Mises argues that only the availability of money prices allows people to use arithmetic as a guide to much of their activities. This is not to say that arithmetic itself is dependent on money; even people living in a community of barter can understand how to add, subtract, multiply, and divide. However, without money prices, Mises says, the results of arithmetical computations would provide little guidance for people when they made their plans for the future or when they evaluated the success (or failure) of previous plans.

Action by itself yields only subjective, ordinal rankings, applicable to the individual performing the action. When a person chooses an apple over an orange, all we can say is that she valued the apple *more than* the orange; we can't say anything about how much more value she attributes to the apple, and we certainly can't make statements such as, "She derived as much utility from one apple as she would have derived from two oranges." Similarly, if a teenage boy trades ten hours of his labor to paint a farmer's fence in exchange for 20 pounds of bacon, we can conclude, "This boy valued an additional 20 pounds of bacon more than his first 10 hours of leisure," and that "the farmer valued the boy's 10 hours of labor *more than* he valued his first 20 pounds of bacon." The fact that cardinal units of measurement are involved on both sides of the transaction doesn't by itself allow us to apply division or other arithmetical operations. For example, it would be very misleading to say, "The farmer and boy agreed that his labor was worth 2 pounds of bacon per hour." Only in the very special circumstances afforded in a market economy using money is it appropriate for people to apply arithmetical operations in economic affairs.

More than any economist before him, Mises underscored just how crucial economic calculation was in mobilizing the achievements of other fields of thought. Scientific discoveries, technological advances, capital accumulation, and better trained workers could be coordinated into a steadily rising standard of living only with the institutional backdrop of readily available market prices. Mises claimed that most of his colleagues had taken the function of money— and economic calculation, which was dependent upon it—for granted and erroneously supposed that they could analyze the economy as a world of barter without money prices. This intellectual mistake ironically paved the way for the dangerous idea that a socialist society could use its resources as efficiently as, or even better than, a market economy. Through his understanding of the importance of economic calculation in a market economy, Mises was able to write his devastating critique of socialism—a topic we will cover in depth in Part Five of this book.

Using the New Subjective Marginal Utility Theory to Explain Barter Prices

Although the labor theory of value—the idea that the market value of goods is related to the amount of labor power that went into their construction—is associated with Marxism, free-market classical economists such as Adam Smith developed the doctrine. In their approach, value was an objective feature inherent in the good, like its weight or height.

In contrast, the marginal revolution of the early 1870s ushered in a subjectivist approach to value and market prices. In this new approach—where the founder of the Austrian School, Carl Menger, was one of the three acknowledged pioneers—the economist didn't care about the historical origin of a good. When trying to explain its price in the marketplace, the economist started with the fact that the individuals haggling over it had subjective preferences for units of this good, as well as units of other goods. Menger's tremendous accomplishment, shared by those following in his wake, notably Eugen von Böhm-Bawerk, was to give a satisfactory explanation of how the subjective, marginal preference rankings of each individual in the market could give rise to objective, cardinal barter ratios between the goods.[2]

Today's introductory textbooks to microeconomics will typically explain the formation of market prices using supply and demand, with money prices on the vertical axis. Although it isn't wrong, this treatment obscures the accomplishment of Menger et al., who showed the straightforward way that modern economists could explain barter prices.

---

2. A classic exposition of using the new marginal utility theory to explain barter prices is Eugen von Böhm-Bawerk, *Positive Theory of Capital* [1889], "Book III—Value and Price," contained in Volume II of Böhm-Bawerk's *Capital and Interest*, three volumes (South Holland, IL: Libertarian Press, [1884, 1889, 1909] 1959). Even Böhm-Bawerk's treatment at times treated utility as if it were a cardinal, psychic quantity, but his basic approach did not need such baggage. Our treatment in the text will show that we can explain objective and cardinal market prices merely using subjective and ordinal preference rankings.

On the other hand, today's more advanced textbooks can do without money, explaining the formation of prices using *indifference curves*, often in a graphical framework. Again, this type of approach is consistent with the insights of the marginal revolution—after all, Léon Walras used a mathematical approach in his own pioneering work in the 1870s—but its focus on assumptions made for geometrical convenience can lead many students to overlook the actual economics underlying the procedure.

For our purposes, we will walk through a simple market consisting of first two, and then three children who are trading their Halloween candy.[3] We will show how to determine equilibrium barter prices relying only on each child's subjective, ordinal rankings of various combinations of units of Halloween candy. This demonstration will be useful, first of all, in illustrating the great achievement of the post-1871 approach to explaining market prices, and it will also clarify why Mises placed so much emphasis on the role that money prices, as opposed to barter prices, played in civilized life.

Our example revolves around three siblings—Alice, Billy, and Christy—who arrive home on Halloween after an evening of trick or treating. They bring home different amounts of Snickers and Milky Way candy bars. Because of their different holdings and different tastes, the children will be able to reap gains from trade. In other words, through voluntary exchanges, the children will all walk away from their small market happier than when they entered it. In our hypothetical example, we want to show why a specific exchange rate between Snickers and Milky Ways emerges. In other words, we want to understand how the children's initial holdings and their preferences will lead to a specific Snickers-price of Milky Ways or a specific Milky-Way-price of Snickers. Note that no money is involved; we are showing how exchange ratios develop in a world of barter.

Here we will illustrate barter price formation using the same style of exposition that Böhm-Bawerk used in his classic treatment and which Murray Rothbard used in his own rendering of the technique.[4] First, suppose that Alice comes to the bargaining table with six Snickers bars and zero Milky

---

3. The Halloween candy example is adapted from the discussion in Chapter 6 of Robert P. Murphy, *Lessons for the Young Economist*. However, the exposition in *Lessons* is based on the ordinal preference rankings from neoclassical utility theory. In the present text, we describe the basic Halloween story using the type of exposition favored by Murray Rothbard.

4. See Chapter 2 of Murray Rothbard's *Man, Economy, and State*, [1962] 2009.

Ways, while her brother Billy shows up with zero Snickers and one Milky Way. To see if the siblings can make any possible gains from trade, we need to examine their preference rankings. We can illustrate them as shown in Table 7.1, which mirrors the treatment in Rothbard, where items shown in parentheses indicate units that the person does not yet possess:

Table 7.1. Rankings of Various Units of Candy Bars for Alice and Billy

Alice's Subjective, Ordinal Ranking	Billy's Subjective, Ordinal Ranking
6 Snickers	(6 Snickers)
(1 Milky Way)	(5 Snickers)
5 Snickers	(4 Snickers)
4 Snickers	(3 Snickers)
3 Snickers	(2 Snickers)
2 Snickers	1 Milky Way
1 Snickers	(1 Snickers)

In Table 7.1, we see that Alice would be willing to trade for Billy's Milky Way so long as he asked for one to five Snickers bars in exchange. This follows from the fact that Alice places the yet-unobtained Milky Way higher on her preference ranking, or scale of values, than up to five of her currently possessed Snickers. However, if Billy insisted on receiving all six of Alice's Snickers in exchange for his single Milky Way, she would reject the offer.

Similar reasoning shows that for his part, Billy would be willing to trade away his Milky Way so long as the price were in the range of two to six Snickers bars. Putting the two ranges together, we find scope for trade between the children, with the equilibrium barter price being at least two Snickers but no more than five Snickers for a Milky Way. We can take the analysis no further at this point, without bringing in further assumptions, for example, about the bargaining strength of the children.

By adding an individual to the market, however, we can reduce the zone of indeterminacy. For example, suppose Christy comes to the bargaining table with four Snickers bars of her own and with her own preference ranking or scale of values that allows us to construct Table 7.2:

Table 7.2. Preference Rankings for Candy among Three Children

Alice	Billy	Christy
6 Snickers	(6 Snickers)	
(1 Milky Way)	(5 Snickers)	
5 Snickers	(4 Snickers)	4 Snickers
4 Snickers	(3 Snickers)	(1 Milky Way)
3 Snickers	(2 Snickers)	3 Snickers
2 Snickers	1 Milky Way	2 Snickers
1 Snickers	(1 Snickers)	1 Snickers

The presence of Christy will reduce the range of possible equilibrium barter prices. With Alice and Billy, the range was anywhere from two to five Snickers bars for one Milky Way. However, Christy has knocked out the potential equilibrium price of two because if she saw such a trade about to unfold, she would object, "Stop! Billy, rather than trade your only Milky Way to Alice for two Snickers bars, I would gladly offer you three of mine."

However, similar reasoning shows that the price of three is knocked out, too. For example, if Billy were about to trade his Milky Way to Christy for three of her Snickers, Alice would interject, "Stop! Billy, don't give your Milky Way to Christy for three, when I would gladly give you four of my Snickers."

This type of reasoning shows that with the revised table above, the zone of potential equilibrium prices has been reduced to four or five Snickers bars in exchange for one Milky Way. We know that Alice will be the one to end up with Billy's Milky Way, we just don't know whether she will surrender four or five of her initial holdings for it. Compared to our original scenario with just two children, the addition of Christy has knocked out the lower prices.[5] Intuitively, by increasing the supply of Snickers on the market, the exchange value of a Snickers bar fell relative to a Milky Way. Or, equivalently, by increasing the Snickers demand for Milky Ways, the Snickers price of a Milky Way was bolstered.

---

5. A more complete analysis would show that adding additional people to the market can cause the zone of potential prices to converge to a unique equilibrium price.

The purpose of this simplistic example was to illustrate the power of Mengerian price theory. Modern textbooks often skip crucial steps by assuming money prices or by assigning utility functions to consumers. Yet the revolutionary marginal utility theory Menger developed doesn't need such crutches. It can explain the formation of equilibrium exchange ratios—barter prices— in a world without money, relying only on ordinal rankings of units of goods.

Adding Money as an Afterthought

After the work of the previous section we now can explain a situation where, say, two Snickers bars trade against one Milky Way, without having to say anybody "gets twice as much happiness from the Milky Way." Furthermore, notice that we didn't care a whit about how much labor or other resources went into producing or acquiring the candy bars; we took their stockpiles as given at the outset and needed to know only how the children subjectively ranked various units of Snickers and Milky Ways against each other.

In summary, our simple Halloween candy discussion gave just a taste of how economists approach the problem of direct exchange, in which people in the market exchange goods and services directly against each other. Under direct exchange, each party to a transaction directly desires the good he or she is obtaining. With the insights provided by Menger et al., economists after the early 1870s could offer a satisfactory explanation of how equilibrium prices arise in a world of direct exchange.

Ironically, this new approach was so appealing that economists actually fell into a trap; they overrated their ability to understand and explain the real-world market economy with the theoretical tools they were using. As Mises explains:

> The elementary theory of value and prices employs . . . the construction of a market in which all transactions are performed in direct exchange. There is no money; goods and services are directly bartered against other goods and services. This imaginary construction is necessary. One must disregard the intermediary role played by money in order to realize that what is ultimately exchanged is always economic goods of the first order against other such goods . . . . But one must carefully

guard oneself against the delusions which this construction of a market with direct exchange can easily engender.

A serious blunder . . . was the assumption that the medium of exchange is a neutral factor only . . . . The whole theory of catallactics [i.e., market exchange], it was held, can be elaborated under the assumption that there is direct exchange only. If this is once achieved, the only thing to be added is the "simple" insertion of money terms into the complex of theorems concerning direct exchange. However, this final completion of the catallactic system was considered of minor importance only. It was not believed that it could alter anything essential in the structure of economic teachings. The main task of economics was study of direct exchange. What remained to be done besides this was at best only a scrutiny of the problems of "bad" money.[6]

Mises is here alluding to the fact of a great divide in economic theory. On the one hand, when trying to explain the relative prices of goods and services in the marketplace, economists would resort to the type of barter analysis we sketched out in our Halloween story. For example, we could imagine an economy consisting just of the candy bars and conclude that, in equilibrium, a Milky Way bar had twice the market value of a Snickers bar.

However, in the real world, most prices are quoted not in kind but in units of money. Here is where the other leg of economic theory would come in. Rather than treat units of money with the same tools that would be used to handle units of candy, now a completely different theoretical apparatus was adopted. Originally the economist might say that a Snickers bar had a price of $1, while the Milky Way had a price of $2. Then, if the quantity of dollars held by the children were to double, maybe the price level would double, too, driving the Snickers price up to $2 and the Milky Way price up to $4. Regardless of the specific details, the crucial point is that the relative price of a Milky Way—quoted in terms of Snickers bars—would be determined in a conceptual framework that lacked money altogether. Then, to come up with absolute prices quoted in money, the revolutionary marginal utility theory would go out the window; economists didn't try to explain the equilibrium exchange ratio between dollar bills and Milky Way bars the same way they

---

6. Mises, *Human Action*, 203.

would explain the equilibrium barter ratio between Snickers bars and Milky Way bars.

It is not surprising that Mises should dwell on this inconsistent and unsatisfactory procedure since it was Mises himself who solved the problem—thereby unifying micro- and macroeconomics into a seamless framework—in his pioneering 1912 book, translated as *The Theory of Money and Credit*. Later on in the present book, we will sketch out the main stumbling blocks that had tripped up prior economists and how Mises was able to overcome them. In essence, Mises figured out how to use the new tools of subjective marginal utility analysis to explain not just barter prices, but money prices too.

Money Prices Solve the Problem of Economic Calculation

Mises was not chastising the economists simply to be pedantic. Because they thought they could adequately explain a modern market economy with a mental framework lacking money, most economists didn't really understand the importance of monetary calculation. Recall that economic calculation involves aggregating various inputs and outputs according to their prices, quoted in money, in order to evaluate a course of action. To repeat, most economists thought they could solve a model of the economy that involved only barter and then just plug in the absolute money prices as an afterthought to reflect the relative prices that would exist in a world of barter. Mises explains that this mindset led many theoretical economists to support socialism because they were not equipped to grasp its fundamental defects.

Later in this book, we will discuss Mises's famous critique of socialism, which focuses on its inability to rationally allocate scarce resources. For now, we will pinpoint the specific problem of economic calculation and how money prices solve it. As usual, it is best to first quote Mises himself and then elaborate on his remarks:

> Technology and the considerations derived from it would be of little use for acting man if it were impossible to introduce into their schemes the money prices of goods and services. The projects and designs of engineers would be purely academic if they could not compare input and output on a common basis. The lofty theorist in the seclusion of

his laboratory does not bother about such trifling things; what he is searching for is causal relations between various elements of the universe. But the practical man . . . must know whether what he wants to achieve will be an improvement when compared with the present state of affairs and with the advantages to be expected from the execution of other technically realizable projects which cannot be put into execution if the project he has in mind absorbs the available means. Such comparisons can only be made by the use of money prices.

Thus money becomes the vehicle of economic calculation. This is not a separate function of money. Money is the universally used medium of exchange, nothing else. Only because . . . most goods and services can be sold and bought on the market against money, and only as far as this is the case, can men use money prices in reckoning. The exchange ratios between money and the various goods and services as established on the market of the past and as expected to be established on the market of the future are the mental tools of economic planning. Where there are no money prices, there are no such things as economic quantities.[7]

A specific example will clarify Mises's argument. Suppose we are considering oranges in the United States. Surely most people would agree that in any sensible use of resources, at least some American farmers ought to be planting some oranges so that some Americans can eat them. Furthermore, most people would agree without much thought that if oranges are going to be planted in the United States, it makes more sense to do so in Florida and California, rather than Montana and Alaska. Yet beyond such vague generalities, what can we say about how we ought to handle the issue of growing U.S. oranges?

Notice that science and technology alone can't provide the solution; they can merely provide a range of options. For example, even if we assume that the oranges should be planted in the states with favorable natural conditions, it's still not obvious how many should be planted. At some point, people would get sick of eating oranges and drinking orange juice. But the primary problem is that the more land that is devoted to orange production, the less is available

---

7. Mises, *Human Action*, 209–10.

for other crops, or for houses. The agronomists and architects could inform us of the physical tradeoffs involved, for example, by explaining that an extra so-and-so pounds of oranges per year would mean one fewer apartment building able to house thirty families. But these technicians and scientists couldn't explain the proper decision in light of these physical tradeoffs.

Even if we provisionally assumed we had the solution for the amount of oranges to grow, we would then be left with the problem of distributing them to Americans around the country. Again, the technical experts could give options but not solutions. The oranges could be shipped by rail, truck, plane, or ship. More fancifully, it would be technically possible to transport the oranges by mule or bicycle, too. These latter methods seem ludicrous for an American scenario, but they are still in use in certain parts of the world. The right way to distribute products to consumers is not a mere technical problem that can be answered by scientists. It is above all an economic problem that requires the evaluation of each technical possibility in terms of its expected revenues and expenses, quoted in terms of money.

Consider: In the United States, it would seem obviously primitive to transport oranges from groves to the ultimate consumers using bicycles. It is surely much more sensible to, say, ship them by truck since they will get to their destination much faster. Yet this reasoning by itself might lead us to recommend shipping all oranges by supersonic jets—a procedure that would be obviously absurd on the other end of the spectrum. Although these extreme examples may seem patently silly, the intermediate cases are not as clear. Indeed, the actual solution in the market economy involves a combination of the various technological options, with some oranges being shipped in massive amounts by rail to central distribution points, where they are divided into smaller batches and sent out in trucks. Furthermore, at least some of the oranges destined for Alaska go by plane. There is no technical answer or explanation for this pattern; this is an economic problem, involving the alternative uses that people can make of the same resources.

Yes, it would be obviously wasteful to ship all oranges around the country on supersonic jets because it eats up many resources to produce and use supersonic jets. The gain in delivery speed is not sufficient to compensate for the greater loss in alternative enjoyments from the resources used up by the delivery mechanism. In the real world, this consideration jumps out as a huge discrepancy in revenues versus expenses. In short, the reason Americans don't ship all of their oranges via supersonic jets is that it's too expensive to do it that way. "Too expensive" is not a technological concept but a strictly economic one.

Our consideration of orange production and distribution shows the inadequacy of relying on a mental framework using only direct exchange. To make sensible decisions in a modern market economy, people in their roles as entrepreneurs, resource owners, workers, and consumers need to rely on a single unit of account into which they translate the natural units (such as pounds of oranges, gallons of gasoline etc.) of other items.

In understanding and explaining how people in the real world generate money prices and use them to guide their actions, economists cannot resort to the harmless fiction of a model assuming barter.

As Mises showed, there is a fundamental difference between a world in which people trade goods directly against each other and a scenario where one side of most transactions involves the good called money. In this special type of scenario—and only in it—economic calculation is possible. The development of money and fading away of barter exchange allowed for the economical use of scarce resources.

8

What Economic Calculation Can and Can't Do

Describing the Monetary Entries That Enter into Economic Calculation

ECONOMIC CALCULATION GUIDES individuals by quantifying in monetary terms the revenues and expenses of various possible actions. Loosely speaking, it puts dollars and cents figures on the costs and benefits of various plans to help the acting individual organize his or her deliberations. Yet what exactly are these monetary entries that are the ingredients in economic calculation?

There are two broad types of *monetary entries*, as Mises calls them: prices that were actually paid in the market in the past and prices that are expected to be paid in the market in the future. Past prices can be useful in helping to mold expectations of future prices, but conditions can suddenly change, causing prices to swing violently; action is always inherently speculative. Contrary to the approach of some other economists, in Mises's framework, prices are not given to the individuals in the market but instead are dependent on each person's subjective estimates of the future.

Even something as apparently rock solid as a corporate balance sheet, prepared by a meticulous accountant, is largely based on speculation about future economic conditions as they pertain to the company in question. Consider the hypothetical balance sheet shown in Table 8.1.

The balance sheet (on the next page) seems so precise and objective—both sides balance perfectly. The owners of our hypothetical company believe they have $2,157,000 in shareholder equity. In principle, this means that if they liquidated the company—through selling off all of its assets and paying off all of

Table 8.1. Hypothetical Balance Sheet

As of January 31, 2014			
Assets		**Liabilities & Equity**	
Cash	$308,000	Wages Payable	$95,000
Accounts Receivable	$85,000	Accounts Payable	$64,000
Inventory	$545,000	Bonds	$865,000
Office Supplies	$87,000	Tax Liability	$24,000
Vehicles	$60,000	Total Liabilities	$1,048,000
Plant & Equipment	$2,120,000	Shareholder Equity	$2,157,000
Total Assets	**$3,205,000**	**Total Liability & Equity**	**$3,205,000**

its creditors—they would be left with $2,157,000 free and clear, which could be split among the shareholders according to how much stock they held.

Yet following Mises's discussion, we can see that this apparently objective and precise figure is driven by subjective speculation. On the asset side, the only entry that is fairly objective is cash at $308,000. For example, if this business has a checking account with a commercial bank, with $308,000 on deposit, the owners of the company can be fairly sure—though even here, not absolutely certain—that the $308,000 figure is accurate and will not change.

Yet moving on, things become much less reliable. For example, the accounts receivable figure of $85,000 refers to money that the company's customers owe it for work or product already delivered. The figure of $85,000 is not an estimate of what people might be willing to pay for the company's output; the prices were already agreed to, and the company's side of each transaction was completed. Even so, the owners of this business cannot treat that $85,000 asset as certain as the $308,000 in cash. Suppose $35,000 of the accounts receivable is owed by a client that is about to go bankrupt. Even though everybody agrees that this client owes $35,000, this debt might not be paid or, if it is, only with pennies on the dollar.

Next consider the $545,000 in inventory. We can suppose that for this particular company, inventory refers to product that the company has already produced and is holding in anticipation of being able to sell to customers down the road. How should it be appraised on the balance sheet? Accountants have developed various procedures for valuing inventory based on cost of production to satisfy tax authorities and creditors. Yet if the balance sheet is to serve as a guide to the owners' future action, the inventory should ideally be appraised based on their ability to sell at certain prices in the future.[1] However, this correct method of appraisal is necessarily speculative. For example, suppose the company in question produces cigarettes, and the $545,000 figure refers to thousands of cartons in the warehouse awaiting distribution to retailers. Then a new health movement sweeps the country, with celebrities and other influential people urging people to quit smoking. The drop in consumer demand for cigarettes leads to a fall in demand from retailers, meaning the cartons in the warehouse would plummet from their originally estimated wholesale market value of $545,000.

Similar problems plague the estimates of the other assets. If the plant and equipment includes highly specialized machinery that has been customized to fit into this company's assembly line, it may be impractical to remove those specific items and sell them to another firm. So long as the owners expect to remain in operation and continue to use the pieces of machinery, the proper approach is probably to estimate how much they contribute to the production of goods or services intended for future sale—meaning that once again, the appraisal of the business asset depends crucially on speculative expectations about the future demand for the company's output.

In light of our discussion, it might seem that Mises is denigrating accountancy and the use of balance sheets. On the contrary, Mises endorses Goethe's remarkable claim that double-entry bookkeeping is "one of the finest inventions of the human mind."[2] Mises's remarks on the nature of the monetary entries going into economic calculation are simply intended to ensure that the reader understands exactly what economic calculation can—and can't—do. In Mises's words:

> It is not the task of economic calculation to expand man's information about future conditions. Its task is to adjust his actions as well as possible to his present opinion concerning want-satisfaction in the future. For this purpose acting man needs a method of computation,

1. See Mises's discussion in *Human Action*, 213–14.
2. Mises, *Human Action*, 231.

and computation requires a common denominator to which all items entered are to be referable. The common denominator of economic calculation is money.[3]

No social institution can provide acting humans with a view of the future. The misguided attempts to create a money of stable value were based on a faulty understanding of value and what it is that money gives us in economic calculation. Value is ultimately subjective in the minds of acting individuals. Market value, as expressed in monetary terms, simply refers to the number of money units that are exchanged against units of another commodity. Market prices are not measured in money, but rather market prices consist in money.[4] Mises insisted on such precision of language because he wanted to drive home the point that monetary figures were not analogous to the readings on a thermometer, where the number of degrees in Celsius is an arbitrary social convention, corresponding to a more fundamental physical reality. Precisely because value is ultimately in the minds of individuals, it is subjective and ordinal; it cannot be measured. Historical market prices merely record the ratios at which goods traded against units of money, and even in principle, there could be no such thing as a money possessing "stable value."

Whenever people make choices—whether as entrepreneurs, resource owners, workers, or consumers—they necessarily have to make speculative predictions about what the future holds and which course of action is best, in light of these fallible judgments. No social institution can remove the possibility of error. However, if they operate in a framework of private property and money, these inherently speculative judgments will be as informed as possible.

Economic Calculation Doesn't "Reduce Everything to Money"

In extolling the virtues of market prices and double-entry bookkeeping as mental tools to guide action on the marketplace, we run the risk of implying that people in a capitalist society care only about the bottom line. We apparently justify the caricature of *homo economicus*, a mythical creature motivated

---

3. Mises, *Human Action*, 215.
4. Mises. *Human Action*, 218.

ultimately by the desire for financial gain. Amartya Sen is an economist in a long line of thinkers to deride the all-too-typical assumption among advocates of a market economy that people are utilitarian calculators. Sen mocked this notion as not only distasteful but also empirically false, in his quick description of what life would be like in such a world: "'Where is the railway station?' he asks me. 'There,' I say, pointing at the post office, 'and would you please post this letter for me on the way?' 'Yes,' he says, determined to open the envelope and check whether it contains something valuable."[5]

Although it is regrettably true that the work of some economists lives up to the caricatures, it is most emphatically not true that Ludwig von Mises in particular—or the Austrian School of economics more generally—assumes that people in a market economy are just out to make money. Economic principles or laws as conceived by Mises apply to action as such, which is the intentional use of means in the pursuit of ends. Mother Teresa placed the aid of orphans above the lifestyle she could enjoy if she worked at an office job in New Jersey and consequently maximized her utility by the actions she chose.

When it comes to economic calculation, here, too, we must not overstate Mises's argument. Money prices and the profit and loss test merely clarify the consequences of various possible choices. For example, there is nothing irrational or noneconomical about a man buying a $40,000 sports car, when a more modest $20,000 vehicle would solve his need for transportation. However, it is important for the man to know how much more expensive the sports car is, so that he realizes just how much in other potential goods and services he is forfeiting by buying the car that will give him more subjective enjoyment.

Even business owners can deviate from the profit-maximizing strategy to cater to their subjective preferences. For example, a bookseller may refuse to stock "adult" magazines he considers immoral, even if he would earn a higher monetary income by carrying them. Or, if the owner of a fast food chain believes everyone deserves a second chance, she might hire an ex-convict for $10/hour even though she reckons he will actually increase the net income of her restaurant by only $9/hour. She implicitly is giving a gift of $1 to the man for every hour he works at her restaurant, which she may be happy to

---

5. Amartya K. Sen, "Rational Fools: A Critique of the Behavioral Foundations of Economic Theory," *Philosophy & Public Affairs*, 6, no. 4, (Summer 1977): 332.

do in order for him to have a shot at leaving his previous life of crime. Yet she probably wouldn't hire the man initially as a manager, as this would be far too expensive—as her accountant could demonstrate.

Economic calculation, by its very nature, can attach monetary values only to those elements of our lives that are sold against money. Many things are quite valuable subjectively but do *not* enter the market nexus directly and consequently cannot be quantified in dollars and cents. Nonetheless, economic calculation is still an indispensable mental tool of action because it shows individuals—with as much precision as possible, given the nature of the situation—the monetary implications of various possible choices. This makes it possible for the individuals to focus their attention on the tradeoffs involved between the monetary and nonmonetary elements of their decision.

PART IV

Catallactics

Economics of the Market Society

9

Defining and Studying
the Market Economy

Introduction

IN PARTS ONE THROUGH THREE of *Human Action*, Mises explained and defended the legitimacy of the scientific study of human action, a field he called praxeology. Now, in Part Four, Mises turns to *catallactics*—which literally means the study of exchanges—and is what the layperson probably has in mind when thinking about economics.

In Mises's framework, catallactics is the study of action that can rely on monetary calculation and is thus a subset of praxeology. This means that everything that is true of action in general is also true of action embedded in a market economy with private property and money. For example, the law of marginal utility applies to Robinson Crusoe, but it also applies to a speculator in a trading pit in Chicago. However, in Part Four, Mises derives additional results that are applicable only to a market economy. For example, in Chapter 10, we will explain the process by which prices are determined for consumer and producer goods. Obviously, this explanation has no relevance for Robinson Crusoe deserted on his island or for the comrades living under a completely socialist regime.

The reader should be clear that Mises still employs the logical, deductive approach when focusing his attention more narrowly on the market economy. He is not making empirical assumptions in the same way that most other economists would describe their own approach. In particular, it is still true that Mises does not think that we must derive economic principles or laws through testing of hypotheses. Rather, Mises is specifying the conditions under which his deductive conclusions are true.

To understand the subtle position, let us again return to the analogy of Euclidean geometry. All triangles have interior angles that sum to 180 degrees. However, we can go further and derive results that are applicable only to right triangles, which have one angle equal to 90 degrees. The Pythagorean theorem is one such result. Geometry professors still prove the Pythagorean theorem through the axiomatic, deductive approach, starting with assumptions and definitions and then logically deriving the conclusion in a step-by-step process. However, when asking if the result is applicable to a particular geometric shape, one must ask, "Is it a triangle? If so, does it have a right angle? If so, then yes, we know that the Pythagorean theorem applies, and so we conclude that the square of the hypotenuse is equal to the sum of the squares of the other two sides." To summarize: In geometry, every theorem that we can prove regarding a triangle is necessarily true of any right triangle. However, some theorems can be proved only about right triangles.

Our geometry discussion is analogous to Mises's understanding of catallactics as a subset of praxeology, or in other words, of the scientific study of the market economy being a subset of the broader scientific study of human action. In Part Four of *Human Action*, Mises will, for example, derive theorems concerning the purchasing power of money. Such results presuppose the existence of human action and the widespread use of a medium of exchange. But given these assumptions, the results concerning money are necessarily true. Thus the only empirical issue is whether we have human action and the existence of money; we don't need to further test whether the economic principle or law is actually valid.

What Is the Market Economy?

Since we will devote Part Four of this book to the study of the market economy, it is important to define it upfront. The following quotation captures Mises's definition of the market and his understanding of its most important features:

> The market economy is the social system of the division of labor under private ownership of the means of production. Everybody acts on his own behalf; but everybody's actions aim at the satisfaction of other

people's needs as well as at the satisfaction of his own. Everybody in acting serves his fellow citizens . . .

This system is steered by the market. The market directs the individual's activities into those channels in which he best serves the wants of his fellow men. There is in the operation of the market no compulsion and coercion. The state, the social apparatus of coercion and compulsion, does not interfere with the market . . . . It protects the individual's life, health, and property against violent or fraudulent aggression on the part of domestic gangsters and external foes . . . . Each man is free; nobody is subject to a despot. Of his own accord the individual integrates himself into the cooperative system. The market directs him and reveals to him in what way he can best promote his own welfare as well as that of other people . . .

The market is not a place, a thing, or a collective entity. The market is a process, actuated by the interplay of the actions of the various individuals cooperating under the division of labor. The forces determining the—continually changing—state of the market are the value judgments of these individuals and their actions as directed by these value judgments. The state of the market at any instant is the price structure, i.e., the totality of the exchange ratios as established by the interaction of those eager to buy and those eager to sell . . . . Every market phenomenon can be traced back to definite choices of the members of the market society.

The market process is the adjustment of the individual actions of the various members of the market society to the requirements of mutual cooperation. The market prices tell the producers what to produce, how to produce, and in what quantity. The market is the focal point to which the activities of the individuals converge. It is the center from which the activities of the individuals radiate.[1]

In Mises's vision, the market economy is a process through which individuals coordinate their activities in a voluntary fashion. In the market, no one can force anybody else to serve him, but ironically the price signals of

---

1. Mises, *Human Action*, 258–59.

the market—sometimes called market forces—indicate to individuals the appraisal that others make of their possible actions, as reckoned in monetary terms. To give a simple example: In the market economy, nobody can force a musician to tour the world and perform her hit songs for her fans. However, her agent can estimate for the musician just how much she would be able to earn if she *were* to go on a world tour. She always retains the freedom to retire and never sing another note, but the market process gives an indication to the musician of just how much other people would benefit from her decision to continue performing.

The "Pure" Market Economy and Other Unrealistic Thought Experiments

To study the operation of a market economy as it exists in the real world, the economist must rely on hypothetical thought experiments or imaginary constructions as Mises called them. Chief among these artificial thought experiments is the pure market economy, which is a market economy that is completely unfettered by government intervention. In the pure market economy, the government acts to ensure the operation of the market only by punishing domestic criminals and foreign aggressors. Such a government is sometimes called a "night-watchman state" or a minimal state. Logically, it makes sense to first study a pure market economy before contrasting such a scenario with a market economy that is heavily influenced by government policies that seek to alter incomes and other market outcomes.

Critics of orthodox economics often criticize this procedure. Because many economists walk away from their studies with laissez-faire policy recommendations, the critics are suspicious that the economists are simply smuggling in their desired conclusions at the outset. In other words, the critics argue that the laissez-faire economists simply assume that the economy is the pure market that they personally desire and then derive their laissez-faire outcomes accordingly. However, the critics continue, it is more scientific and objective to study the economy as it actually is, namely one with heavy government involvement.

As Mises points out, this type of criticism—though extremely popular—makes absolutely no sense. If we are trying to decide whether government intervention in a particular area—such as the minimum wage, for example—

is something we support or oppose, the only possible way for economists to shed light on the issue is to describe what the world would be like (a) with minimum wage laws and (b) without them.

To put the same point differently, supporters of minimum wage laws also have to resort to an unrealistic thought experiment if they want to explain why it's important to keep such laws in place: namely, by warning everyone of how awful conditions would be for the unskilled workers, supporters of minimum wage laws must resort to describing an economy where wages are set solely by the market forces of supply and demand. Of course, laissez-faire economists and supporters of minimum wage laws would probably paint much different pictures of the world (a) with and (b) without minimum wage laws, but the crucial point here is that they would both be using hypothetical thought experiments.

Mises explains other mental devices to help study the market process.[2] The plain state of rest occurs whenever the market comes to a temporary standstill because no one perceives any advantage from further trading. Notice that this is an actual situation that occurs again and again in the real world. In contrast, the final state of rest is a hypothetical unrealistic scenario in which all of the effects of a particular change (or "shock" in the language of mainstream economists) have worked themselves out. In the real world, the market never achieves a final state of rest because new disturbances continually upset the original trajectory of the market. The evenly rotating economy is an even more fictitious scenario in which there is no longer any genuine change in the market; every production and consumption process repeats itself day in and day out, so that in the plain state of rest every price is equal to its final price.

An example will help clarify these different conditions. Suppose we are in an initial equilibrium situation where oil is $100 per barrel. Suddenly an energy company discovers vast new crude deposits off the coast of South America, which eventually will allow for a large increase in global annual oil output. After the news of the discovery spreads across financial markets, the spot price of oil falls to $80. Once everyone has adjusted to the news, the oil market will again be in a plain state of rest. The new price of $80 per barrel fully takes into account the oil discovery.

---

2. Mises describes the plain state of rest, final state of rest, evenly rotating economy, and stationary economy on pages 245–52 of *Human Action*.

However, the situation doesn't stop there. For example, deep-sea platforms may not be profitable when oil is less than $90 per barrel. The platforms continue with their previous operations because they had already scheduled the personnel months in advance, but given the new reality in the oil market, the owners of the platforms are gradually rotating the personnel out and slowing down extraction, waiting for oil prices to rise. In a longer term adaptation to the oil discovery, the sharp fall in crude prices may lower the retail price of gasoline at the pump. Motorists in the market for a new vehicle end up buying more gas-guzzling SUVs and fewer fuel-efficient hybrids and compact cars than they would have if crude had remained at $100 per barrel. Consequently the demand for gasoline grows more quickly than it otherwise would have done. Changes such as these put upward pressure on the world price of crude oil, so that eventually—years after the new oil discovery—it would settle into the final price of $88 per barrel, if no other outside disturbances affected the oil market in the meantime.

In an evenly rotating economy, the crude price of oil would forever be $88 per barrel, and every other price would be constant as well. Not only is the oil market free from outside disturbances, but so is every other market. People still go to work, natural resources and capital goods are still transformed into finished consumer products, and consumers still go to the store to buy things, but there is no uncertainty about the future. Everything repeats itself in a perfectly predictable pattern, so that none of the quantitative data of the market change.

Finally, not to be confused with the evenly rotating economy is the concept of the stationary economy. In the stationary economy, things change—some businesses thrive, while others flounder. Consumers are fickle and switch their loyalty from one brand to another. The reason the economy is stationary, however, is that the two forces exactly counterbalance each other in the aggregate. That is to say, the economic profits of the expanding industries or firms are exactly matched by the losses of the shrinking industries or firms. Thus, it's true of both the evenly rotating economy and of the stationary economy that aggregate profits are zero and the amount of capital goods per person is constant. However, in the evenly rotating economy these aggregates occur because even at the individual firm and household level, there is no profit or net capital investment. In contrast, in the stationary economy one firm can suffer losses, and a particular industry can use up more of its machinery than is replaced by new investment, just so long as net profits and investment in other industries offset the change in the economy-wide totals.

The various mental devices we have just described are important for understanding how the market process in the real world adapts to changes. Recall that to understand the effects of government intervention in the market, and even full-blown socialism, we first need to study the pure market economy. By the same token, if we are to understand the real world in which thousands of changes to consumer preferences, resource availability, and technological know-how strike the system daily, the only way to proceed is to mentally isolate the impact of just one change and see how it plays out in market prices and quantities of output. Thus the point of defining and studying the artificial constructions of the final state of rest, the evenly rotating economy, and the stationary economy is not that these are realistic descriptions of the actual market, but rather that they act as foils against which we can understand the real economy, which is constantly in flux and is most definitely not stationary.[3]

Different Roles People Play in the Economy

In real life, a particular person may be a consumer, a capitalist, a worker, a landowner, and an entrepreneur. However, in economic theory, we conceptually separate these distinct functions to understand the role each type of person plays in the operation of the market. As we will see, each role is associated not only with a particular function, but also with a particular type

---

3. In Mises's framework (see *Human Action*, 252), an economy in which losses exceed profits—and consequently the net amount of wealth and income per person shrinks—is a retrogressing economy. On the other hand, a progressing economy is one in which there are aggregate net profits, and the amount of wealth and income per person, measured in monetary terms, increases. Note that Mises classifies even these constructions as imaginary. Even though we can logically think through the implications of such constructions, in practice we can never actually measure total wealth or income in an economy, and therefore, we could never actually determine whether it was retrogressing, stationary, or progressing. It makes sense to ask, "What are the total assets of a particular firm?" since, in principle, the owners of the firm could sell everything on the market and raise a definite sum of money. In contrast, it doesn't really make sense to ask, "What are the total assets of the country?" let alone of the planet, since even in principle such a large-scale and complete sale would either be impossible or would at least fundamentally alter the economic structure so as to change the concept allegedly being measured.

of income. However, modern economic theory doesn't always agree with the everyday layperson's understanding of what type of person earns which type of income, so we need to be precise in explaining the payment accruing to each category of person.

The most obvious is the worker, who sells labor services on the market. No matter the production process, there is always the need at least for human oversight; labor is an essential ingredient in every operation. In exchange for their productive labor services, workers receive income in the form of wages.

Next consider the *landowners*, who own the natural resources, meaning those productive factors given by nature that are not the result of human toil. In modern economics, the concept of land includes not only the actual soil and parcels of real estate, but also fisheries, coal mines, and timber. Now consider the *capitalists*, who own all of the capital. Recall that capital goods are produced means of production.[4] Capital goods include tractors, microscopes, assembly lines, hammers, and the cardboard boxes used to hold apples as they are shipped to a grocery store.

We have grouped the landowners and capitalists together, because their contribution to the market economy is quite similar, and consequently their income is of the same form. From this perspective, the only real distinction between landowners and capitalists is the history of the productive goods that they own. Since action is concerned primarily with using today's resources to cope with the future more effectively, the history of a particular good's origin is a bit of trivia. As we will see in greater detail in the next chapter, the market determines the prices of natural resources and capital goods in the same way. Specifically, the landowners and capitalists can rent their property out and earn a specific gross income per unit of time, which is due to the marginal productivity of the natural resource or capital good. However, after accounting for the wear and tear of their property—what economists and accountants call *depreciation*—the only net income the landowners and capitalists earn is

---

4. For the purist, we note that for Mises, an individual's capital includes the money he or she owns, but strictly speaking money itself is neither a consumer nor a producer good. Rather, money is best classified as a medium of exchange. However, these are subtleties of monetary theory that Mises doesn't even discuss in *Human Action*, and so we will not pursue them further. The interested reader should refer to chapter 5 of Mises's *The Theory of Money and Credit*.

interest, which has nothing intrinsically to do with physical productivity, but instead is entirely due to the way people subjectively value goods differently as they pass through time.

The relationship between rental income and interest and our claim that landowners and capitalists are functionally comparable are characteristically Austrian issues and so deserve more discussion at this point to lay the foundation for a more detailed treatment in the coming chapters. One of the major stumbling blocks in this effort is that the layperson may already have a notion that the landowner earns rents, while the capitalist alone earns interest. Historically, the classical economists adopted this framework, too. However, the modern theory of value and price shows that this classification scheme simply won't stand up to scrutiny. If we are going to associate specific economic functions or roles with specific types of income, we can only conclude that landowners and capitalists serve the same role and are financially compensated according to the same principles. To repeat, both landowners and capitalists earn both rental income and interest income; we can't assign one type of income to one of the roles, the way we can say that wage income is exclusively paid to workers for their labor.

A numerical example will help illustrate this crucial point. Suppose a wealthy tycoon who owns a large parcel of arable farmland rents it out to tenant farmers in exchange for a total of $1 million per year. For simplicity, further suppose that the tycoon doesn't need to spend any money on maintenance; he structures his contracts such that the soil is kept in good condition. Under these assumptions, the $1 million in annual payments are clearly rent paid to a landlord.

However, if the market rate of interest is 5 percent, and if the tycoon were absolutely certain that he would be able to find tenant farmers willing to pay such rents for years to come, then the market price of his land would be $20 million.[5] That would mean that at any moment, the tycoon would have the option of liquidating his farmland and turning it into $20 million in cash,

---

5. This must be the case because the farmland acts like a safe bond that promises to pay a perpetual stream of $1 million annual payments. If the market rate of interest is 5%, then the present discounted value of that stream of payments is $20 million, and consequently it will be the market price of such a bond. Since the farmland offers the same stream of payments, it must have the same market price as the bond.

which he could use to buy all sorts of goods offering immediate enjoyments, such as tropical cruises, fancy meals, and so forth. If the tycoon refrains from selling, he is effectively keeping his $20 million in financial capital invested in the farmland. That $20 million of invested capital earns a return of $1 million per year. That is clearly a 5% rate of interest on the tycoon's capital.

As our simple example of the tycoon demonstrates, there is no hard and fast distinction between rental income and interest income; the same $1 million flowing to the tycoon could be classified as either one, depending on the interpretation. On the one hand, the tenant farmers were paying $1 million to the landowner for his scarce natural resource, since they were able to raise more crops with his land than without it. Clearly, then, this $1 million constituted a rental payment for the services of the land. However, on the other hand, it is just as valid to view the $1 million as a 5 percent annual return to the tycoon on his $20 million of financial capital invested in the real estate project. Since we are assuming that this return was absolutely certain, the $1 million is clearly interest income, accruing to the capitalist for his willingness to postpone consumption and keep his $20 million rolling over in the productive enterprise, rather than liquidating it to spend on short-term frills. To drive home the point, consider: If the original tycoon had lent the $20 million to a developer at a contractual 5% interest rate, and then the developer used the money to go buy an identical farm and rent it out to raise the necessary $1 million annual payments, then clearly the $1 million payments from the developer to the tycoon would be interest income since they would be contractual payments due to a loan of money. In our scenario, we have simply collapsed the two people into one; the tycoon and developer are the same person, meaning the $1 million flowing annually from the tenant farmers into his pocket is quite legitimately a form of interest income to the tycoon.

Finally consider the entrepreneur, the person who adjusts the factors of production in anticipation of the future. In the everyday sense of the term, the entrepreneur is the leader of a firm, who borrows money from the capitalists to hire workers and buy natural resources and capital goods and to give instructions to the workers on what goods or services to produce for the firm's customers. If the entrepreneur has successfully anticipated the state of the market and has done a good job in hiring the right workers, buying the correct resources, and so forth, then he or she will earn a profit. If, however, the entrepreneur is unable to sell the resulting goods or services for enough money to cover the expenses, including interest owed on any borrowed money, then the entrepreneur suffers a loss.

The entrepreneurial function is thus bound up with the fact that the market economy is always in flux. The future is uncertain; different entrepreneurs will have different ideas about what goods and services the consumers will want and the best techniques for producing these items. The only way a particular entrepreneur can earn a profit is if his or her peers overlooked the opportunity, meaning that the market's use of scarce resources had previously been imperfect until this particular entrepreneur made some adjustments.

However, once we realize that entrepreneurship is fundamentally concerned with the problem of uncertainty—as opposed to the administrative techniques of managing employees and buying raw materials—then we must admit that every individual acts entrepreneurially. Capitalists who lend money to a business venture may be contractually guaranteed a certain percentage return, regardless of the success of the company, but they know that if the company fails badly enough, it may default on its loan and repay only pennies on the dollar. Thus capitalists who lend funds to a business are acting entrepreneurially and must make a judgment on the profitability of the venture before entrusting it with their money.

The situation is similar even for workers who perform a set task for a definite wage, even though at first glance it would seem that such safe action is the furthest thing from entrepreneurship. This is because workers, just like any corporate CEO, are making a judgment about the best course of action to take in light of an uncertain future. By taking jobs with one company, workers have set their career on a particular trajectory. This choice will affect the types of skills they acquire and will influence their ability to take future jobs at different companies. Consider: Someone in the midst of a job search may receive a very lucrative offer from a firm in the industry in which the person wishes to specialize. Even so, should the person take the offer? Perhaps by continuing the search process—which involves sending out more applications and going on more interviews—the job seeker will receive an even better offer in two weeks. By taking the first offer, the worker will never know what opportunities he or she forfeited by this choice. Thus even a worker in the actual market economy must act entrepreneurially, deploying resources (in this case, the worker's own labor services) in a course of action that seems best, amid uncertainty about the future.

Now that we have walked through the various functions or roles that people play in economic theory, and the corresponding types of income that they earn in these capacities, we are in a position to understand Mises's succinct summary:

> In the context of economic theory the meaning of the terms concerned is this: Entrepreneur means acting man in regard to the changes occurring in the data of the market. Capitalist and landowner mean acting man in regard to the changes in value and price which, even with all the market data remaining equal, are brought about by the mere passing of time as a consequence of the different valuation of present goods and of future goods. Worker means man in regard to the employment of the factor of production human labor. Thus every function is nicely integrated: the entrepreneur earns profit or suffers loss; the owners of means of production (capital goods or land) earn originary interest; the workers earn wages.[6]

In later chapters, we will return to the difficult but critical issue of interest and how it is driven by time preference. Understanding the Austrian perspective on this topic is essential not merely to understand the exact process by which capitalists and landowners earn income, but also to understand the theory of the business cycle that Mises and his followers, notably Friedrich Hayek, developed.

Capital, Income, and Saving

The central intellectual concept in economic calculation is capital. In this respect, the Marxists were right to call the market economy capitalism, though of course they intended the label as derogatory rather than complimentary. The Marxists wanted to brand the market economy as one that served only the interests of a small group of exploiters, whereas Mises appreciates the term

---

6. Mises, *Human Action*, 255.

because it recognizes that only in a market economy can individuals resort to the indispensable mental tool of economic calculation.

It's important to note that Mises defines capital in the way that an accountant or businessperson would: Capital is quoted in monetary units, and is equal to the total market value of all assets minus the total market value of all liabilities. Loosely speaking, to calculate how much capital is invested or tied up in a particular business entity, the accountant estimates how much money would be left over after first selling all of the business assets and then paying off all of the business debts.[7]

Although Mises's definition of capital is orthodox enough, it actually represents a departure from the usage of modern economists, who tend to think of capital not as a financial or monetary concept, but as a physical and real concept. This difference in perspective on the meaning of capital goes back to the fundamental difference in the way certain economists understand the role that money plays in a market economy: Economists who think they can solve for an equilibrium assuming barter prices and then add on money as an afterthought are also the ones who think of capital as a collection of physical things that aid in production.

In contrast, remember that Mises thought it was important to integrate the crucial role of money in a market economy from the ground floor, as it were. Money is not neutral, and it is misleading to conceive of the market economy as if it were a giant network of barter exchanges. The crucial concept of capital makes sense only in a monetary economy since capital could be computed only by resort to adding and subtracting the money prices of various assets and liabilities. It's true, the indispensable tool of economic calculation refers to physical things and how they are deployed; such considerations are necessary for Robinson Crusoe, as well as a socialist state. But the point is that a complex society requires a market and its attendant money prices for the various means of production and consumer goods, if there is to be any

---

7. In practice, it might not make sense to sell certain business assets, such as pieces of specialized equipment, to separate buyers, and accountants have developed procedures to appraise such items when listing them on the asset side of the balance sheet. We discussed such subtleties when explaining Mises's understanding of balance sheets and how they too are driven by speculation about future market prices.

hope of efficient use of resources; the socialist dictator wouldn't be able to objectively tell whether he were increasing or decreasing the amount of wealth at his disposal. In Mises's succinct statement: "In a socialist economy there are capital goods, but no capital."[8]

Closely related to the concept of capital is another familiar term, *income*, which is defined as the amount of consumption in monetary terms that can occur over a defined period without reducing the capital. Notice that both capital and income are defined in units of money, but that capital is a stock concept while income is a flow concept. We can further define *saving* as the difference between income and consumption, while *dissaving* or *capital consumption* is the opposite, namely the amount by which consumption exceeds income. For Mises, capital is the starting point, whereas income, saving, and dissaving are derivative concepts.

To appreciate the guidance offered by economic calculation, we'll walk through two simple numerical examples, the first dealing with an individual household and the second with a business owner. Consider Table 9.1, summarizing five years of capital, income, and consumption for an individual who has a salaried position.[9]

Table 9.1 illustrates the basic concepts of capital, income, saving, and dissaving. How much capital or wealth the individual has at his disposal is a stock concept; it is a snapshot that is true at a particular moment in time. In contrast, income, saving, and dissaving make sense only as a flow concept, over a period of time. These flow concepts explain the change in the stock concept from the beginning to the end of the period in question. For example, in Year 4 the man lives beyond his means and consumes $4,000 more than he earns

---

8. Mises, *Human Action*, 264.

9. Table 9.1 assumes that the individual's capital consists only of his bank balance. In particular, it ignores the fact that he doesn't possess an infinite capacity to produce labor income; eventually, his body will grow old so he will not be able to earn $100,000 from his salaried job perpetually. Some economists might want to include this consideration in the calculations of capital—by broadening the concept to include human capital—but we are not following this practice here, because (a) it is not how most accountants would describe a typical household's finances and (b) it relies on a hypothetical appraisal of the market price of a worker's entire lifetime flow of future labor services, which is not a real monetary item outside of a slave economy.

Table 9.1. Individual Household's Financial History over Five Years

Item	Year				
	1	2	3	4	5
Starting Bank Balance	$0	$0	$10,000	$10,000	$6,000
Interest Income (5% of Balance)	$0	$0	$500	$500	$300
Labor Income	$100,000	$100,000	$100,000	$100,000	$100,000
Total Income	$100,000	$100,000	$100,500	$100,500	$100,300
Consumption	$100,000	$90,000	$100,500	$104,500	$100,300
Saving (Dissaving)	$0	$10,000	$0	($4,000)	$0
Ending Bank Balance	$0	$10,000	$10,000	$6,000	$6,000

in total income for that year, which is why his ending bank balance is $4,000 lower than his beginning bank balance for that period.

The usefulness of economic calculation in guiding action may be more apparent when we next consider a business owner. Suppose she owns a factory producing electronic devices. Over the course of a year, her business receives $1 million in gross revenues from its sales to customers, out of which she pays $600,000 in wages and another $100,000 for raw materials. How much can the business owner take as net income from the business to spend on her household affairs? She wants to take out of the business only as much as she can without impairing its ability to generate income in the future.

With the numbers we have seen thus far, it would appear the business owner can afford to take out $300,000 over the course of the year, since that's how much more she collects from her customers compared to how much she pays for labor and other inputs. Yet her accountant updates the balance sheet and reminds the owner that she must account for the depreciation of the machinery in her plant. Specifically, every five years the business owner must buy a new piece of equipment that is necessary for her factory to continue operating in the same way. The piece of equipment has a market price of $500,000 when it is purchased brand new. Therefore, out of her $300,000 left over from paying the workers and buying raw materials, the business owner must also dedicate a portion of it to replacing the machinery that is slowly wearing out. If the interest rate is 5 percent, this depreciation expense is about $90,500 annually, meaning that the true net income of the business is only about $209,500 each year.[10] This lower amount is how much the business owner can safely spend on her individual household, without impairing the ability of the business to continue generating the same level of income.

As even this simple example demonstrates, individuals in the real world are utterly dependent on market prices and economic calculation to guide their choices. No rule or principle of economics states that individuals must act to preserve their capital; it may be perfectly sensible, for example, for a retired individual to consciously draw down the principal of his savings, consuming more than his earnings and effectively selling off assets to go on cruises, send birthday money to his grandchildren, and so forth. Yet to be sure, he isn't surprised on his eightieth birthday by the limited options at his disposal, and to know how much of his paycheck to save during his prime working years, such a man also relies on market prices and economic calculation.

The guiding light of economic calculation—and its fundamental notion of capital—makes possible all of the wonders of capitalism. In the words of Mises:

> The system of market economy has never been fully and purely tried. But there prevailed in the orbit of Western civilization since the Middle Ages by and large a general tendency toward the abolition of institutions hindering the operation of the market economy. With the successive progress of this tendency, population figures multiplied and the masses' standard of living was raised to an unprecedented and hitherto undreamed of level. The average American worker enjoys amenities for which Croesus, Crassus, the Medici, and Louis XIV would have envied him.[11]

As the last sentence in the above quotation indicates, Mises utterly rejects the Marxist claim that capitalism is a social system that exists to serve the capi-

---

10. If the owner puts aside $90,500 for five years in a row, with the first payment rolling over at 5 percent for four years, the second rolling over for three years, and so on, then the total sum after the fifth payment is about $500,000, which is how much the owner needs to spend after five years to replace the now completely worn-out equipment. Note that in our example we are ignoring price inflation, taxes, and other real-world complications.

11. Mises, Human Action, 265.

talists. On the contrary, Mises conceived of the market economy as a system in which not the entrepreneurs or capitalists were in charge, but ultimately the consumers. We explain this perspective in the next section.

Mises's Doctrine of Consumer Sovereignty

One of the standard objections to the market economy is that it allegedly allows the wealthy elite to control everyone else. In the Marxist framework, the system is dubbed capitalism since the capitalists control the means of production; they are running the show. In contrast, the hapless workers are "wage slaves" who have the nominal freedom to quit their jobs, yes, but hardly enjoy true freedom since they will starve if they lose their paycheck. Just as the old aristocratic system had been swept aside by the movement for political democracy, the Marxists tried to sell the masses on the idea that socialism represented economic democracy that would complete the emancipation of man.

Mises sought to turn this typical view of the market on its head with his notion of consumer sovereignty. For Mises, the notion that the factory owner or landowner controlled the economy was absurd and reflected a naïve understanding of economics. In his words:

> The direction of all economic affairs is in the market society a task of the entrepreneurs. Theirs is the control of production. They are at the helm and steer the ship. A superficial observer would believe that they are supreme. But they are not. They are bound to obey unconditionally the captain's orders. The captain is the consumer. Neither the entrepreneurs nor the farmers nor the capitalists determine what has to be produced. The consumers do that. If a businessman does not strictly obey the orders of the public as they are conveyed to him by the structure of market prices, he suffers losses, he goes bankrupt, and is thus removed from his eminent position at the helm. Other men who did better in satisfying the demand of the consumers replace him.[12]

Later Mises turned the tables on the socialists calling for economic democracy when he writes:

---

12. Mises, *Human Action*, 270.

The consumers determine ultimately not only the prices of the consumers' goods, but no less the prices of all factors of production. They determine the income of every member of the market economy. The consumers, not the entrepreneurs, pay ultimately the wages earned by every worker, the glamorous movie star as well as the charwoman. With every penny spent the consumers determine the direction of all production processes and the minutest details of the organization of all business activities. This state of affairs has been described by calling the market a democracy in which every penny gives a right to cast a ballot. It would be more correct to say that a democratic constitution is a scheme to assign to the citizens in the conduct of government the same supremacy the market economy gives them in their capacity as consumers.[13]

The notion of consumer sovereignty helps to explain why Mises was so passionate in his defense of the market economy. Not only did the institutions of private property and money allow for a higher standard of living, but they also secured individual autonomy as much as is humanly possible. In truth, there was no tradeoff between efficiency and equity, or between output and individualism: The same system that drew forth the maximum effort from society's most talented members was also the one that best protected the interests of the weakest members.

Because the doctrine of consumer sovereignty was so essential to Mises's understanding of the market, we will elaborate on it to clarify what Mises meant and what he didn't. We can imagine the entrepreneurs as standing in between the consumers on the one hand, and the owners of the factors of production—the owners of natural resources, labor, and capital goods—on the other. The consumers spend their money on final goods and services sold to them by the entrepreneurs, who in turn use those revenues to enter the various factor markets to hire workers and to buy natural resources and capital goods.

The consumers know what they want and can look at the various goods and services available at the retail level—with their corresponding prices—to determine the best way to spend their limited budgets. Through these spending

---

13. Mises, *Human Action*, 271.

decisions made by the consumers, the entrepreneurs receive their marching orders and have the means to enter the various factor markets and bid away scarce resources to devote them to a particular consumer product. Only through the competitive market process—where multiple entrepreneurs bid on the different land, labor, and capital goods offered for sale—can genuine prices emerge for these inputs. These factor prices are then compared with the output prices to determine if a given operation is turning a profit or loss. This is the method of economic calculation by which a market economy ensures that resources are being devoted efficiently to various uses.

A specific example will help clarify Mises's understanding of how entrepreneurs act as the representatives for the consumers as they bid on various resources. Suppose that Ms. Jewell operates a jewelry store. She buys gold and silver at wholesale prices and then uses them to make necklaces and earrings. Although the gold and silver are expensive, Ms. Jewell can afford to buy them because she receives enough in revenue from her customers when selling the gold and silver jewelry. Ms. Jewell can stay in business even though she regularly uses gold and silver in her operation.

In contrast, Mr. Mason is a homebuilder who would never incorporate gold or silver into his building designs. It's true, his customers would pay more for a house with an interior coated in gold or silver; it would feel like living in a royal palace. However, his customers wouldn't be willing to pay enough extra to cover the higher expenses of building such an exquisite home. If for some reason Mr. Mason foolishly insisted on building and selling houses with interiors coated in gold or silver, he would eventually go out of business because he would lose large amounts of money on each unit.

These two entrepreneurs—Ms. Jewell and Mr. Mason—may not know each other, but they are related. The reason Mr. Mason can't afford to use gold or silver for homebuilding is that those precious metals are more urgently needed in jewelry production. The relatively high prices of gold and silver serve as signals saying, "Use with extreme caution!" to any entrepreneur. However, the prices aren't so high as to make these metals too expensive for everyone because otherwise no buyer would be supporting the high prices in the first place. Rather, the competitive market process allows entrepreneurs such as Ms. Jewell to bid up the prices of gold and silver to ensure that these precious metals flow into jewelry production and a few other lines to the exclusion of other possible outlets where they would be valued as well.

The crucial point in our simple story is that the consumers ultimately steer the gold and silver into jewelry and away from housing. Of course, the consumers don't realize they are doing this, and literally speaking, the entrepreneurs are the ones making the decisions about whether or not to use gold and silver in their operations. Yet Mises's insight is that Jewell and Mason are guided by market prices, which in the final analysis are determined by consumer spending patterns. If, for some reason, people decided that they didn't care much whether necklaces were made out of gold or plastic, while they suddenly decided that having a gold-plated coffee table was extremely fashionable and a social necessity, then market prices would adjust to bring about this new configuration. Gold would no longer flow into the production of new necklaces, and in fact, people would sell their existing gold necklaces to buy cheaper plastic ones and pocket the difference. Gold would then begin flowing into the production of extremely expensive coffee tables.

As our simple story illustrates, most resources can serve a variety of possible uses. The challenge is to determine the best pattern of deployment, which means using resources in a way that not only beats doing nothing but is also better than any other possible use of the resources. This problem, Mises claims, can be adequately addressed only through economic calculation, which itself is only possible in a society with private property and money.

Before leaving this section, we should address two loose ends in Mises's view of consumer sovereignty. First: Is Mises really arguing that entrepreneurs have to obey orders from the consumer? After all, can't the entrepreneur ignore market prices, at least within limits?

This is certainly true, but Mises handles such cases by claiming that the entrepreneur is acting as a consumer. For example, suppose a man owns a vast forest in the middle of which sits his house. The trees are centuries old. The man reckons that if he were to cut down all of the trees and allow a developer to build a shopping mall with large parking lots, he would be able to charge $50,000 per year in rental payments from the developer. In a sense, then, the consumers with their spending decisions are voting $50,000 per year to convince the man to allow the developer to tear down the trees and build the shopping mall.

However, suppose the man decides that he prefers the tranquility of the forest and the sheer knowledge that the trees are centuries old to the potential stream of $50,000 annual payments. He therefore refrains from bringing in the logging crews, and no one else ever sets foot on the land. Does this mean he has selfishly ignored the wishes of the consumers and has hoarded the land to himself?

No, this is *not* the conclusion Mises would draw. Rather, the man is himself one of the consumers. He is implicitly spending $50,000 per year to live in a pristine, old-growth forest, rather than living next to a shopping mall. There is nothing irrational or uneconomical about this decision; it is analogous to a worker who prefers a job as a librarian that pays $30,000 annually to a stressful job as a lawyer that pays $80,000 annually. In both cases, the market prices are crucial for the resource owner to make an informed decision, but Mises would say that ultimately it is still the consumers' preferences that guide resource allocation. By making decisions that reap them less monetary income, our hypothetical landowner and laborer are implicitly spending their potential money on consumption that they buy from themselves.

The second loose end in our discussion of consumer sovereignty is the possibility of a *monopoly price*. This was the one exception Mises saw to his default position; if a producer could restrict production to earn a monopoly price, then the incentives of the marketplace would fail to guide such a producer into obeying the desires of the consumers. For example, if a producer controlled a large enough share of the coffee harvest that he could actually make more total revenue by burning some of the crop, this would clearly be, in Mises's view, a violation of consumer sovereignty: It doesn't free up resources to produce other goods or services. We hasten to add that Mises's follower, Murray Rothbard, criticized Mises's view on monopoly price from within the Austrian framework, claiming that even conceptually there was no way to distinguish a monopoly price from the free-market price.[14] In any event, Mises himself acknowledged that his concerns were largely theoretical. In the real world, Mises knew that the true problem of monopoly price came from government restrictions on domestic producers and foreign imports, not from genuine market forces.

---

14. See Murray Rothbard, *Man, Economy, and State*, Chapter 10.

Competition, Freedom, and (In)Equality

Virtually all commentaries on economics and politics champion the virtues of competition, freedom, and equality, as most people endorse these attributes and will be more likely to endorse a proposed social institution if it yields them. The problem is that different writers mean different things by the same terms; what is freedom to Karl Marx is different from the freedom envisioned by Thomas Jefferson. The classical liberal endorses equality of rights under the law, whereas the socialist may demand equality of income distribution. Even among professional economists, the term competition means something different.

In the view of Mises and most Austrian economists, the only notion of freedom that is coherent is the degree of individual autonomy consistent with an unbiased enforcement of property rights under the rule of law. Mises, though not all of his followers, believed that the government had a vital role to play in the maintenance of civilization by protecting property rights from domestic criminals and foreign invaders. Yet he recognized all too well the danger— borne out by history time and again—in granting policing, legal, and military powers to a political body. The function of constitutions and bills of rights is precisely to restrain the government, to prevent it from growing beyond its proper sphere. This bourgeois conception of liberty is negative; people can be free only if the government is tightly restricted in what it can do *to* them, as opposed to what some might want it to do *for* them.

Although economics is a value-free and objective science of how the world is, Mises nonetheless drew a connection between the market economy and political liberty. In his words, "No government and no civil law can guarantee and bring about freedom otherwise than by supporting and defending the fundamental institutions of the market economy."[15] Furthermore, the specific mechanism by which the market delivers freedom is competition. Workers are not wage slaves, as the Marxists claim, because of competition among employers; if their current boss becomes intolerable, workers can quit and seek employment elsewhere. By the same token, consumers are not at the mercy of the company selling food or medicine because they can always

---

15. Mises. *Human Action*, 283.

switch to a different seller if they don't like the price or quality provided by current vendors.

Austrian economists are not alone in recognizing the importance of competition to reap the benign fruits of a market economy. However, the mainstream economics profession in the twentieth century developed a notion of "perfect competition" as a theoretical ideal against which to judge the actual degree of competition in the real-world market. The mainstream approach to competition looked at a snapshot of a given industry to see how competitive it was, for example, by looking at the market share held by the leading firms in the industry or by seeing whether the firms produced identical versus distinct goods. In this approach, the industry for running shoes is not perfectly competitive because a few large firms dominate the market, and furthermore each has pricing power because it has differentiated products. On the other hand, the mainstream approach would classify the milk industry as very close to perfectly competitive because many producers are offering a fairly standardized product. No single dairy farmer has the ability to cut back production and charge a slightly higher price for his milk because the consumers of milk don't respect name brands.

In complete contrast to this typical mainstream approach, Mises and subsequent Austrians viewed competition not as a static condition or state but as a process. In order for the market to live up to its role of steering resources into those ends most desired by consumers—and thereby providing the only type of individual freedom possible in a society based on the division of labor—it is not necessary that every industry have dozens or hundreds of firms. Rather, the only requirement is that the government places no arbitrary obstacles in the way of potential entrants into an industry. To insist on more than this would be to impair the market economy in its task of allocating resources most efficiently:

> Entrance into a definite branch of industry is virtually free to newcomers only as far as the consumers approve of this branch's expansion or as far as the newcomers succeed in supplanting those already occupied in it . . . . If the existing plants are sufficient, it would be wasteful to invest more capital in the same industry. The structure of market prices pushes the new investors into other branches.

It is necessary to emphasize this point because the failure to grasp it is at the root of many popular complaints about the impossibility of competition. Some fifty years ago people used to declare: You cannot compete with the railroad companies; it is impossible to challenge their position by starting competing lines; in the field of land transportation there is no longer competition. The truth was that at that time the already operating lines were by and large sufficient. For additional capital investment the prospects were more favorable in improving the serviceableness of the already operating lines and in other branches of business than in the construction of new railroads. However, this did not interfere with further technological progress in transportation technique. The bigness and the economic "power" of the railroad companies did not impede the emergence of the motor car and the airplane.[16]

We have seen a similar pattern in more recent times. In the 1960s, IBM was considered an invulnerable giant in the computer industry, such that the U.S. government engaged in a lengthy antitrust litigation against "Big Blue." Yet in hindsight, we now know that its days as a Goliath were numbered, as it would largely miss out on the personal computing revolution ushered in by Apple and Microsoft. In a similar twist, Microsoft was itself the target of an antitrust prosecution at a time when it was viewed as an unstoppable force. Yet here, too, we know in hindsight that Microsoft's alleged monopoly did not eliminate competition among web browsers.

Finally, we come to the vexing issue of (in)equality. For many critics, it is an intolerable defect of the market economy that it results in vastly different outcomes of income and wealth. Rather than endure a system that allows some people to own vacation homes while others are homeless, these critics advocate large-scale government redistribution of income, if not outright socialism.

However, once we understand Mises's principles of economic calculation and consumer sovereignty, we realize that inequality of income and wealth is an unavoidable feature of a market economy. Money prices mean something when they are generated in a market process, and therefore, they must be

---

16. Mises, *Human Action*, 275–76.

allowed to do their important work. For a simple example, suppose there are one hundred individuals in a market, where two of them are singers and the other ninety-eight are fans. Left to their own devices, each individual can grow enough food on his own land to sustain himself. However, the ninety-eight fans would be willing to work harder to grow slightly more food in order to give singer A enough food that he would rather sing full-time than grow food for himself. At the same time, the ninety-eight fans would be willing to work much harder to grow enough extra food to give singer B an exorbitant amount of food, such that she could sing full-time and live in abundance. If everyone is free in the sense of respect for property rights, then the ninety-eight fans work very hard in order to grow enough extra food to induce the two singers to voluntarily give up farming and sing full-time. By their offer of food, the ninety-eight farmers convinced the other two that the best use of their labor was in producing songs, not crops. Yet in this outcome, singer B is far more successful than singer A, who in turn is more successful than the average farmer. If the government were to interfere with this outcome, it might impair the satisfaction of the consumers, not to mention that it would prevent people from voluntarily exchanging their property.

Although it might seem possible to efficiently plan a simple economy with one hundred individuals and only two occupations, in a real-world market, we need economic calculation, which in turn relies on accurate prices. Recall in our discussion of consumer sovereignty how the market prices of gold and silver were signals to homebuilders to refrain from purchasing the precious metals, as they were more urgently needed in the production of necklaces and earrings. A corollary of these high prices is that the owners of gold and silver mines will enjoy large revenues when selling their output, and the mines themselves will constitute assets of great wealth. To try to soften or round out this outcome—perhaps through a luxury tax levied at the retail level or an excess profits tax levied on the mine owners—would impair the flow of precious metals from the mines to the necks and earlobes of the consumers, which is where they want the gold and silver to end up. Furthermore, the type of freedom that the individual enjoys in a market economy is circumscribed when the government decides that certain patterns of consumption are conspicuous and can safely be taxed in order to alter behavior. The individual has less control over his or her life if the authority waits in the wings to impose a stiff tax or regulation on those with whom the individual wishes to trade.

The connection between high income and satisfaction of the consumers is most obvious in the case of entrepreneurial profit. The only way the entrepreneur can earn a profit is by better anticipating the future state of the market. In the classic formula, the entrepreneur wants to buy low, sell high. This is possible only if the entrepreneur realizes that today's resources can be deployed in a particular outlet that others have overlooked. If others hadn't overlooked the opportunity, after all, then they would have bought the necessary resources, pushing up their prices, to provide more of the desired good or service down the road, pushing down its price. Thus the spread or markup between input and output prices would be reduced back to the level consistent with the going rate of interest, leaving no additional margin of pure profit for the entrepreneur.

Economists often warn that income redistribution and other interventionist policies run the risk of reducing incentives. However, Mises's notion of economic calculation—and its relationship to inequality in market outcomes—runs much deeper. To repeat, the specific market prices attached to each factor of production and consumption mean something as they enter into the calculations of entrepreneurs, resource owners, and consumers. Even the slightest deviation from the genuine market prices thereby impairs economic calculation; people are now getting the wrong information from the false prices. Once we understand the pivotal role of economic calculation, we can see why income redistribution and other schemes will cripple the operation of the market. For an analogy, if the referees in an NBA game decided to award points on the basis of dribbles, rather than according to how many times the ball went through the hoop, it would be odd to say such a move would reduce the incentives to score. On the contrary, the players would no longer really be playing the game of basketball at all.

If an individual's flow of income in a market is a reflection of the flow of services he provides to the consumers, then the individual's stock of wealth is a reflection of the consumers' evaluation of his stewardship of a collection of resources. The market effectively channels control over scarce resources into the hands of those whom the consumers decide—indirectly and metaphorically, of course—are the most likely to use them effectively. Consider: An investor who consistently anticipates changes in consumer tastes and technological development better than her peers will enjoy a growing fortune over time. This growing fortune will in turn give her a much greater ability to influence the market's trajectory. On the other hand, if a prodigal son inherits his father's fortune, he can quickly fritter it away through foolish investments and riotous living. Soon enough, even though the son started out rich, he will no longer be able to influence the allocation of resources, save for his own labor services and the goods he can buy with his wages.

The hostility aimed at the rich—especially the "1 percent," as they were dubbed after the 2008 bailouts of the financial sector—often overlooks the fact that much of their wealth does not consist in mansions and yachts but rather takes the form of shares of stock in a company that the billionaire founded. The only way for such a billionaire to maintain his enormous wealth is to continually prove to others in the market that he is exercising wise stewardship over the resources owned by the company. If Bill Gates suddenly announced that Microsoft would be focusing all of its research and development on producing computers that relied only on abacuses, rather than circuit boards, the share price of Microsoft would collapse immediately, and Gates's fantastic net worth would disappear with it. Although this example is farfetched, it serves to underscore the point that nobody in a market economy has guaranteed wealth or status; even the 1 percent must constantly subject themselves to withering criticism in the market.

Private Management versus Government Bureaucracy

Mises's famous critique of socialism can also be applied in a more piecemeal fashion, allowing us to understand the nature of government bureaucracy and at the same time to see how it's possible for large enterprises in the market to sidestep these problems. The crucial difference between a manager working for a private firm and a bureaucrat working for a government agency is that the manager's actions can be evaluated with the same tools of monetary calculation that apply to the firm as a whole. In contrast, profit and loss calculations are meaningless—and might even be perverse—if applied to government bureaucrats. As Mises explains:

It is the system of double-entry bookkeeping that makes the functioning of the managerial system possible. Thanks to it the entrepreneur is in a position to separate the calculation of each part of his total enterprise in such a way that he can determine the role it plays within his whole enterprise. Thus he can look at each section as if it were a separate entity and can appraise it according to the share it contributes to the success of the total enterprise. Within this system of business calculation each section of a firm represents an integral entity, a hypothetical independent business, as it were. It is assumed that this section "owns" a definite part of the whole capital employed in the enterprise, that it buys from other sections and sells to them, that it has its own expenses and its own revenues, that its dealings result either in a profit or in a loss which is imputed to its own conduct of affairs as distinguished from the result of the other sections. Thus the entrepreneur can assign to each section's management a great deal of independence. The only directive he gives to a man whom he entrusts with the management of a circumscribed job is to make as much profit as possible.[17]

Consider, for example, the operation of a large grocery store chain. In the hierarchy of command, the owners appoint a manager for each store. The owners insist on certain standards for each store, including the logo, layout, and general rules for what types of products the store must and must not carry, but beyond this framework, each store manager is given a wide degree of latitude to be as profitable as possible. The store manager, in turn, interviews and hires department managers to head up the grocery, meat, dairy, pharmacy, and other departments. Thus, in practice, the dairy manager decides how much shelf space in the cooler to devote to 2% half-gallons of milk versus 16 oz. containers of blueberry 1% fat yogurt. The dairy manager would know that her performance will be evaluated primarily on the profitability of the department and act accordingly. As a result, the dairy manager would charge other departments—perhaps a restaurant for customers—if they used butter and milk, even though the two teams were working for the same company.

---

17. Mises, *Human Action*, 301–02.

On the other hand, the dairy manager would still be just a manager, not the actual entrepreneur. The worst that could happen is that she would be fired for poor performance; she wouldn't be personally $1 million poorer if she somehow managed to cause such a loss to the company. This is why the dairy manager would not have total discretion in her activities. For an exaggerated example, she would not have the authority to unilaterally borrow money on the company's behalf to have Elton John sing about the wonders of cottage cheese; that would simply be too large of an expense, with too uncertain of a return, to be justifiable. On the other hand, if the dairy manager examined the books and wanted to stop carrying milk altogether—because the profit per square foot of shelf space was much lower for milk than for other dairy products—the store manager would presumably say, "Are you kidding? No, customers expect to be able to get milk when they go shopping for groceries, so we need to always have milk, even if you think it's not worth the shelf space. You can stop carrying pints of milk if you want, and let me know how many complaints you get, but you have to maintain a basic selection in quarts, half gallons, and gallons. Otherwise you could wreak havoc on the sales of other departments."

As our fanciful discussion illustrates, a for-profit business enterprise can grow quite large without suffering from the problems typically ascribed to bureaucracy because each unit can be isolated and evaluated in terms of profitability. The millions of decisions that must be made on a daily basis to run a large enterprise can be divided and delegated to various subordinates, who are free within a general framework to make these decisions on their own initiative and judgment.

In total contrast, a typical government agency cannot be run in this fashion. As Mises explains:

> *Bureaucratic management*, as distinguished from *profit management*, is the method applied in the conduct of administrative affairs, the result of which has no cash value on the market. The successful performance of the duties entrusted to the care of a police department is of the greatest importance for the preservation of social cooperation and benefits each member of society. But it has no price on the market, it cannot be bought or sold; it can therefore not be confronted with the

expenses incurred in the endeavors to secure it. It results in gains, but these gains are not reflected in profits liable to expression in terms of money. The methods of economic calculation, and especially those of double-entry bookkeeping, are not applicable to them. Success or failure of a department's activities cannot be ascertained according to the arithmetical procedures of profit-seeking business. No accountant can establish whether or not a police department or one of its subdivisions has succeeded.[18]

It is precisely because of the lack of an objective metric of success—which is profitability in a private business enterprise—that a typical government operation must be run bureaucratically. The head of the agency must lay down precise rules specifying how his subordinates are to act in various situations. When a problem occurs, the important thing for the subordinate is to establish that he has acted in accordance with the procedures—that is all that can be expected of him—even if the procedures yield absurd results in particular scenarios.

The fundamental differences between profit management and bureaucratic management are that business enterprises in the market (a) must convince their customers to voluntarily pay them and (b) cannot prevent competitors from offering a similar product or service. These two conditions do not hold for most government services; the differences explain why self-interested motivation in the private sector is benign but can be sinister in the public sector.

For example, in the private sector, airlines may offer their customers the option of joining an "elite" club, in which they have access to fancy lounges at the airports, ride in nicer seats on the planes, and can check-in and board in special lines while the passengers flying coach must wait in usually longer lines. Although this state of affairs might cause resentment among some of the people flying coach, ultimately the outcome is socially beneficial: The two-tiered framework allows the airlines to extract more revenue from those customers willing to pay more for such conveniences, which translates into lower ticket prices for the people flying coach. Competition also provides the ultimate safety valve on such schemes, as well: If enough customers disliked

---

18. Mises, *Human Action*, 305.

the two-tiered approach strongly enough, then one or more airlines would refrain from offering such programs and would advertise accordingly.

In contrast, suppose a city's police department adopts an implicit two-tiered scheme, whereby squad cars respond much more quickly to calls coming from households that have contributed to that year's Police Benevolence Fund Drive. This is by no means a socially beneficial outcome, but instead reeks of corruption and a shakedown of the citizenry. The citizens of the community are not free to withhold a portion of their taxes if they don't think the police department is earning its budget, and they can't even hire outside firms to perform police services if they are not getting enough from the government provider. Thus the situation of a flying customer vis-à-vis an airline is completely different from a citizen vis-à-vis the police department.

10

How Prices Are Formed
on the Market

Introduction

IN CHAPTER 7, we used the simplified example of children trading Halloween candy to illustrate how modern economics can start with subjective, ordinal preference rankings and end up with objective, cardinal exchange ratios or barter prices. In this chapter, we will elaborate on the method by which prices are formed on the market, not only for consumer goods, but for producer higher order goods as well.

The exposition in this chapter assumes the existence of money. Following Mises's treatment, we will postpone the explanation of the origin of money until the next chapter. In other words, we will simply take it for granted that most transactions involve money on one side of the exchange and that individuals have access to a wide array of money prices for every good and service available in the economy. Given this array of money prices, we will explain how the individual consumer or entrepreneur spends his or her money on the various consumer and producer goods. In the next chapter, we will investigate how money emerged from an initial state of barter, and we will also analyze in much greater depth why money has a particular purchasing power.

Explaining the Prices of Consumer Goods and Services

The basic techniques we used in Chapter 7 to explain barter prices also work when it comes to money prices. The one significant difference is that one of the items happens to be a commodity called money. For example, let

Table 10.1. Rankings of Money and Candy Bars for Alice and Billy

Alice's Subjective, Ordinal Ranking	Billy's Subjective, Ordinal Ranking
6 dollar bills	(6 dollar bills)
(1 Milky Way)	(5 dollar bills)
5 dollar bills	(4 dollar bills)
4 dollar bills	(3 dollar bills)
3 dollar bills	(2 dollar bills)
2 dollar bills	1 Milky Way
1 dollar bill	(1 dollar bill)

us adapt our Halloween candy discussion from a barter to a monetary framework, as shown in Table 10.1 above.

Thus, given the preferences described in the table above, we see that Alice would be willing to pay $5 or less for Billy's Milky Way, but she wouldn't be willing to pay $6. Billy, on the other hand, would not be willing to sell his Milky Way for $1, but he would be happy to trade it in exchange for $2 or more. There is thus an opportunity for mutual gains from trade. We don't have enough information to pin down the price in this example; all we can say from the table is that if a trade occurs, Billy will sell his Milky Way bar to Alice for more than $1 but less than $6. Just as with our barter discussion, if we added more people to this market, the zone of indeterminacy of the equilibrium dollar-price of a Milky Way would shrink.

Although the explanation—at least superficially—seems just as straightforward as it was in the case of barter, there is a problem. Why does Billy prefer two or more dollar bills to his Milky Way? Back in the barter discussion, when we were dealing with Snickers bars instead of dollar bills, the answer was clear: Billy wanted to acquire Snickers bars because he derived happiness or utility from eating them.

Yet things are different when it comes to money. In its role as money, the money good provides no direct service at all. In short, you can't eat a dollar bill or use it to physically produce desirable goods or services. So again we ask: Why would Billy give up a perfectly tasty Milky Way bar, in exchange for green pieces of paper that are virtually useless to him directly?

The answer, of course, is that Billy expects to be able to use those green pieces of paper to buy goods and services from other people in the future. Therefore, what Billy is ultimately comparing is the value he places on his Milky Way versus the value he places on other items that he expects to be able to purchase with various amounts of dollar bills. For example, if it just so happened that the market price for a Snickers bar were $1, and if Alice and Billy expected this to remain the case for the foreseeable future, then our table would represent the same preferences for candy bars as our first table in the Halloween candy barter discussion.

At this point, we should clarify two important points to avoid possible misunderstanding. First, the mere introduction of a good that we call money and that has a familiar unit—in the United States, dollars—does not change the nature of subjective valuation. If, say, Alice ends up spending $3 in order to buy Billy's Milky Way, it is not accurate to say, "Alice measured the amount of value in the Milky Way at $3." Rather, what happened in this exchange is that Alice valued the Milky Way more than her sixth, fifth, and fourth dollar bills, while Billy valued the collection of his first, second, and third dollar bills more than his Milky Way.[1] If we want, we can say that the Milky Way has a market value of $3, but such language may be misleading: All we really mean is that a Milky Way will fetch $3 on the marketplace. In this example, the objective price of the Milky Way was $3, but its value is subjective to Alice and Billy. Money is not a measuring rod of an intrinsic value embedded in the Milky Way. In the modern approach to value and price theory, value is ultimately a subjective phenomenon that is ordinal in nature; all we can say is that people prefer *a* to *b*, meaning that they value *a* more highly than *b*.

The second clarification we should make is that there is something odd about our explanation of how Alice and Billy place dollar bills in their preference rankings. We argued that they would evaluate dollars based on the dollars' ability to fetch them other goods in the market. In other words, Billy is willing to sell his valuable candy bar for dollars because other people in the community are willing to sell their valuable candy bars for dollars. But if we pushed the issue and asked why are they willing to do so, we would give the

---

1. To be clear, our discussion assumes that Alice starts out with six dollar bills and no Milky Way bars, while Billy starts out with one Milky Way bar and zero dollar bills.

same answer. We get the uneasy feeling that we may be moving in a circle in our explanation, in which we're basically saying, "People are willing to sell useful goods for money because people are willing to sell useful goods for money."

At this point, we are not ready to handle this subtle concern for it actually represented a major stumbling block in the development of marginal utility theory. Solving this particular problem was one of Mises's early scholarly contributions to economic theory. We will elaborate on the problem and provide Mises's solution in the next chapter.

For our purposes now, we're satisfied with explaining the general process by which consumers spend their money on the various goods and services available to them. Because all of the potential goods and services in which they are interested have money prices, the consumers can easily evaluate various possibilities in terms of the direct happiness that they would yield. For example, if a woman is considering whether to buy a blouse with a price of $50, she contrasts the satisfaction it would give her against the satisfaction she could achieve from buying other goods and services with a total price of $50. The use of money allows the woman to quickly assess the various tradeoffs involved—such as one blouse versus two $25 lunches at her favorite restaurant near work—but her decisions in light of the tradeoffs can be explained using the exact same principles from our barter discussion.

Valuation versus Appraisement

Before explaining how the prices of producer goods—also called factors of production or goods of a higher order—are formed, we first must make the distinction between valuation and appraisement. Valuation refers to the significance that an individual places on a good or service because of its ability to confer happiness or utility on the individual. Valuation occurs whenever there is action; Robinson Crusoe and members of a socialist community engage in valuation. In contrast, appraisement assesses the amount of money for which a good or service can be sold. As such, appraisement can occur only in a market economy. For yet another difference between the two concepts, there is a sense in which appraisals are objective whereas valuations are inherently subjective.

Although valuation and appraisement are distinct concepts, they are closely connected in a monetary economy. In order for a consumer to decide whether she wants to make a specific purchase, she must have a basic familiarity with the money prices of the other goods and services she might desire to buy instead. This is not a question that can be answered solely by her subjective preference rankings; she needs to have some idea of the market prices of other goods, and this is an objective fact of the world in which she lives.

Also, even if people have little use for a good themselves, they would still attribute a high subjective valuation to it if they knew it had a high objective appraisal value. For example, a blind man has little use for a Ferrari. But if he somehow found himself in possession of a Ferrari—perhaps he won it through a contest—the blind man would presumably value it quite highly. This is not because it would directly satisfy his goals, but because he could sell it for a large sum of money, which in turn he could spend on the things he wants. Notice that the man really does value the Ferrari while he owns it; if some punk teenagers wrecked it during a joyride, the man would be devastated, assuming his insurance didn't cover it.

The widespread use of money in a market economy creates a complex feedback cycle in which individuals' subjective valuations are the ultimate basis of objective market prices, but these market prices in turn influence people's subjective valuations. Our succinct statement may seem circular since we are claiming that valuation is the prerequisite to appraisement, while appraisement in turn influences valuation. Yet there is no logical circularity; the early Austrian theorists explained the entire process methodically.[2] The crowning achievement of this line of thought was Mises's explanation of the subjective valuation of money itself, a process that crucially depends on appraisement of money's objective exchange value in the market. We will return to this topic in the next chapter.

Explaining the Prices of Producer Goods (and Services)

For any acting person—whether a nun, stock trader, or Robinson Crusoe—the subjective valuation of the means is derived from the subjective valuation of the end. For example, Robinson Crusoe's valuation of a boat and net

2. See, for example, Eugen von Böhm-Bawerk, *Basic Principles of Economic Value* (Grove City, PA: Libertarian Press, [1886] 2005).

is dependent on his valuation of the fish they will help him catch. If Crusoe discovered that the fish of the island made him ill, the boat and net would lose all significance for him.

In a market economy using money, the entrepreneurs buy factors of production to create goods that they then sell for money on the market. Thus, when the individual entrepreneur evaluates a particular factor of production—a worker's labor, a kilowatt-hour of electricity, a new tractor, and so on—he must engage in two different sorts of speculations or forecasts. First, he needs to understand the physical processes involved well enough to predict what good or service the particular factor will help to create. Second, the entrepreneur must also predict how much money he will be able to fetch when he sells this output to his customers. On the basis of these judgments, the entrepreneur is in a position to place the factor in his preference rankings and can decide how many units of money he would be willing to offer for it. As Mises describes the process:

> The prices of the goods of higher orders are ultimately determined by the prices of the goods of the first or lowest order, that is, the consumers' goods. As a consequence of this dependence they are ultimately determined by the subjective valuations of all members of the market society. *It is, however, important to realize that we are faced with a connection of prices, not with a connection of valuations.* The prices of the complementary factors of production are conditioned by the prices of the consumers' goods. The factors of production are appraised with regard to the prices of the products, and from this appraisement their prices emerge. Not the valuations but the appraisements are transferred from the goods of the first order to those of higher orders. The prices of the consumers' goods engender the actions resulting in the determination of the prices of the factors of production. These prices are primarily connected only with the prices of the consumers' goods. *With the valuations of the individuals [i.e. the consumers—RPM] they are only indirectly connected, viz., through the intermediary of the prices of the consumers' goods*, the products of their joint employment. (italics added)[3]

---

3. Mises, *Human Action*, 330–31.

To repeat, the prices of consumer goods are determined by the consumers' subjective valuations between various units of each good and various units of money. Entrepreneurs anticipate these prices when they enter the market to bid on units of land, labor, and capital goods. In one sense, then, the consumers ultimately determine all prices, both for consumer goods and for the factors of production; this is the basis for Mises's notion of consumer sovereignty. It's why Mises argues that ultimately the consumers determine who is rich and who is poor in a market economy.

On the other hand, Mises is clear in the above quotation that subjective consumer preferences do not directly explain or determine the prices of land, labor, and capital goods. Rather, consumer preferences work through consumer prices and then the appraisement of entrepreneurs to influence the prices of producer goods.

We can get a sense of just how important this point is to Mises, when he later brings up "Professor Schumpeter's dictum according to which consumers in evaluating consumers' goods 'ipso facto also evaluate the means of production which enter into the production of these goods.'" At first blush, Schumpeter's statement seems consistent with Mises's discussion of consumer sovereignty, and yet Mises has more to say about Schumpeter's point: "It is hardly possible to construe the market process in a more erroneous way."[4] Mises's harsh judgment of an apparently innocuous statement by Schumpeter revolves around a central theme in *Human Action*, namely the importance of economic calculation in *monetary* terms. This crucial procedure—which, we recall, Mises thanked for the existence of modern civilization—is possible only in an institutional setting that allows entrepreneurs to bid on the various factors of production. By claiming that the consumers, in evaluating consumer goods, were by that very act evaluating the importance of producer goods, Schumpeter removed entrepreneurs from the scene entirely. He brushed aside the role that entrepreneurs and economic calculation play in the real world. Indeed, it was precisely this type of thinking—believing that knowledge of consumer preferences and technological recipes would be enough to rationally allocate resources—that Mises attacked so strongly in his famous critique of socialism.

---

4. Mises, *Human Action*, 354.

The general principle, then, for explaining the prices of factors of production is that entrepreneurs bid on them in accordance with the prices they expect to charge for the goods and services these factors eventually will produce. However, there are two complications when we try to apply this principle to specific cases.

First, entrepreneurs would not be willing to spend the full amount of revenues expected on a future sale of product on the inputs needed today to create it. For example, suppose a home builder thinks he can hire laborers and buy the wood, glass, tiles, and other materials necessary to build a house, which will take him one year to create, market, and finally sell for $100,000. To the extent that he views his homebuilding operation as a way to earn income, the builder won't spend more than $100,000 on the various ingredients necessary to build the house. However, we can go further and say that he will spend less than $100,000 because of positive interest rates. For example, if the going rate of interest on a very safe one-year bond is 5 percent, then our home builder could invest about $95,238 today in order to receive $100,000 in twelve months. Looking solely at monetary considerations, therefore, it would be foolish of him to spend more than $95,238 total on buying wood, glass, and other materials to build a house; he would earn a greater return on his money by buying the safe bond.

Thus if we want to say that entrepreneurs pay prices on factors of production that reflect the prices of the products they will eventually create, we have to take account of the fact that goods today are more valuable than goods in the future. This concept of time preference is such an important element of the Austrian perspective that we will devote Chapter 13 to it. In the meantime, we note that these considerations explain why Mises says in his discussion of entrepreneurship that

> Entrepreneurial profits are not a lasting phenomenon but only temporary. There prevails an inherent tendency for profits and losses to disappear . . . . If new changes in the data were not to interrupt this movement and not to create the need for a new adjustment of production to the altered conditions, the prices of all complementary factors of

production would—due allowance being made for time preference—finally equal the price of the product, and nothing would be left for profits or losses.[5]

In other words, Mises is arguing that if there were no changes in the data of consumer preferences, resource supplies, technological know-how, and so on, then eventually profits and losses would be weeded out of, say, the housing industry. If builders had to spend $105,000 on materials in order to produce houses that sold for only $95,000, they would suffer monetary losses and would presumably scale back their operations.[6] The lower demand for homebuilding materials would push down their price, while the reduced supply of finished houses would push up their price. On the other hand, if the homebuilders could spend, say, $80,000 on materials in order to produce houses that they were sure they could sell for $120,000, then they would be earning monetary profits and would presumably expand their operations. The higher demand for homebuilding materials would push up their price, while the increased supply of finished houses would push down their price. Yet because of time preference, and its corollary of a positive rate of interest, this process won't stop at literal equality of the two numbers. Even in a stable, long-run equilibrium—what Mises calls the evenly rotating economy—we would expect a perpetual gap or markup in the price structure, reflecting the fact that the goods of higher orders can produce goods of lower orders only after the passage of time. Thus capitalists would still earn interest on their investments in the evenly rotating economy, even though entrepreneurs could neither earn pure profits nor suffer pure losses.

Besides the phenomenon of time preference, as well as interest, another complication to our general principle of factor pricing is the decomposition of the total factor payments into the individual inputs. In our homebuilder

---

5. Mises, *Human Action*, 293.

6. In this discussion, we use the caveat *presumably* because, strictly speaking, a homebuilder might enjoy the enterprise for nonpecuniary reasons. Thus he might be willing to produce houses for low-income individuals even though the builder could earn more money by directing his resources elsewhere.

example, we argued that if a house can be sold for $100,000 in one year, then a market rate of interest of 5 percent means that in equilibrium, a homebuilder will pay about $95,238 to hire the workers and buy the other materials necessary to build the house. Yet we didn't explain how much of that sum would go to the workers, how much would go to the people selling wood, how much to the people selling glass, and so on.

To explain how much each particular input gets paid, economists invoke the concept of marginal productivity. Just as consumers spend their money guided by marginal utility, entrepreneurs spend their funds according to marginal productivity. Note that this isn't really a different explanation; rather, the marginal productivity approach to factor prices is simply the marginal utility theory supplemented with the extra step of appraisement. Ultimately, it's correct to say that an entrepreneur spends his money in accordance with considerations of marginal utility; it's just that we can say much more about how he values various units of factors in terms of the revenue each is expected to yield. For example, if an entrepreneur buys a $1,000 machine but refrains from buying a $500 tool, then we can say he gets more utility from the machine than from the tool. Yet we gain insight into why his subjective preferences are ranked in this fashion when we learn that he believes the machine will generate $1,050 in extra revenue for his business, while the tool would generate only $450 in extra revenue.

Note that the principle of marginal productivity explains the hire-price or rental rate of labor, which is simply a resource by which the entrepreneur can increase future revenues. If adding a worker to the staff will boost revenue by $50 per hour, then competition among employers will provide a tendency for the worker to earn $50 per hour.

The reason starting pitchers earn a higher income in a market economy than elementary schoolteachers is that their marginal productivity is higher. Recall that marginal utility explains the water-diamond paradox. By the same token, even though education is—according to some people!—more valuable than Major League Baseball, the services provided by any individual elementary teacher are not nearly as scarce as those provided by any individual starting pitcher. The disparity in income is not a reflection of the ethical status of one occupation versus the other.

What about the Supply Side?

It may seem from our discussion thus far that we are focusing only on the buyers in a market, or the demand side. What about the sellers, or the supply side?[7] Isn't it a staple of modern economics that the market price for a good—whether a consumer or a producer good—is set by the interaction of demand and supply?

The quick answer is that in Mises's exposition, he can adequately explain all market prices by referring only to the entrepreneurs and the consumers. Because the entrepreneur buys factors of production to create products for consumers, the entrepreneur sits on the demand side of the factor markets and the supply side of the consumer good markets.

However, it is worth mentioning that compared to most other economists, the Austrians tend to focus more on subjective demand considerations than on objective cost considerations when explaining market prices. Although it is certainly true that we can illustrate price formation using supply and demand concepts and diagrams, this approach can be misleading as it suggests that different types of forces are influencing the market price, when in fact the seller is simply the buyer with the goods reversed. For example, if we understand Jim's motivations as a potential milk buyer when he considers spending $3 on a gallon, then we can use the exact same apparatus to understand Sally's motivations as a potential milk seller, when she considers spending a gallon of milk to buy three dollar bills. This kind of equivalence between buyers and sellers is most evident in a barter transaction: When Alice trades two Snickers bars to Billy for one Milky Way, Alice can be considered both as a seller of Snickers and a buyer of Milky Ways. Similarly, Billy is a seller of Milky Ways and a buyer of Snickers. The same framework by which we understand Alice's actions obviously applies to Billy's actions as well.[8]

---

7. To avoid confusion, we should clarify that in this section we are not contrasting supply side economics (as associated with Arthur Laffer, Jude Wanniski, and Ronald Reagan) with demand side economics (as associated with John Maynard Keynes, Paul Krugman, and Barack Obama). Rather, we are talking about the much more simple ideas of supply and demand in the explanation of a market price.

8. Indeed, in his treatise on Austrian economics, Murray Rothbard first develops the conventional supply/demand approach to explaining prices but then lays out a completely

The reason there appears to be a qualitative gulf between the supply and demand sides is that the suppliers are often physically creating the goods while the demanders are consuming them. Yet even in a case where the seller created the goods in question over a long period, once the goods are completed and in the seller's possession, we can analyze the situation as if it were Alice starting with her two Snickers bars. It is irrelevant how much the seller spent in the past to get to this moment. Bygones are bygones; these are "sunk costs," as economists would say.

To illustrate this point about sunk costs, suppose at the start of the 2015 baseball season, someone spent $100,000 printing up 20,000 T-shirts that said, "Yankees 2015 World Series Champs." Thus the monetary expenses would be $5 per shirt. The person did this because he was confident the Yankees would win, and he expected that in such a scenario he would be able to sell all 20,000 shirts at $15 each, for a hefty profit of $10 per shirt or $200,000 total. Unfortunately, as it turns out, the Yankees make it to the World Series but get swept, losing the first four games to the Atlanta Braves. Now, our T-shirt vendor could market his wares to Braves fans, who might buy the shirts at $1 each as a joke reflecting the arrogance of Yankee fans. Should the vendor go ahead with the $1 sales? After all, if he does this, he will lose $4 per shirt. But he is sitting on 20,000 T-shirts and his $100,000 expense is a sunk cost, the vendor can sell the shirts to Braves fans to bring in $20,000 in revenue *or* he can refuse and bring in $0 in revenue. Maybe he decides to donate them to a clothing drive or he sells them for a dime apiece to an auto body shop to use as rags, but if he wants to maximize his monetary return from the project, selling them at a loss for $1 each is the best option. Note that whatever he does with the shirts once they have been produced, he cannot restore the $100,000 that he spent to make them. That's what economists mean by sunk costs. When the vendor is holding 20,000 T-shirts and is surveying his options, he acts exactly the way Alice acts when she holds her two Snickers bar and surveys the market composed of her siblings. The vendor and Alice both engage in trades according

---

equivalent "total demand to hold" approach in which the unsold portion of a fixed stock of goods is demanded by the seller and therefore remains in his possession. See Rothbard, *Man, Economy, and State*, Chapter 2, section 8.

to whether they allow them to move to a higher position on their preference rankings, in other words to achieve a higher subjective utility. As Mises says:

> The task incumbent upon the businessman is always to use the supply of capital goods *now* available in the best possible way for the satisfaction of future needs. In the pursuit of this aim he must not be misled by past errors and failures the consequences of which cannot be brushed away.[9]

Now it is certainly true that going forward, our vendor will not—unless he's motivated by nonpecuniary objectives—continue creating and selling T-shirts in a market where the shirts must always be sold for less money than he has to spend in producing them. This is the sense in which it appears that suppliers are influenced by marginal cost, in complete contrast to consumers, who are influenced by marginal utility. Indeed, undergraduate textbooks will often devote much space to showing students how to draw various diagrams containing cost curves to explain producer behavior, whereas they rely on indifference curves to explain consumer behavior.

However, the Austrian insight is that both sides of the market—buyer and seller—are motivated in the final analysis by subjective marginal utility. It's true, if the market price of a TV falls, leading many suppliers to exit the market, they might say, "We had to stop producing because we could no longer cover our costs." But those costs to which they refer are simply prices for the factors of production necessary for making TVs. Furthermore, the reason people on the supply side want to maximize monetary profit by producing where marginal revenue equals marginal cost is that they are anticipating the subjective happiness they will derive from the goods and services they will buy with their newly acquired profits.

Perhaps the most obvious way to explode the typical distinction made between subjective utility and objective costs is to remind the reader of the definition of cost as an opportunity cost of a decision, which is the value of the next-best alternative that is now unattainable because of the decision. As Mises puts it:

---

9. Mises, *Human Action*, 344.

If costs were a real thing, i.e., a quantity independent of personal value judgments and objectively discernible and measurable, it would be possible for a disinterested arbiter to determine their height and thus the correct price. There is no need to dwell any longer on the absurdity of this idea. Costs are a phenomenon of valuation. Costs are the value attached to the most valuable want-satisfaction which remains unsatisfied because the means required for its satisfaction are employed for that want-satisfaction the cost of which we are dealing with. The attainment of an excess of the value of the product over the costs, a profit, is the goal of every production effort. Profit is the pay-off of successful action. It cannot be defined without reference to valuation. It is a phenomenon of valuation and has no direct relation to physical and other phenomena of the external world. Economic analysis cannot help reducing all items of cost to value judgments.[10]

Neither Mises nor his followers oppose splitting the market up into a demand and a supply side when analyzing the market price.[11] The purpose of this section was to explain to the reader that Mises conceives of the market economy not as individual markets composed of suppliers and demanders, but rather as a group of entrepreneurs entering the various factor markets to produce goods and services for the consumers. During his exposition, Mises deals with many of the more orthodox concepts (such as fixed, average, and marginal costs),[12] but his focus on the role of monetary costs in guiding entrepreneurs to serve consumers is quintessentially Misesian.

Mises's Critique of Mathematical Economics

Because the actions of producers involve many quantitative elements, economists have developed mathematical models to describe the equilibrium

---

10. Mises, *Human Action*, 393.

11. For example, in *Human Action* on pages 329–30, Mises uses the conventional terminology to discuss the effect of changes in supply and demand on the market price (though he dismisses the drawing of supply and demand curves as "mere byplay").

12. See section 4 on "Cost Accounting" in Chapter XVI on "Prices," beginning on page 336 of Mises, *Human Action*.

relationships between prices and costs. Mises criticized such an approach quite vehemently:

> The mathematical method must be rejected not only on account of its barrenness. It is an entirely vicious method, starting from false assumptions and leading to fallacious inferences. Its syllogisms are not only sterile; they divert the mind from the study of the real problems and distort the relations between the various phenomena.[13]

When confronting such bold statements, many economists are baffled by Mises's position. Is he rejecting the use of math completely in economics? However, part of the dispute arises from Mises's distinction between economic theory and economic history:[14]

> Statistics is a method for the presentation of historical facts concerning prices and other relevant data of human action. It is not economics and cannot produce economic theorems and theories. The statistics of prices is economic history. The insight that, *ceteris paribus* [other things equal—RPM], an increase in demand must result in an increase in prices is not derived from experience. Nobody ever was or ever will be in a position to observe a change in one of the market data *ceteris paribus*. There is no such thing as quantitative economics. All economic quantities we know about are data of economic history. No reasonable man can contend that the relations between price and supply is in general, or in respect of certain commodities, constant . . . . Nobody is so bold as to maintain that a rise of *a* per cent in the supply of any commodity must always—in every country and at any time—result

---

13. Mises, *Human Action*, 347.

14. When evaluating Mises's comments on mathematical economics, part of the problem is that formal economics has evolved since he wrote *Human Action*. Even professional economists who are well-versed in Mises's writings currently disagree on exactly what his target really is in this section (e.g., merely the assumption of general equilibrium or all nonverbal economics?). There is a similar problem in Mises's harsh treatment of game theory. In context, it is clear that Mises has in mind zero-sum games, which is understandable because that was how von Neumann and Morgenstern originally tackled the subject. But since the work of John Nash, what economists mean by game theory is broader and not necessarily vulnerable to the specific critique Mises lays out in *Human Action*.

in a fall of *b* per cent in its price. But as no quantitative economist ever ventured to define precisely on the ground of statistical experience the special conditions producing a definite deviation from the ratio *a* : *b*, the futility of his endeavors is manifest.[15]

Therefore, Mises does not disparage the work of those who explore the impact of a financial crisis on consumer spending or who calculate the price elasticity of demand for potatoes in Ireland during a famine. His point, however, is that such explorations are economic history. The results of these types of inquiries could never lead the economist to discover a general law. Going the other way, the actual laws that economists use—such as the law of demand—can't be tested, even in principle. The law of demand states that if the price of a good goes up, consumers will buy the same amount or less of it, other things equal. In practice, therefore, the law of demand isn't threatened if, say, the price of gasoline goes up even as people buy more gallons. In such a case, the economist would conclude that something else had changed, perhaps the arrival of summer, when people go on vacations and drive more.

Conclusion

We will return in Chapter 13 to give a more detailed treatment of wage rates for labor, as well as rental rates/purchase prices for capital goods and natural resources, in light of time preference and interest rates. At this stage in our development of Mises's economic theory, the important insight is that the consumers' subjective valuations direct the entire economy because the value of producer goods is ultimately derived from the value of the consumer goods that they produce. However, the actual mechanism by which consumers steer resources is the entrepreneurs entering the factor markets on the consumers' behalf, armed with their appraisement of future prices of consumer goods.

We should emphasize that the explanation of price formation outlined in this chapter is the result of the subjectivist marginal revolution of the 1870s. The classical economists embraced variants of a cost theory of value in which the long-run equilibrium price of a consumer good was explained by the cost

---

15. Mises, *Human Action*, 348.

of the factors going into its construction. For example, if a necklace contains a half an ounce of gold, and gold is selling for $2,000 per ounce, then a classical economist might point out that, in the long run, jewelers will produce only a limited quantity of necklaces that they can sell for at least $1,000 each. Although this is true insofar as it goes, with the new approach economists reverse the direction of the explanation: Consumer demand is the ultimate cause of the high price of gold necklaces, and this price in turn allows jewelers to bid up the price of gold. To put the matter simplistically but succinctly: The classical economists explained the high price of necklaces by the high price of gold, whereas the modern post-1870s economists explain the high price of gold by the high price of necklaces. Among modern economists, the Austrians have pushed this revolution further than most; they do not dwell on cost factors when explaining market prices but instead point to subjective marginal utility as the ultimate cause of prices.

In contrast to the logical, deductive method of Mises, many economists approach economic issues by building mathematical models. Yet Mises dismissed such efforts, claiming that the "mathematical description of various states of equilibrium is mere play." In Mises's view, for the economic theorist, the "problem is the analysis of the market process."[16]

Finally, in this chapter, we took it for granted that there is a certain commodity that is used in almost every transaction; it is called "money." We explained the general principles behind the formation of consumer and producer prices, from the point of view of an individual consumer or entrepreneur deciding how much money to spend on various goods and services. However, this explanation is incomplete because it essentially explains prices by assuming that consumers and entrepreneurs already have a knowledge of prices. We will explore this apparently circular argument, and Mises's solution, in the next chapter.

---

16. Mises, *Human Action*, 353.

11

Indirect Exchange and Money

Introduction

IN CHAPTER 7, we showed how modern subjective marginal utility theory could explain the formation of barter exchange ratios. In other words, economists could explain *relative* prices—why three bananas traded for one orange, for example—in a much more satisfactory way, compared to the earlier classical economists who had relied on a labor or cost theory of value. Carl Menger, founder of the Austrian School, was one of the three pioneers credited with discovering subjective marginal utility theory.

As we will explain in this chapter, Carl Menger also gave a coherent account of the origin of money itself. Rather than relying on a wise intellectual or powerful ruler to invent money, Menger explained its emergence from a pre-existing state of barter in a step-by-step fashion that did not require any extraordinary foresight or altruism from the individuals involved. The institution of money was thus another example of a spontaneous order that was the product of human action, but not of human design.

However, we have also alluded earlier to the ironic situation in which the new theory of marginal utility of Menger et al. was not used initially to explain the absolute money prices of goods and services in the market. Instead, economists viewed the market as if it consisted of barter transactions, and then they would overlay a money commodity on top of these trades, almost as an afterthought. In this chapter, we'll explore why economists went down this route. We'll also explain how Mises evaded the problems involved and provided a truly coherent explanation of actual market prices, quoted in money.

By expanding Menger's marginal utility approach to include the money commodity itself, Mises unified micro- and macroeconomics. In this way, Mises completed the revolution in economic thought that Menger had initiated.

Direct versus Indirect Exchange

Although it is common to contrast a monetary economy with a barter economy, Austrian theory requires the more precise concepts of direct exchange versus indirect exchange. In a direct exchange, the two parties to a trade both intend on directly using the item obtained. For example, if Sally trades her bologna sandwich for Jim's peanut butter sandwich at lunch, the two children have engaged in a direct exchange.

Note that a direct exchange can include a producer good, not just a consumer good. For example, suppose Farmer Anderson trades his ax in order to receive a bull from Farmer Brown. Neither farmer will consume these new goods but instead will use them to produce other items that they value: Anderson will use his new bull to father new calves, while Brown will use his new ax to acquire firewood for the winter. Yet even though there's a sense in which these goods will provide only indirect benefits to their new owners, our hypothetical exchange of Anderson's ax for Brown's bull would still be classified as a direct exchange because each farmer plans on directly using the newly acquired good.

In contrast, an indirect exchange occurs when at least one party to the transaction acquires a good with the intention of trading it away again. Thus, the person views the newly acquired good not as a potential consumer good or even producer good but rather as a medium of exchange. (Just as air or water can serve as the *medium* through which sound waves travel, so too can a particular good serve as the medium through which multi-person exchanges occur.)

We can tweak our previous example to illustrate the concept of indirect exchange. Suppose Farmer Anderson starts with an ax, which he values less than Farmer Brown's bull; Anderson would therefore like to trade his ax in order to receive the bull. However, in this new scenario, suppose that Brown does not value the ax more than his bull. If these were the only two individuals involved, there would be no gains from trade.

However, suppose there is a third farmer, Chambers, who has some chickens that he would gladly give up in exchange for an ax. Even if Anderson has little direct use for the chickens—he would prefer to keep his ax rather than trade it to acquire the chickens for his personal use—he would go through with the trade if he knew that Brown would be willing to give up his bull in exchange for the chickens. In this case, there would be two rounds of exchange, so that by the end, Anderson ended up with the bull, Brown ended up with the chickens, and Chambers ended up with the ax. (See Figure 11.1.)

If the ordinal preferences of each farmer were as depicted in Figure 11.1, there would be no gains from direct exchange. However, indirect exchange opens up new possibilities. Farmer Anderson approaches Farmer Chambers, offering his ax for the chickens. Chambers agrees, as he would personally prefer to the ax to the chickens. However, Anderson does not directly prefer the use of the chickens to his ax. The reason he agreed to the exchange is that

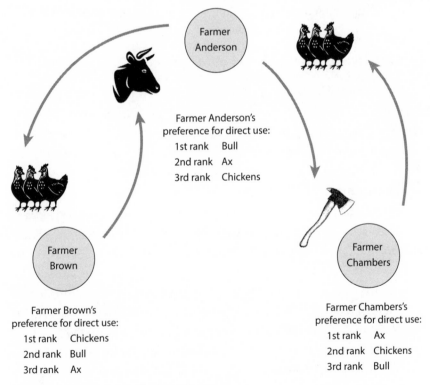

Figure 11.1. Direct versus Indirect Exchange

he correctly anticipated that Farmer Brown would directly prefer the use of the chickens to his bull. This simple example shows how indirect exchange can widen the scope for a rearrangement of property in a market economy, in such a way that every participant ends up better, according to his or her subjective preference rankings, than before the trading commenced and, moreover, where the rearrangement cannot be implemented with individual trades, each of which is mutually beneficial considered in isolation.

In our example involving the three farmers, Anderson engaged in indirect exchange when he traded away his ax for Chambers's chickens, planning to use them to acquire a bull in further exchange. In this example, the chickens served as a *medium of exchange*.

Once we understand the sharp distinction between direct and indirect exchange—and how indirect exchange is accomplished using a medium of exchange—we can give a crisp definition of money: Money is a medium of exchange that is nearly universally accepted in a given community. This definition will be clearer in the next section, where we explain the origin of money.

Carl Menger on the Origin of Money

On the face of it, the use of money is an extremely odd practice, especially when using fiat money, a commodity that serves no other purpose. Consider: In a monetary economy, people regularly give up valuable goods and perform irksome labor in exchange for items that they don't personally plan on using. The reason they do this, of course, is that they expect other people in the future to reciprocate this behavior by giving up valuable goods and performing irksome labor to acquire these same items. At the same time—as our exploration of Mises's views thus far has proven—the use of money is an indispensable element of modern civilization itself, for it makes possible economic calculation. Thus, the widespread use of money is a great thing, but it makes sense for any individual to use money only if just about everybody else is using it, too.

These considerations lead to an obvious question: Where did money come from? Obviously, at some point in the distant past, people must not have used money. How then did humanity get over the hump, as it were, since it seems that the use of money is an all-or-nothing proposition? In other words, it would make no sense for an American today to sell his used guitar for a green piece of paper featuring a picture of Benjamin Franklin if nobody else used dollars anymore. So if we go back in time to the point when nobody used money of any kind, what was the process by which we arrived at today's world, in which just about every human on planet Earth is familiar with some kind of money?

When faced with a social phenomenon that requires large-scale coordination, many people naturally assume that a wise leader or strong ruler conceived of the idea and then persuaded or forced everyone else to adopt the new procedure. Indeed, there is a long tradition of the state theory of money, which holds that money's origin can be traced to mandates from political authorities.[1]

However, there are problems with the state theory of money. For one thing, there's no record of any wise ruler truly inventing money from a preceding condition of barter.[2] Second, it is implausible that starting in an initial state of purely direct exchange, any individual would have had the imagination to perceive the benefits of adopting a common medium of exchange. It is obvious to us, with the benefit of hindsight, that money is a monumental development in human history, but it would not have been obvious to people living before the development of money. Suppose some wise elder told everyone in his tribe, "From now on, rather than trading for things you actually want, I suggest everybody first works through the medium of, say, these smooth rocks I found in the forest. Trust me, if you all do this, we'll all be phenomenally richer in a few years." They would probably conclude that his wisdom had been greatly exaggerated.

Third, even if a leader could persuade or force his people to move from a state of barter[3] into accepting some designated item as money, he would then

---

1. A classic work in this genre is Georg Knapp, *The State Theory of Money* (Simon Publications, [1905] 2003).

2. Modern critics of the Mengerian explanation of the origin of money have claimed to produce historical evidence that ruling officials determined the initial choice of money. See, for example, David Graeber, *Debt: The First 5,000 Years* (Brooklyn, NY: Melville House, 2012). Yet upon closer examination, Graeber's historical evidence is consistent with the orthodox Mengerian account, in which the precious metals first were embraced as money through voluntary market exchanges and only later were incorporated into official political and/or religious decrees.

3. In this section, we are using the term *barter* to mean an economy using only direct exchange. In everyday usage, people often use barter in a much weaker sense, meaning an economy that does not use money. As our discussion of Austrian theory has shown, this casual and wider sense of barter could include indirect exchange, so long as the medium or media

face the problem of knowing which prices to set in terms of the new money. For example, the tribal chief could perhaps threaten execution to force every person to always trade away his or her goods in exchange for the smooth stones he had gathered in the forest. But even though they would do so—under penalty of death—the people wouldn't know how much to charge when selling. For example, a woman who had been in the habit of trading berry juice for blankets might try to sell the juice for stones instead, intending to use the stones to buy the same amount of blankets. But before agreeing to part with her berry juice for an offer of, say, 10 stones, the woman would need to know whether 10 stones would be enough to buy the number of blankets she would have gotten using a direct exchange. But she can't know that because the seller of the blankets is in the same position—he can't make the first move since he doesn't know how many stones he will need to buy the amount of berry juice he normally received under barter when trading away his blankets. Thus the leader would need not merely to compel the use of the stones as money but might also have to force people to sell at a particular price to get things rolling.

Our brief remarks should underscore the conceptual and logistical difficulties in moving from a state of barter to a monetary economy in one fell swoop. Fortunately, we can avoid such implausible accounts because there is a much more satisfactory alternative. Among his other accomplishments, the founder of the Austrian School, Carl Menger, provided one of the most compelling explanations to our question, refining the narrative that classical economists had given.[4]

Menger starts with the observation that even in an initial state of purely direct exchange, different goods would have different degrees of saleability

---

of exchange involved were not commonly accepted in the community. In other words, in between a society using strictly direct exchanges, on the one hand, and a full-blown monetary economy, on the other, we can imagine an intermediate case of a money-less community that nonetheless practices indirect exchange. It is unclear from common usage whether such an intermediate scenario should be called barter or not because the layperson doesn't usually think in terms of direct versus indirect exchange, but rather in terms of money versus nonmoney.

4. An English translation of Menger's explanation is available in Carl Menger, "On the Origins of Money," *Economic Journal*, 2 (June 1892): 239–55, http://mises.org/Books/origins money.pdf.

or marketability or liquidity.[5] Note that a good's liquidity or marketability is a completely different aspect from its market price. For example, a person could own a house with a market value of $100,000, as well as corporate bonds with a current market price of $100,000. They are both worth $100,000, but the bonds are far more marketable or liquid than the house. Specifically, the person would not have to spend much time finding a buyer willing to pay $100,000 for the bonds. In contrast, selling a house for its full market value is typically a time-consuming process, requiring a month or longer. With a liquid good, the owner can find a buyer willing to pay the highest likely price in a very short time. In contrast, with a very illiquid good, if the owner must sell in a very short time, he will have to discount the price; if the owner is allowed to spend time marketing the good and searching for the right buyer, he eventually will be able to sell on much better terms. With an illiquid good, the convention is to report its market value as the price the owner would receive after a period of searching for buyers.

Back to Menger's explanation: Even in a state of purely direct exchange, various goods would have different degrees of liquidity because some goods, such as eggs and tobacco, would have a wide market, meaning that many people in the community regularly want to acquire them in trade. On the other hand, some goods, such as horses or spears, would have a narrow market, meaning that only a few people would be seeking to acquire such goods on a given trading day.

Menger argued that someone going to market with relatively illiquid goods would—as an intermediate stepping stone to his ultimate objective—trade them away for goods that were more liquid, even if the person didn't really desire those particular goods. In other words, Menger simply generalized the specific story we told above concerning the farmers Anderson, Brown, and Chambers. Whenever the first person had such a eureka moment and accepted something in trade not because he wanted to use it personally but because he realized it would be easier to get what he really did want with the newly acquired goods—at that moment, indirect exchange was born, and the goods in question were the first medium of exchange.

---

5. We are using various terms in the text because Menger's actual argument was written in German, and the direct translation of his term does not help the modern reader very much.

Yet Menger didn't stop there. He pointed out that this process would constitute a positive feedback loop. Those goods that were initially relatively liquid because people wanted to use them would see their liquidity enhanced as a new batch of people sought to acquire them for trading purposes. Even in a world of direct exchange, the tobacco farmer heading to market is in a strong bargaining position because plenty of smokers are probably at that very moment heading to market, too, looking to acquire tobacco. However, once people grasp the advantages of indirect exchange, the demand for tobacco will increase. Even nonsmokers heading to market may be willing to trade their goods for tobacco, so long as the goods they start with, such as horses, are less liquid than tobacco. Thus, the number of traders willing to accept tobacco has increased, precisely because tobacco has so many people willing to accept it. This is the logic behind Menger's claim that goods enjoying an initial superiority in liquidity will see that superiority enhanced.

However, other factors are at work. A good's liquidity is only one factor a trader will consider when deciding whether it makes sense to treat the good as a medium of exchange. Let's imagine a hypothetical horse breeder, heading to market with a fine new stallion. Let's further suppose that he is interested in acquiring a powerful telescope because he is an amateur stargazer. Now his horse is valuable in the sense that if he can find the right buyer, he will be able to acquire a plentiful stockpile of various goods in exchange for it. Yet the problem, of course, is that not many people on a given day are in the market for a fine new stallion. What's worse, even those who are interested in buying are almost certainly not going to be selling the powerful telescope that our horse breeder wants to acquire. Economists refer to this situation as a lack of *double coincidence of wants*, which is a problem under direct exchange because a trade can take place only if one party happens to want and have the goods that the other has and wants.

The obvious solution for our horse breeder is to be willing to accept a medium of exchange, or media of exchange, for his stallion. He still faces the problem of locating the few buyers who are interested in a fine stallion, but when he finds them—assuming they can offer goods that are more liquid than his horse—it will make sense for him to go through with the trade. However more than mere liquidity is at stake: Suppose the horse breeder encounters one buyer who offers a large quantity of eggs, while he encounters a different buyer who offers a large quantity of tobacco. Both the eggs and tobacco are far more liquid and marketable than his stallion, but the horse breeder will clearly prefer to trade for the tobacco. This is because a large quantity of tobacco is much more convenient to carry around than a large quantity of eggs—and he still has to find someone selling a telescope. After all, the eggs can easily break, and even if the horse breeder handles them gently, they will soon spoil. In contrast, tobacco is much sturdier and will last for much longer while the horse breeder searches for his elusive object.

As our tale illustrates, the desirability of a good as a medium of exchange depends only partly on its initial liquidity in a state of direct exchange. People will be more willing to adopt it as a medium of exchange depending on its physical durability and longevity. Some other desirable properties would be its divisibility— tobacco can be divided into smaller quantities for smaller purchases much more easily than cattle can be divided—its homogeneity, and its convenient market exchange value relative to its physical weight.

In light of these desired attributes, it is not surprising that people from various cultures and states of development often turned to the precious metals of gold and silver as excellent media of exchange, as they score well on all criteria. Gold and silver are easily divisible and can be recombined again. Unlike eggs, gold and silver are not fragile and will never spoil. Gold and silver are also preferable to tobacco because they have a more convenient market exchange value relative to their weight; our horse breeder would find it easier to trade his stallion for a few ounces of gold or pounds of silver rather than for hundreds or even thousands of pounds of tobacco. Yet gold and silver are also better media of exchange than precious stones such as diamonds and rubies because the latter come in different sizes and qualities and must be evaluated on a stone-by-stone basis; a large diamond is more valuable than two smaller diamonds that have the same combined weight, whereas a hunk of gold weighing an ounce is roughly the same market value as two smaller hunks weighing a half-ounce each.[6]

---

6. Naturally, we simply mean that one ounce of gold is equivalent to another according to the subjective preferences people have concerning gold. It is always subjective preferences and the uses to which people put goods that matter, not the intrinsic properties of the objects themselves.

For all of these reasons, people tended to voluntarily embrace gold and silver as the most excellent media of exchange. Nothing in economic principles or laws says gold and silver must be chosen, and indeed throughout history, many types of goods, including cattle and tobacco, were used as the pre-eminent media of exchange for a given culture and time period.

Menger's general narrative said that eventually the entire community would settle on just one or a few goods as the medium or media of exchange. This was not because of a committee or group vote; it was the natural end result of the positive feedback loop described above. As certain goods became acceptable in trade to an ever-widening group of people, the process was amplified because now these goods were that much better as media of exchange. Eventually, only a few of them rose to the top and were embraced by just about everyone. These media of exchange were now money because by definition, money is a medium of exchange that is almost universally accepted within a community.

We have now summarized Menger's explanation of the origin of money, adapted with different examples to be more understandable to a modern reader. To be clear, Menger was not engaged in a historical inquiry, but rather he was walking through the economic logic of how a community could start in an initial state of purely direct exchange and then step by step arrive at a situation where everyone used one good as the universally accepted medium of exchange. As Menger demonstrated, we don't need to posit a wise leader or powerful ruler to explain the origin of money. Instead, the use of money is another example of a spontaneous order, in which individuals acted in their narrow self-interest to bring about a complex and socially beneficial result that no single person could have imagined beforehand. Menger explained how everyday commodities—which were initially valued solely for their direct usefulness, either in consumption or production—could begin to do double duty as media of exchange and how some of these media of exchange eventually rose to the status of money.

Analyzing Money Using Supply and Demand, Not Velocity of Circulation

When Mises wrote his famous work on money,[7] there was a bifurcation in economic theory. In the wake of the intellectual revolution of the 1870s, most economists used subjective marginal utility theory to explain the formation of relative exchange ratios between goods and services in a barter framework. This was a micro approach, which looked at the motivations of each individual and determined what prices would look like when the system achieved equilibrium and all individuals were content with the combination of goods they held.

Yet when trying to add money to the system, many economists used a different theoretical apparatus. Rather than looking at things from the perspective of each individual, and then deducing properties of an equilibrium where all individuals were content, these economists took a macro approach and made statements about the total stock of money as it circulated around the economy.

The best example of this mindset is the famous equation of exchange, often denoted by $MV = PT$. In this equation, M represents the total quantity of money, V is the velocity of circulation (how often on average a dollar bill changes hands in a given time frame), P is the average price level, and T is the total number of transactions during a given time frame. Once we spell out the elements of the equation, we see that it must necessarily balance; it is an accounting identity. M times V gives us the total amount of money spent during a period of time, while P times T yields the same answer. Analytically, the equation of exchange serves as the foundation for versions of what is called the *quantity theory of money*, which allows an economist to make statements such as, "So long as the velocity of turnover stays roughly constant and the underlying 'real' activity in the economy stays roughly constant, an increase in the quantity of money will increase the general level of prices proportionately."

Although the equation of exchange—and the various formulations of the quantity theory of money based on it—are famous and serve as the starting framework for many economists when they think about money, most Austrian economists reject it on methodological grounds. Simply put, the equation of

---

7. Recall that we refer to Mises's 1912 book with the English title of *The Theory of Money and Credit*.

exchange is a mechanistic approach that conceives the economy as a mindless system, with money circulating about as if it were water in a river. While individuals' subjective preferences can be incorporated indirectly into the model through their impact on the four variables—if people fear that money will lose its purchasing power in the near future, they will try to spend it more quickly and V will increase—these are not central elements in the equation itself. Moreover, the equation of exchange relies on concepts, such as the average price level, that have no relevance to anyone in action. People make decisions based on particular prices, while the P in the equation of exchange really means nothing except MV divided by T. It cannot be defined as an independent concept that has causal power along with the other elements of the equation. As Murray Rothbard says in his own critique of the equation of exchange: "It is absurd to dignify any quantity with a place in an equation unless it can be defined independently of the other terms in the equation."[8]

So if Mises and most other Austrians don't use the velocity of circulation approach to understanding money, what do they use? They approach money just as any other good: They look at individuals and their desires to supply or demand various units of money. For Mises, individuals demand money just as surely as they demand other types of goods and services; in contrast to the approach of some other economists, Mises didn't conceive of the demand for money balances as a residual that popped out after the demand for all of the other assets was satisfied.

It is admittedly odd to conceive of individuals demanding money, for it is not a consumable good, like an orange or a candy bar. Rather, money is a durable good that provides a flow of services to its owner, merely by being in his or her possession; in this respect, money is more like a mint condition Babe Ruth rookie card than an orange. We therefore don't view an individual as wanting to consume money but rather as wanting to hold money, at least for the time being.

Once we figure out how much money an individual wants to hold, we sum across all individuals and find the total demand to hold money in the economy. In equilibrium, the entire stock of money must be held, and so

---

8. Murray Rothbard, *Man, Economy, and State*, 841, italics in original.

the price of money adjusts until that is the case. Again, this is exactly analogous to how economists would handle the determination of the price of Babe Ruth rookie cards: We would figure out the quantity demanded by each individual in society at various hypothetical prices in order to sum up the total market demand. Then we would look at the fixed quantity of mint condition Babe Ruth rookie cards in existence in order to determine what the market-clearing or equilibrium price had to be, such that each rookie card ended up in someone's possession and everyone was content with the quantity he or she possessed at that price.

There is one glaring problem with our analogy: The price of a Babe Ruth rookie card is quoted in money, so we can ask, "At $1,000 per card, how many units would Bob Smith demand? At $900 per card, how many would he demand?" and so forth. Yet what does such a procedure look like when it comes to money? In other words, what does it mean to adjust the price of money and thereby move along an individual's demand curve for money?

Because money is the generally accepted medium of exchange, it stands on one side of all transactions. Whenever people trade in a monetary economy, they trade away their goods and services to acquire money. This is why we can quote the prices of these goods and services in terms of money.

In light of money's special role in the economy, its price is not a single number but is strictly speaking a list or vector of the reciprocal of all other prices in the economy. For example, if bubble gum sells for 50 cents a pack, oranges sell for $2 per pound, and bicycles sell for $200, then a unit of money—one dollar bill—has the price of two packs of gum, one half pound of oranges, or one two-hundredth of a bicycle. If the price of money—perhaps more naturally thought of as the purchasing power of money—goes up, people who want to acquire money must give up more of their goods and services to get units of money.[9] This means that the prices of these goods and services quoted in

9. The admittedly odd concept of the price of money might make more sense to the reader in the context of the foreign exchange market. If the price of a dollar goes up, in terms of euros, it clearly means that the dollar buys more euros and that the dollar has strengthened against the euro. Moreover, the euro price of a dollar is simply the inverse of the dollar price of a euro; if $1 trades for two euros, then a euro trades for 50 cents. Finally, notice that at any given time, there is a distinct dollar price for every currency in the foreign exchange market.

money will go down. The opposite holds as well: If the price or the purchasing power of money goes down, then it becomes easier to buy money with other goods and services, meaning that their price tags will go up.

When first encountering the idea of applying a demand curve to money—where people want to hold less money as its price rises—some readers are confused because they don't understand why people would be less willing to hold money as its market value increases and the owners apparently become richer. We can clear up the confusion by reminding the reader of the distinction between money and wealth. Imagine that the price of money is increasing: Its purchasing power increases, and the prices of all other goods drop. As we move up and to the left along the demand curve, we know that in the aggregate, people are willing to hold less and less money. But this doesn't mean that these people are merely trying to buy pizzas and other consumer goods; they may also be changing the composition of their financial assets to shift out of cash and into other investments.

For example, if a man starts out with $100 in cash in his wallet and another $900 in his bank checking account, this represents $1,000 in money in his possession. If the prices of most goods and services go down for several years in a row, however, the man might decide to carry only $90 in his wallet, and only $810 in his checking account. This is because the types of purchases the man previously wanted to make with the $100 in his wallet and the additional $900 at the bank, he can now make with the $90 in his wallet and $810 at the bank. There is nothing magical about the particular numbers; the reason the man enjoys holding cash is that it gives him the flexibility to make purchases on the spot. Now, with the extra $100 that he freed up from this reduction in his cash holdings, the man might buy a few extra shares of corporate stock or perhaps a bond yielding a certain interest return. As this example illustrates, a downward sloping demand curve for money doesn't at all imply that at some point, people have no desire for further *wealth*. Rather, it simply means that given the pros and cons of holding wealth in the form of money, a higher purchasing power of money means that the same number of dollar bills can go further and therefore a person will not want to hold as many in equilibrium.

To sum up: Mises and most other Austrians approach money just as they would other goods, from the perspective of individuals demanding it. Because it is not consumed or used up in production, the demand for money is the demand to hold money. The price or purchasing power of money adjusts so that in equilibrium, the total quantity of money demanded across all individuals is equal to the total quantity of money in existence at that moment. To say that the price of money goes up is equivalent to saying that the money prices of other goods and services go down, and vice versa.

Stepping back, notice that Mises's preferred approach to money is radically different from the equation of exchange approach. He uses the same tools of micro analysis based on subjective individual preferences that economists used for all other goods and services in the wake of the 1870s revolution. This is the sense in which the demand-to-hold-money approach unified micro- and macroeconomics and completed the marginal revolution. In Mises's words:

> The deficiency of the equation of exchange and its basic elements is that they look at market phenomena from a holistic point of view . . . . On a market there are only individuals or groups of individuals acting in concert. What motivates these actors is their own concerns, not those of the whole market economy. If there is any sense in such notions as volume of trade and velocity of circulation, then they refer to the resultant of the individuals' actions. It is not permissible to resort to these notions in order to explain the actions of the individuals. The first question that catallactics [i.e. economics] must raise with regard to changes in the total quantity of money available in the market system is how such changes affect the various individuals' conduct. Modern economics does not ask what "iron" or "bread" is worth, but what a definite piece of iron or of bread is worth to an acting individual at a definite date and a definite place. It cannot help proceeding in the same way with regard to money. The equation of exchange is incompatible with the fundamental principles of economic thought. It is a relapse to the thinking of ages in which people failed to comprehend praxeological phenomena because they were committed to holistic notions. It is sterile, as were the speculations of earlier ages concerning the value of "iron" and "bread" in general.[10]

---

10. Mises, *Human Action*, 397.

What Mises here derides as a sterile and holistic approach to money—crystallized in the equation of exchange—has permeated even the layperson's understanding. People routinely talk of money in circulation, when in fact money is never in circulation; at any moment, money is in someone's possession. Every piece of money is always the property of someone in the market economy; it is never in between owners. Money does its job when it sits idle in people's cash balances, not merely when it is being spent. These considerations also show that the common discussion of money hoards is equally dubious:

> Every piece of money is owned by one of the members of the market economy. The transfer of money from the control of one actor into that of another is temporally immediate and continuous. There is no fraction of time in between in which the money is not a part of an individual's or a firm's cash holding, but just in "circulation." It is unsound to distinguish between circulating and idle money. It is no less faulty to distinguish between circulating money and hoarded money. What is called hoarding is a height of cash holding which—according to the personal opinion of an observer—exceeds what is deemed normal and adequate. However, hoarding is cash holding. Hoarded money is still money and it serves in the hoards the same purposes which it serves in cash holdings called normal. He who hoards money believes that some special conditions make it expedient to accumulate a cash holding which exceeds the amount he himself would keep under different conditions, or other people keep, or an economist censuring his action considers appropriate.[11]

In this section, we have sketched out Mises's approach to money, which is the same supply and demand framework that Mises and most other economists use for all other goods besides money. Once we adjust for the unusual nature of the price of money, everything else in the analysis flows straightforwardly. We can analyze money on the basis of individual preferences and action, rather than from an economy-wide perspective that eschews purposeful behavior and incentives. People specifically decide how much money they wish to hold, just as they specifically decide the size of their bond and stock

---

11. Mises, *Human Action*, 399.

holdings, as well as the amount of bottled water and paper towels they keep in their pantry. Naturally the particular reasons people hold money are usually different from the motivations for holding other types of assets and consumer goods, but the economist should still use the same framework when explaining the process.

In light of the obvious advantages of Mises's approach to money, why should there have been any controversy? Indeed, why didn't all economists naturally apply the framework of the marginal revolution to money? We will explain the roadblocks—and Mises's solution—in the next section.

Applying Subjective Value Theory to Money: Mises's Regression Theorem

Money is a medium of exchange. People hold money in their cash balances because they expect to be able to use it to buy other goods and services in the future, which will be directly useful. If the money in question happens also to be a regular commodity in its own right—such as tobacco or gold—then individuals will demand it because of its direct usefulness but also because of its ability to serve as a medium of exchange. On the other hand, when money is useful only as a medium of exchange—such as dollars, euros, yen, and pounds in today's world—then individuals hold it solely because of the services it provides as a medium of exchange. People will be willing to trade away goods or their own labor services to acquire units of money because they expect these units of money will allow them to acquire other goods and services down the road. Thus money *qua* money is valued because of its purchasing power. And, once we understand why an individual would subjectively value money and would trade units of other goods away to obtain units of money in the marketplace, we can explain the resulting exchange ratios between units of money and units of other goods. The explanation is identical to what we did in our hypothetical Halloween candy scenario except that instead of Snickers bars, one of the commodities is "money."

Yet there is a problem with this line of attack, and it caused many economists in the immediate wake of the marginal revolution to pause in their application of the new subjectivist framework to handle the market exchange value of money. When it came to explaining the relative prices of eggs, milk, cigarettes, and dresses, economists didn't need to explain why individuals valued them; it was enough to assert that individuals placed the units of these goods in various places on their subjective preference rankings. Economists would take the valuations of consumer goods as given and then could explain how equilibrium price ratios among them would emerge in a barter economy. With the relative prices of the consumer goods so specified, then economists could also explain the prices of the factors of production. Everything was internally consistent and derived logically from the starting point of the consumers' preferences for various amounts of different types of goods and services.

Yet when it came to money, something seemed fishy about this procedure. As we have seen, the only reason people value money is that it has purchasing power. So yes, an economist could incorporate money into the same framework by simply assuming at the outset that the consumers valued units of money in a particular way and then all else would follow. But such a move seemed arbitrary in a way that was not so in the case of consumer goods. With consumer goods, we started with the bedrock assumption of subjective preferences over various units and built up the objective exchange ratios from there. The reasons for the specific rankings of consumer goods in an individual's subjective preferences are outside the scope of economics; an individual might want to acquire goods for matters of health, vanity, religious beliefs, parental commands, and so on. Yet with money, the only reason to hold it is that it possesses purchasing power. Thus, it seems odd to invoke the demand to hold money as the cause of the purchasing power of money. Subjective value theory, when applied to the case of money, seems to run in a circle. We seem to be saying: Individuals value units of money because individuals value units of money. Such a framework is consistent with units of money having a high purchasing power or a low purchasing power. The whole procedure seems circular and arbitrary, in a way that doesn't occur when it comes to explaining the exchange ratio between apples and bananas.

Here is how Mises summarizes the apparent problem and provides the solution:

> The demand for a medium of exchange is the composite of two partial demands: the demand displayed by the intention to use it in consumption and production and that displayed by the intention to use it as a medium of exchange . . .

Now the extent of that part of the demand for a medium of exchange which is displayed on account of its service as a medium of exchange depends on its value in exchange. This fact raises difficulties which many economists considered insoluble so that they abstained from following farther along this line of reasoning. It is illogical, they said, to explain the purchasing power of money by reference to the demand for money, and the demand for money by reference to its purchasing power.

The difficulty is, however, merely apparent. The purchasing power which we explain by referring to the extent of specific demand is not the same purchasing power the height of which determines this specific demand. The problem is to conceive the determination of the purchasing power of the immediate future, of the impending moment. For the solution of this problem we refer to the purchasing power of the immediate past, of the moment just passed. *These are two distinct magnitudes.* It is erroneous to object to our theorem . . . that it moves in a vicious circle. (italics added)[12]

Thus Mises introduced the time element to escape the apparent circularity of his position. It is not specific enough to say that using subjective value theory, one explains the purchasing power of money by reference to the purchasing power of money; that statement is indeed circular. Rather, a more accurate statement is this: We explain the purchasing power of money today—meaning how many units of milk, eggs, horses, and so on a unit of money will fetch on the market today—by reference to what people today expect the purchasing power of money will be tomorrow. For example, to understand why someone *today* would trade eight hours of her labor for $160, we invoke her expectation that tomorrow she will be able to trade that $160 for a new purse. Then, to explain how people could come to form expectations about the purchasing power of money tomorrow, we cite the fact that they easily observed money's purchasing power yesterday. In our example, the woman saw yesterday that the purse she desired had a price tag of $160. In summary: Today's purchasing power is derived from individuals' expectations about tomorrow's purchasing power, expectations that are themselves based

---

12. Mises, *Human Action*, 405–06.

on yesterday's purchasing power. By introducing the time element, we have thus broken out of the vicious circle; we are not explaining the purchasing power of money by the purchasing power of money because the purchasing power at one time is explained by the purchasing power of an earlier time.

This move is fine as far it goes, but it seems to open Mises to an equally devastating objection: Yes, it is true that his explanation no longer moves in a vicious circle. But now, doesn't it suffer from an infinite regress? Mises explains today's purchasing power of money by yesterday's purchasing power. But where did yesterday's purchasing power come from? Why, from the purchasing power of the day before yesterday, and so on forever. So it still seems as if there are serious, logical problems with applying subjective value theory to money.

Here is Mises's statement of this new objection, along with his solution:

> But, say the critics, this is tantamount to merely pushing back the problem. For now one must still explain the determination of yesterday's purchasing power. If one explains this in the same way by referring to the purchasing power of the day before yesterday and so on, one slips into a *regressus in infinitum*. This reasoning, they assert, is certainly not a complete and logically satisfactory solution of the problem involved. What these critics fail to see is that the regression does not go back endlessly. It reaches a point at which the explanation is completed and no further question remains unanswered. If we trace the purchasing power of money back step by step, we finally arrive at the point at which the service of the good concerned as a medium of exchange begins. At this point yesterday's exchange value is exclusively determined by the nonmonetary—industrial—demand which is displayed only by those who want to use this good for other employments than that of a medium of exchange.[13]

Thus we see that Menger's theory of the origin of money is useful not merely for its own sake but also to put the finishing flourish on the application of subjective value theory to the case of money. As Mises indicates in the quotation above, we avoid the accusation of an infinite regress by showing—logi-

---

13. Mises, *Human Action*, 406.

cally, not historically—that at some point in our explanation, the purchasing power of a medium of exchange[14] on Tuesday is explained by the exchange value of that same good on Monday, even though on Monday the community was in a state of purely direct exchange. Mises called his solution the regression theorem.

For example, if we are talking about gold—which was the world's money during most of Mises's career—then we can trace its purchasing power back to the point at which people valued gold because of its beauty or because of its use as a metal. We already know how to explain the objective market exchange ratios between various goods in a state of purely direct exchange. Gold would have been one such good. On our Monday—the last day of purely direct exchange—gold would have had a market value, and people would have seen that it was very liquid, as well as divisible, durable, and all of the other properties making it an excellent medium of exchange. Then on our Tuesday—the day that indirect exchange was born—one person accepted gold in exchange for what he was offering in trade, not because he wanted the gold for his own use, but because he knew it would be easier to find a trading partner who wanted gold. When making this decision, the person knew what a certain weight of gold would fetch in the market because he had just observed various transactions involving gold the day before, on Monday. But by his very willingness to accept gold on Tuesday, the man adds to gold's purchasing power; gold is now more valuable on Tuesday than it had been on Monday, in the days of direct exchange. The snowball process thus begins, with more people accepting gold on Wednesday because it is now an even better medium of exchange, in light of what they saw on Tuesday. And so on, up until Mises's early career when gold was the undisputed money of planet Earth.

Our exposition here is simplistic in order to isolate the important conceptual issues involved in Mises's theory of money. To satisfactorily use marginal utility analysis with money, it was necessary to refer to the history of the commodity. This is not to say that actual historical work had to be performed by economists. Rather, their theory itself contained within it the notion of the monetary good's history. This was not a necessary feature of the economic

---

14. We are referring to this good as a medium of exchange, and not as money, because on the first day of indirect exchange, clearly it had not yet attained the status of money.

explanation of the valuation of other goods and services, and it helps shed light on why Mises had to fill the gap in the scholarship with his own pioneering work, which first came out in 1912. To see this distinction clearly, let us quote again from Mises:

> [A person] who considers acquiring or giving away money is, of course, first of all interested in its future purchasing power and the future structure of prices. *But he cannot form a judgment about the future purchasing power of money otherwise than by looking at its configuration in the immediate past. It is this fact that radically distinguishes the determination of the purchasing power of money from the determination of the mutual exchange ratios between the various vendible goods and services.* With regard to these latter the actors have nothing else to consider than their importance for future want-satisfaction. If a new commodity unheard of before is offered for sale, as was, for instance, the case with radio sets a few decades ago, the only question that matters for the individual is whether or not the satisfaction that the new gadget will provide is greater than that expected from those goods he would have to renounce in order to buy the new thing. . . . As has been mentioned already, the obliteration of the memory of all prices of the past would not prevent the formation of new exchange ratios between the various vendible things. *But if knowledge about money's purchasing power were to fade away, the process of developing indirect exchange and media of exchange would have to start anew.* It would become necessary to begin again with employing some goods, more marketable than the rest, as media of exchange . . . . The acceptance of a new kind of money presupposes that the thing in question already has previous exchange value on account of the services it can render directly to consumption or production. *Neither a buyer nor a seller could judge the value of a monetary unit if he had no information about its exchange value—its purchasing power—in the immediate past.* (italics added)[15]

In the quotation above, Mises refers to a thought experiment he conducted on pages 334–35 of *Human Action*, in which he showed that a sudden bout of

---

15. Mises, *Human Action*, 407–08.

amnesia—where everyone forgot the exchange ratios between various goods and services—would provide a mere hiccup to the market economy. People would soon enough re-establish the equilibrium exchange ratios, although the new equilibrium might be different because of changes occurring during the adjustment process. Nothing is needed from the history of exchange ratios to explain the formation of barter prices. Thus, Mises's point in this thought experiment and in the quotation is that consumers need to consult only their subjective preference rankings to decide how much they value units of different consumer goods. But when it comes to evaluating units of money, it is crucial to have a memory of what these units of money could fetch in the market in the recent past.[16]

Let us restate Mises's point: If everyone suddenly forgot the ballpark price of a Ferrari and had no idea if it would trade for a pack of gum or a house, it would not take very long for Ferraris to regain their relative exchange value against everything else. Blind people and others without drivers' licenses would not initially be interested in acquiring Ferraris, even if offered for a pack of gum, because they would have no use for them. But those driving vehicles would be able to inspect a Ferrari and know immediately that it was a desirable item. Soon enough, Ferraris would once again command a high price in the market relative to other goods.

On the other hand, if Americans somehow suddenly forgot what $100 could buy in the marketplace, then the dollar would cease to be money. People couldn't inspect a dollar bill and realize its usefulness, restoring the demand for dollars back to its previous height in a matter of days. The problems of direct exchange would once again manifest themselves, and individuals would experiment with various media of exchange until a new money emerged—which in all likelihood wouldn't be dollars in this new timeline.

Our discussion naturally leads to a major stumbling block for modern readers when they encounter Mises's regression theorem: How can Mises claim—as he does for example on page 423 of *Human Action*—that "nothing can enter

---

16. Although it is clear what Mises is trying to convey with his two thought experiments, there is a technical problem with his argument in that the two situations are actually equivalent: If people lost all memory of exchange ratios between the various goods, then they also must have forgotten the purchasing power of money. Thus, it's not correct for Mises to contrast the two scenarios as if they are qualitatively different.

into the function of a medium of exchange which was not already previously an economic good and to which people assigned exchange value already before it was demanded as such a medium"? After all, in today's world, dollars, euros, yen, and so on are all examples of fiat money. They serve no useful purpose except in their roles as media of exchange, and there was never a time when people used green pictures of Andrew Jackson for some other purpose. So doesn't modern fiat money derail Mises's famous regression theorem for explaining the value of money?

The answer is no. Even though gold was still the world's money for almost all of Mises's life,[17] Mises had conceived of the theoretical possibility of fiat money, even in his 1912 work.[18] With the benefit of hindsight, today's economists can easily apply the regression theorem to the fiat currencies of the world. For example, as of this writing, the U.S. dollar is the commonly used medium of exchange in the United States. People today sell goods and services for dollars because of expectations derived from their observations of the dollar's purchasing power yesterday. We can push this regression back until August 15, 1971, the day President Richard Nixon closed the gold window and formally ended the Bretton Woods agreement formed at the close of World War II. Before this day, the U.S. government was obligated to redeem U.S. dollars for gold at the rate of $35 per ounce, if other central banks requested such redemption. Going back even earlier, just before President Franklin Roosevelt's initiatives upon taking office in the spring of 1933, anyone, not just other governments, could turn in dollars to the U.S. government and receive gold at the rate of $20.67 per ounce. Going back even further in U.S. history, there were periods where the government pledged to redeem dollars in specific weights of either gold or silver.

A similar story could be given for all of the other fiat currencies in today's world.[19] Even though they never served themselves as useful commodities in a

---

17. Mises died in 1973, while U.S. President Richard Nixon formally closed the gold window—thus severing the last link of major currencies to a commodity money—in 1971.

18. In *Human Action*, Mises admits to the reader that fiat money is theoretically possible on page 426.

19. The euro was originally introduced with a fixed exchange rate between the various European fiat currencies such as the deutschemark and franc, so that a Misesian can explain the euro's purchasing power by reference to the histories of these respective currencies.

nonmonetary world, their purchasing power can be traced, step by step, back until they were legally redeemable for a genuine commodity money such as gold. Then the application of the regression theorem proceeds just as Mises describes in *Human Action* and other works.[20]

The Non-Neutrality of Money

A recurring theme in *Human Action* is that money has a driving force of its own. Mises repeatedly rejects the approach of those economists who conceive of the economy as a giant system of barter—and use such a barter model to determine the "real" exchange ratios between different goods—and then throw in money as an afterthought. One way to describe Mises's position is that he rejected the so-called neutrality of money; on the contrary, Mises thought money was *non-neutral*, and in fact that a neutral money was not only undesirable, but also a nonsensical concept.[21]

A specific difference between Mises and many of his followers, on the one hand, and many other economists is in their analysis of the effects of infusions of new money into the economy. Many modern economists argue that the introduction of new money—especially to the extent that it is expected—doesn't significantly affect the real variables in the economy, such as the amount of goods that a worker can earn by selling an hour of his work. Rather, it only affects the nominal variables, such as the number of dollars per hour a worker earns. Mises and many of his followers, however, assert that distributional effects always occur with an injection of new money. As Mises explains it:

> Let us assume that the government issues an additional quantity of paper money . . . . The treasury enters the market with an additional demand for goods and services; it is now in a position to buy more goods than it could buy before. The prices of the commodities it buys rise . . . .

20. Although the case of government-issued fiat money poses no problem for Mises's regression theorem, the case of Bitcoin and other "crypto-currencies" has been the subject of debate among modern fans of Mises. Bitcoin is a medium of exchange that has definite purchasing power, even though one could argue that Bitcoin was never valued as a consumer or producer good, and it was never formally redeemable in another good.

21. Mises, *Human Action*, 415.

The prices of some commodities—[namely], of those the government buys—rise immediately, while those of the other commodities remain unaltered for the time being. But the process goes on. Those selling the commodities asked for by the government are now themselves in a position to buy more than they used previously. The prices of the things these people are buying in larger quantities therefore rise too. *Thus the boom spreads from one group of commodities and services to other groups until all prices and wage rates have risen. The rise in prices is thus not synchronous with the various commodities and services.*

When eventually, in the further course of the increase in the quantity of money, all prices have risen, the rise does not affect the various commodities and services to the same extent. For *the process has affected the material position of various individuals to different degrees.* While the process is under way, some people enjoy the benefit of higher prices for the goods or services they sell, while the prices of the things they buy have not yet risen or have not risen to the same extent. On the other hand, there are people who are in the unhappy situation of selling commodities and services whose prices have not yet risen or not in the same degree as the prices of the goods they must buy for their daily consumption . . . . *When the process once comes to an end, the wealth of various individuals has been affected in different ways and to different degrees. Some are enriched, some impoverished.* Conditions are no longer what they were before. The new order of things results in changes in the intensity of demand for various goods. The mutual ratio of the money prices of the vendible goods and services is no longer the same as before. The price structure has changed apart from the fact that all prices in terms of money have risen. *The final prices to the establishment of which the market tends after the effects of the increase in the quantity of money have been fully consummated are not equal to the previous final prices multiplied by the same multiplier.* (italics added)[22]

To put the difference in emphasis in concrete terms: Many economists might argue that if the government doubled the quantity of money, in the

---

22. Mises, *Human Action*, 409–10.

long run, the economy would basically return to its original state, except that all of the prices would be doubled. In contrast, Mises would not make such a claim but would instead never lose sight of the fact that in any actual episode of such inflation, the new money would enter the economy through specific channels. And even if it entered in a neutral way with a proportional injection given to everyone on the basis of his or her original cash holdings, there would still arise distributional effects as some individuals spent the new money more quickly than others. When all was said and done, the economy would not return to its original equilibrium because real transfers of wealth would have occurred. Some people would be enriched during the adjustment process, while some would be impoverished. There is no reason to suppose that the types of things they bought would be identical, meaning that in the new equilibrium, the relative demand for some goods would have increased, while the relative demand for other goods would have decreased.[23]

To take a concrete example from the real world: In the wake of the unprecedented interventions by central banks due to the financial crisis of 2008, all economists discussed the potential impacts on the general purchasing power of the dollar and other currencies. It was commonplace for economists to argue about whether the various rounds of "quantitative easing" (QE) would lead to runaway price increases or whether the Federal Reserve could remove the injections of reserves before this became a problem. However, the Austrian commentators pointed out that not just the size of the various rounds of QE but also the composition was distorting the economy. Specifically, by spending the newly created dollar reserves to buy U.S. Treasury bonds and mortgage-backed securities, the Federal Reserve was enriching certain institutions—such as the federal government and large investment banks—at the expense of individuals holding dollar-denominated assets, who did not benefit from the Fed's actions. These included retired pensioners with little wealth invested in the stock market.

In addition to the non-neutrality of money, another common theme in the work of Mises and many of his followers is the idea that all quantities of money are optimal. As Mises puts it, "The quantity of money available in the

---

23. These effects are often called *Cantillon effects* in honor of the economist Richard Cantillon, who first described them in his 1755 work.

whole economy is always sufficient to secure for everybody all that money does and can do."[24]

Mises is here arguing that there is never any social benefit from enlarging the stockpile of money, if we consider only the monetary function. Notice that this proposition doesn't hold for any other good in the economy. If, say, the stock of rocking chairs or of apples suddenly doubles, there is an obvious sense in which humanity is materially wealthier. It's true, depending on how the increase manifests itself, some people might be harmed—such as the antique dealer holding a collection of rocking chairs, only to see their relative price plummet. But to repeat, an increase in the available rocking chairs, apples, or any other real good will make humanity richer in general.

In contrast, doubling the quantity of money does not make people richer in general. Some people will be enriched, but only at the expense of others who will be impoverished. Doubling the quantity of U.S. dollars will not by itself cause Americans to have a higher standard of living; they will not be able to produce more cars or grow more crops or attend more baseball games, just because there are twice as many green pieces of paper in existence. It's true that the average individual will have twice as much money in her cash holdings as before, but this won't mean the same thing as if she held twice as many cars or twice as many houses. This is because the new money will eventually result in higher prices, so that even though the average cash balance is twice as high as before, she will not be able to buy more goods or services.

To the extent that the monetary good happens to be a commodity that serves other purposes, then an increase in its quantity is beneficial for the community. For example, if people use gold as money, then a sudden increase makes them richer, on average, because people will be able to wear more jewelry, get more gold fillings, and enjoy all of the other goods that use gold in their production. In a case like this, Mises's point is that *in its role as money*, an increase in gold does not benefit the community in general. The annual influx of new gold certainly enriches the mine owners and the workers they employ, but only by reducing the wealth of other people in society.

These considerations explain why many economists—including Adam Smith and David Ricardo—think that the use of gold as money is in a certain sense wasteful or uneconomical. If the mining, distribution, and storage of

---

24. Mises, *Human Action*, 418.

new gold around the world for use as money confers no net advantages on society, then surely the resources used in the mining, distribution, and storage are wasted. It would seem preferable to find a way to economize on the physical gold held in the bank vaults and purses across the world—where the gold could be diluted with only fractional backing, or replaced entirely by fiat money—in order that the resources previously devoted to gold mining could be used to mine coal, for example, or to catch more tuna.

However, although he understood the theory behind such ideas, Mises thought that these proposals reflected a gross miscalculation of the relative dangers of various institutional frameworks:

> One may call wasteful all expenditures incurred for increasing the quantity of money. The fact that things which could render some other useful services are employed as money and thus withheld from these other employments appears as a superfluous curtailment of limited opportunities for want-satisfaction. *It was this idea that led Adam Smith and Ricardo to the opinion that it was very beneficial to reduce the cost of producing money by resorting to the use of paper printed currency.* However, things appear in a different light to the students of monetary history. *If one looks at the catastrophic consequences of the great paper money inflations, one must admit that the expensiveness of gold production is the minor evil . . .*
>
> The choice of the good to be employed as a medium of exchange and as money is never indifferent . . . . *The question is only who should make the choice: the people buying and selling on the market, or the government?* It was the market which in a selective process, going on for ages, finally assigned to the precious metals gold and silver the character of money. For two hundred years the governments have interfered with the market's choice of the money medium. Even the most bigoted étatists do not venture to assert that this interference has proved beneficial. (italics added)[25]

As the quotation above indicates, Mises was particularly fond of the gold standard, not only as a reflection of the voluntary market choice of money, but also for its historical role as a check upon government depredation through

---

25. Mises, *Human Action*, 418–19.

the printing press. In the next section, we will explore the operation of the gold standard more thoroughly.

The Gold Standard

Mises assumes that his readers understand the operation of the classical gold standard, and yet, modern readers have no direct experience with such a system. In this section, we will sketch out the basics[26] so that Mises's remarks in *Human Action* and elsewhere will be more understandable. The recurring theme throughout Mises's work is that gold and silver were chosen by the voluntary market process as the most suitable commodities to serve as money in global capitalism. Such a system had its drawbacks—all human enterprises do—but whenever governments did more than simply issue currency perfectly redeemable for fixed weights of gold or silver, it spelled trouble and often disaster for their citizens.

One of the traditional functions of governments has been to issue currency. Historically, government paper was a redemption claim on commodity money that arose on the market. The very term *pound sterling* for the British currency suggests a weight of silver. Although governments would often renege on their pledges—especially during wars—the various currencies were not worth a particular weight in gold or silver but rather were *defined* as such. For example, when the U.S. abandoned the bimetallic system and formally went on a gold standard in 1900, it defined one U.S. dollar as 23.22 grains (1.505 grams) of gold. The government's role in regulating money was perceived as a matter of establishing uniform weights and measures; a dollar *was* 23.22 grains of gold the same way that one foot is 12 inches. The point wasn't to steer the macroeconomy or create the optimum rate of inflation. Rather, the government's purpose was to provide a uniform standard for citizens to use in their transactions. If a carpenter signed a contract promising to buy a certain number of feet of lumber for so many dollars, those very terms would need

---

26. The discussion in this section is adapted from the treatment given in Robert P. Murphy, *The Politically Incorrect Guide to the Great Depression and the New Deal* (Washington, DC: Regnery, 2009), 91–94.

a commonly accepted definition in case of a lawsuit, lest one party to the contract claim that he was using an unorthodox definition of *feet* or *dollar*.

Throughout the nineteenth century, the governments of a growing number of major trading countries followed Great Britain's example and tied their currencies to gold. The definitions they adopted then implied corresponding, fixed exchange rates between the various currencies. For example, the U.S. dollar was defined as $20.67 to one troy ounce (31.1 grams) of gold, while the British pound was defined as 4.25 pounds to a gold ounce. Thus, many authors write that under the classical gold standard, the British pound had a fixed exchange rate of $4.86.

In actual practice, the British pound didn't literally always trade for exactly $4.86. After all, unlike inches and feet—which were just different units of length—an ounce of gold and a dollar (or pound) were units of different things. In practice, what would happen is that the dollar price of a British pound or the pound price of a U.S. dollar would be set on international currency markets, with floating exchange rates set by supply and demand, not government dictates—just as they are typically set in today's markets. The crucial difference, however, under the classical gold standard was that the British and American governments were obligated to redeem any amounts of currency presented to them according to the stipulated weights in gold, less a small commission. This set a tight band—centered on $4.86—within which the dollar/pound exchange rate would fluctuate.

It is important to remember that ultimately, the vast majority of people in a given country must be paid in their own currencies. If American shopkeepers in 1910 wanted to import British tea, they would first need to obtain British pounds. On the other hand, if British librarians wanted to import back issues of *Poor Richard's Almanac*, they would first need to use British pounds to buy American dollars. The trades would occur in the currency markets, where supply and demand would set the exchange rate between each pair of currencies. If Americans wanted to spend more dollars on British goods and British assets than the British wished to spend on American goods and American assets—when valued at the prevailing exchange rate—then the surplus dollars chasing British pounds in the currency markets would push up the dollar price of a pound, perhaps to $4.88.

However, the classical gold standard set an upper limit on the dollar price of a British pound. If the American trade deficit[27] continued to grow, eventually the dollar price of a pound would rise until it reached the gold export point, which would depend on shipping and other transactions costs involving gold. To give an extreme example, if the dollar depreciated to $10 per pound, then owners of gold could make a killing. They could sell an ounce of gold in England at 4.25 pounds, based on its legally defined value. Next, they could enter the currency markets and receive U.S. $42.50 for the 4.25 pounds. Then they could present the $42.50 in U.S. currency to the U.S. Treasury and demand the legally defined payment of roughly 2.06 ounces of gold. Thus, absent shipping and other costs, the gold owners would be able to more than double their gold holdings through this arbitrage action because they started with an ounce of gold and ended up with roughly 2.06 ounces of gold.

As with other opportunities for almost pure profit in the marketplace, the $10 British pound in our hypothetical scenario would soon correct itself. The near arbitrage operation we described above involves depositing gold with the Bank of England and withdrawing gold from the American government. The transfer of gold from America to England would reduce the money supply in the United States and raise it in England. This would cause domestic prices to fall in America, while domestic prices would rise in England. The change in domestic prices in the two countries would eventually reverse the trade imbalance, as consumers in both countries tried to buy less from British producers and more from American producers. At the exchange rate of $10 per pound, eventually, more pounds would be chasing dollars in the

---

27. Strictly speaking, the term *trade deficit* refers narrowly to an imbalance in goods and services traded between countries. In the text, we are actually referring to an overall *balance of payments deficit* in which all American items for sale, including financial assets such as government bonds and corporate stock, do not attract enough British buyers to offset the desired American purchases of British goods, services, and assets. Thus, a balance of payments deficit, not the more popular trade deficit, would cause the dollar to depreciate against the pound. If the British wanted to invest more in American stocks and bonds than Americans wanted to invest in British assets, then this capital account surplus could finance a trade deficit, with no impact on the dollar/pound exchange rate of $4.86. In fact, this is exactly what happened for most of the late 1800s, as the rapidly industrializing and relatively laissez-faire United States was a magnet for investors the world over. See Gene Smiley, *Rethinking the Great Depression* (Chicago: Ivan R. Dee, 2002), 46.

currency markets, and so the rate would fall back toward the $4.86 anchor point. Therefore, gold would continue to drain out of American vaults and into British ones until the exchange value of the dollar had appreciated back above the gold-export point, at which point the gold drain would cease.

As the discussion above makes clear, the international gold standard served as a check to the expansion of the quantity of money in various currencies. If the U.S. government allowed the number of paper dollars to grow too quickly relative to growth in the number of pounds permitted by the Bank of England, this would lead to an American trade deficit vis-à-vis England and ultimately a drain of gold from U.S. vaults. Such a drain of its gold reserves could not be long ignored. U.S. interest rates would need to rise, and the outstanding amount of dollars held by the public would need to shrink.

Ironically, both the critics and the supporters of the classical gold standard agree that it placed strict limits on the ability of governments to inflate their currencies. For example, Milton Friedman argued that a true gold standard was an unrealistic goal because in cases of emergency—such as a major war—the government would want the flexibility to spend money without the handcuffs of the gold standard.[28]

To Mises, such thinking was precisely why governments should be restrained by the gold standard. He didn't want governments to have the power to resort to monetary inflation when direct taxation or government borrowing would not pass muster with the people.

> It is maintained that inflation is unavoidable in times of war. This, too, is an error. An increase in the quantity of money does not create war materials—either directly or indirectly. Rather we should say, if a government does not dare to disclose to the people the bill for the war expenditures and does not dare impose the restrictions on consumption which cannot be avoided, it will prefer inflation to the other two means of financing, namely taxation and borrowing. In any case, increased armaments and war must be paid for by people through restriction of other consumption. But it is politically expedient—even though

---

28. Milton Friedman, *Capitalism and Freedom* (Chicago: University of Chicago Press, 1962).

fundamentally undemocratic—to tell the people that increased armaments and war create boom conditions and increase wealth.[29]

In the above quotation, Mises argues that resort to inflation to finance war spending is fundamentally undemocratic, because ultimately a nation's people must pay for the war. If the government cannot raise the necessary money through taxation or borrowing, then this is a sign that the people are not willing to bear the costs of waging the war in the manner that the government desires. This opportunity cost, in the sense of other potential goods and services that will now not be available, is not diminished by resorting to the printing press. If anything, the cost of the war is higher when it is financed through monetary inflation because of the ill consequences of credit expansion that we will discuss in Chapter 14.

The classical liberal commitment to sound money went hand in hand with support for a genuine commodity monetary standard, such as the classical gold standard. The benefits of economic calculation could be reaped only in an environment where the purchasing power of money was not subject to violent fluctuations. Yet beyond the narrow economic analysis, Mises looked with favor upon the gold standard as a check on arbitrary government power, to be classified with other limits on government action such as constitutions and bills of rights.

The Changing Meaning of the Term *Inflation*

In modern disputes over monetary policy, the Austrians often emphasize that the meaning of the term *inflation* has subtly evolved since the beginning of the twentieth century and that this evolution was by no means innocuous. Here is how Mises describes what happened, and the implications of the change:

> The semantic revolution which is one of the characteristic features of our day has also changed the traditional connotation of the terms inflation and deflation. *What many people today call inflation or defla-*

---

29. Ludwig von Mises, *Interventionism: An Economic Analysis*, ed. Bettina Bien Greaves (Irvington on Hudson, NY: The Foundation for Economic Education, [1940] 1998), Chapter III.

tion is no longer the great increase or decrease in the supply of money, but its inexorable consequences, the general tendency toward a rise or a fall in commodity prices and wage rates. This innovation is by no means harmless. It plays an important role in fomenting the popular tendencies toward inflationism.

First of all *there is no longer any term available to signify what inflation used to signify. It is impossible to fight a policy which you cannot name.* Statesmen and writers no longer have the opportunity of resorting to a terminology accepted and understood by the public when they want to question the expediency of issuing huge amounts of additional money. They must enter into a detailed analysis and description of this policy with full particulars and minute accounts whenever they want to refer to it, and they must repeat this bothersome procedure in every sentence in which they deal with the subject. As this policy has no name, it becomes self-understood and a matter of fact. It goes on luxuriantly.

The second mischief is that *those engaged in futile and hopeless attempts to fight the inevitable consequences of inflation—the rise in prices— are disguising their endeavors as a fight against inflation. While merely fighting symptoms, they pretend to fight the root causes of the evil.* Because they do not comprehend the causal relation between the increase in the quantity of money on the one hand and the rise in prices on the other, they practically make things worse. (italics added)[30]

We can illustrate both of Mises's points with historical episodes that occurred long after the release of *Human Action*. Regarding his first point, that it is impossible to fight against a policy with no name, we can point to the difficulty Austrian economists had in opposing the expansionary policies of Federal Reserve chairman Ben Bernanke in the aftermath of the 2008 financial crisis. Many Austrian economists instinctively warned the public of the dangers of such massive inflation, referring to the rapid and unprecedented increase in the Fed's balance sheet. However, so long as certain official price indices—such as the core Consumer Price Index—experienced only modest

---

30. Mises, *Human Action*, 420.

growth, the critics derided the Austrians for their false alarms.[31] Yet, as we will see in Chapter 14, Mises in his theory of the business cycle does not regard an increase in prices as the only—or even the primary—harm of monetary inflation.

As an illustration of Mises's "second mischief," consider President Gerald Ford's "Whip Inflation Now" program—launched in 1974 with official pledge forms and WIN buttons—in which Americans were urged to alter their financial decisions in order to contain price increases. This was a classic example of fighting symptoms rather than the disease, which was the reckless increase in the quantity of money made possible by President Richard Nixon's final abandonment of the gold standard in 1971.

To avoid confusion, in this book we will use the terms *monetary inflation* and *price inflation* to distinguish between the old and new meanings of the word.

---

31. In fairness, many Austrian economists and analysts—including the present writer—*did* give explicit warnings about the impact that Federal Reserve policy would have on consumer prices in the years following the 2008 crisis, warnings that in retrospect were at best premature.

12

The Misesian Approach
to Money & Banking

Introduction

SOME OF MISES'S most technical work in pure economic theory is in the realm of money and banking, the most obvious example being his 1912 book, *The Theory of Money and Credit*. Although his presentation of these topics in *Human Action* is much more accessible to the layperson, even here Mises uses professional jargon that will be foreign to the average reader and yet is critical to understanding Mises's broad theory of booms and busts.

Because one of the central aims of the present book is to give the reader a comprehensive explanation of the Austrian theory of the business cycle, in this chapter, we will define Mises's terminology and elaborate on his remarks concerning money and banking. The material in this chapter is the most technical of the present book, but this preparation will make it far easier to understand Mises's theory of the business cycle, which we present in Chapter 14.

Important Definitions Needed to Understand
Mises's Writings on Money and Banking

In the previous chapter, we explained the process by which a community could start in an initial state of direct exchange and eventually end up using a particular good as a commonly accepted medium of exchange. In Mises's framework, this would be a *commodity money* because it served as a good that had nonmonetary uses and originally traded against other goods on this basis.

At this point, we introduce the notion of a *money substitute*, which is a claim on the genuine money that is redeemable upon demand and in which the community has no doubt about its reliability. These two attributes make such a claim "as good as money" and thus a substitute for genuine money. For example, in the United States in 1925, Americans were still on a commodity standard; they used gold as their commodity money. However, the U.S. government had issued pieces of paper—called dollars—that could be redeemed in actual physical gold at the rate of $20.67 per ounce. The dollars served as money substitutes because people could hold dollars rather than physical gold. So long as everyone in the community had no doubt that $20.67 in currency could be exchanged for an ounce of yellow metal, these pieces of paper performed all of the monetary functions of gold, though not of course its industrial or cosmetic functions.

Now we can introduce another distinction: "Money in the broader sense" is a wider concept that encompasses both money in the narrower sense and money substitutes. For example, in the United States in 1925, money in the narrower sense would refer to the actual quantity of physical gold—pieces of metal—being held in various safes around the country and in the form of gold coins in people's pockets. Money in the broader sense would include not just the commodity money of gold itself but also the dollar bills that substituted for, or effectively represented, the underlying commodity money. Note that if the government has issued more pieces of paper than it can redeem, then the quantity of money in the broader sense is larger than the quantity of money in the narrower sense;[1] this is the reason for the terms.

Now suppose the issuing institution suspends redemption of its claims on the genuine money but that the public believes the suspension is only

---

1. The convention in such analyses is to avoid double counting, for example by omitting the reserves in the vaults of the issuing authority from calculations of the stock of money in the broader sense. This will make more sense in the context of a specific example: Suppose the U.S. government simply issued $20,670 in new currency and withdrew 1,000 ounces of gold from the market to put into its vaults. These actions would not be inflationary because the public would simply hold more green pieces of paper instead of yellow metal; on average, nobody's cash balance would be higher. The action therefore would not increase money in the broader sense. However, if the government withdrew 1,000 ounces of gold to add to its vault holdings, while issuing twice as much money as before—a total of $41,340—then the citizenry would indeed experience monetary inflation. Now aggregate cash balances in the private sector would be $20,670 higher than they previously were. Even though the quantity of money in the narrower sense stayed the same—the government didn't alter the amount of physical yellow metal in existence—money in the broader sense increased by $20,670.

temporary. For example, during World War I, the major belligerents, except the United States, abandoned the gold standard because they wanted to use the printing press to pay for the war effort. Mises classified the British pound, the French franc, and other currencies during this period as *credit money*. The British people still used the pound as their currency, even though it could no longer be immediately redeemed for a specified weight of gold. However, they thought that at some point, the British pound would again be redeemable in gold. During the suspension, the pound was no longer a money substitute; it no longer performed the same services to the owner as physical yellow metal. However, people still treated it as a claim, albeit one of uncertain maturity. The British pound still functioned as a medium of exchange, and it was still commonly accepted. Therefore, it was a form of money. In light of all of these considerations, Mises classified it as a *credit money*. When the British went back on the gold standard, the British pound would cease being a credit money and would revert to being a money substitute, where the money in question was gold.

Now push the analysis one step further: Suppose a government (1) has been issuing notes that are instantly redeemable claims on a commodity money, (2) the public uses these claims as interchangeable with the commodity money itself, so that the claims become money substitutes, (3) the government decides to suspend redemption of the claims, (4) the public believes that the suspension is permanent, and yet (5) the public still uses the notes issued by the government as a commonly accepted medium of exchange. In this scenario, Mises would classify the government notes as *fiat currency*. They are neither commodity money, money substitutes, nor even credit money because they are no longer claims on anything at all. Yet they still satisfy the definition of money because the public commonly accepts the government's paper notes in trade, with the intention of using them in the future to acquire other goods and services.

Such a money is called *fiat money* because the government decrees "by fiat" the particular characteristics that an object must possess in order to count as part of this stock of money. For example, ever since Richard Nixon closed the gold window in 1971, the U.S. dollar and other major currencies have been fiat monies. What makes something a genuine dollar—rather than a counterfeit— is determined arbitrarily by the U.S. government. For example, when the $20 bill is periodically altered, the public accepts the new item because they have been assured by the government that the new look of Andrew Jackson on the bill is genuine. Shopkeepers may hold up $20 bills under special lighting and look for tell-tale signs of authenticity, but these signs are completely arbitrary and are designed by the U.S. government. There's no reason for shopkeepers to prefer a genuine to a counterfeit $20 bill, except for the fact that the former is legally defined as being part of the stock of U.S. dollars.

In contrast, under a commodity standard, what matters is whether the object is the commodity that had previously served nonmonetary purposes. For example, under the gold standard, if someone brings a bag of unfamiliar yellow coins—which are in strange shapes and covered with unintelligible foreign writing—into a shop and tries to buy merchandise with them, the shopkeeper only cares whether the coins are in fact gold. In the worst case, they can be melted down and reshaped. The shopkeeper doesn't need to contact the foreign institution that minted the coins in question; if he has the equipment on hand, he can use various tests to determine if the yellow objects on his countertop are indeed gold. The definition of gold relates to chemical and physical properties, not to arbitrary markings placed on coins.

We can illustrate the difference between commodity and fiat money in another way: With a fiat money, no outside agency has the authority to issue more dollars without legal permission, whereas with a commodity money, nobody can restrict new producers from entering the industry. For example, no entity outside of the U.S. government can possibly issue legitimate $20 bills, equivalent to the notes printed by the U.S. Treasury's Bureau of Engraving and Printing. Even if some outsider managed to produce paper notes that were physically indistinguishable from the legitimate bills, they would still be counterfeit legally speaking and would become so economically speaking once the government adapted the design of the dollar to allow banks and merchants to recognize the counterfeit currency and seize it. In contrast, when gold is the money, private mints might issue gold coins of a certain design and stamp the coins with particular symbols, but the purpose would be to alert the public of the authenticity of the coin's weight and fineness in gold content. No single mint could monopolize the industry because the design and markings on its coins wouldn't be defining what the money was; they would simply be identifying particular hunks of metal as genuine weights of gold.

So, for example, the Selgin Mint could build a reputation for issuing quality coins that were hard for counterfeiters to duplicate but only because the Selgin Mint would be stamping actual ounces of gold in ways that made it easy for the public to recognize; the Selgin Mint wouldn't have the power to make something into money. Furthermore, if someone else found an ounce of gold and brought it into the marketplace, it too would serve as money, once others tested it to ensure its authenticity. Thus, the Selgin Mint couldn't prevent outsiders from increasing the quantity of commodity money. To repeat, with a commodity money, the function of private, competing mints would be not to create money, but rather to transform money into a more convenient form.[2]

Before continuing with our catalog of terms in Mises's treatment of money and banking, we should dispose of a common misconception regarding fiat money. Even though the U.S. government, for example, currently has the power to announce the criteria for an object to be a genuine dollar and hence part of the quantity of money in the narrower sense, we must not ascribe too much power to government officials. They cannot simply invent a new fiat money from scratch; recall our arguments detailing the problems with the state theory of the origin of money. Rather, Mises's regression theorem explains how today's fiat currencies achieved their status as a commonly accepted medium of exchange only because of their historical redemption to earlier forms of money. Indeed, Mises went so far as to argue that all media of exchange must have had some type of history through which the economist could trace the evolution of its purchasing power:

> The deliberations of the individuals which determine their conduct with regard to money are based on their knowledge concerning the prices of the immediate past. If they lacked this knowledge, they would not be in a position to decide what the appropriate height of their cash holdings should be and how much they should spend for the acquisition of various goods. *A medium of exchange without a past is unthinkable.* Nothing can enter into the function of a medium of exchange which was not already previously an economic good and to which people

---

2. For an excellent treatment of the theory and history of private mints, see George Selgin, *Good Money: Birmingham Button Makers, the Royal Mint, and the Beginnings of Modern Coinage, 1775–1821* (Oakland, CA: The Independent Institute, 2008).

assigned exchange value already before it was demanded as such a medium. (italics added)[3]

Mises's statements above reinforce his regression theorem and its solution to the alleged problems of circularity and infinite regress in the application of subjective value theory to money. Since Mises had escaped such alleged problems by showing that all forms of money in use today could ultimately be traced back to nonmonetary goods, he obviously thought it was impossible for a medium of exchange to exist without such a link.[4]

Other crucial terms for Mises's view of money and banking involve two types of money substitutes, instantly redeemable claims on money in the narrower sense. First is a *money certificate*, which is a money substitute for which the issuer has set aside in reserve an appropriate amount of the actual money to back up. However, if an issuer creates money substitutes for which it does not keep actual money in reserve, these money substitutes are *fiduciary media*. All money substitutes are either money certificates or fiduciary media, depending on how much of the underlying actual money the issuing body or bodies have set aside to back up the outstanding money substitutes.

To a modern reader, it's easiest to illustrate fiduciary media with the current system of fiat money and *fractional reserve banking*. For a specific example, consider the United States. Money in the narrower sense is the U.S. dollar, in the form of green pieces of paper printed by the Treasury and electronic reserves held on deposit at the Federal Reserve.[5] Now when a regular citizen, Harry, deposits $1,000 in the form of fifty separate $20 bills at his commercial bank, the bank will credit Harry's checking account with $1,000. So if Harry wants to write a check, he can do so up to $1,000. If he goes to an ATM and asks to see his balance, it will show him the $1,000 he just deposited. However, the bank does not keep 100% reserves, holding only a *fraction* of the deposited funds. The bank might grant a loan of $900 to another customer, Sally. Sup-

---

3. Mises, *Human Action*, 423.

4. An interesting controversy among modern fans of Mises is whether privately created crypto-currencies such as Bitcoin violate the regression theorem.

5. Officially, the Federal Reserve is not an agency of the federal government, the way that the Internal Revenue Service or the Environmental Protection Agency is. Rather, the Federal Reserve is a quasi-private organization that has private shareholders but nonetheless is subject to strict government oversight and at the same time enjoys numerous powers and privileges.

pose Sally elects to receive her loan in the form of currency rather than having a checking account at the bank. That means the bank now only has $100—in the form of five separate $20 bills—in its vault, backing up Harry's deposit of $1,000. Nevertheless, Harry is still walking around town with a legal claim on the bank, redeemable upon demand, entitling him to a full $1,000. So long as Harry is patronizing a reputable bank, the community will treat Harry's checking account balance as a money substitute; if Harry has a restaurant bill for $85, he can either pay with green pieces of paper or in most restaurants with his debit card tied to the checking account.[6] Thus Harry's checking account balance is part of money in the broader sense, and in this example $100 consists of money certificates while the other $900 consists of fiduciary media.

As our example illustrates, modern systems of fiat money allow a commercial banking system legally to issue fiduciary media. However, other permutations are possible. For example, back on the classical gold standard, a government might still issue token money in the form of coins that did not contain the requisite weights of gold and silver and for which the government didn't have a 100 percent reserve of gold or silver. These would be fiduciary media, then, in Mises's framework.

In his translation of Mises's book, *The Theory of Money and Credit*, J. E. Batson provided the following diagram in Appendix B[7] that beautifully represents the relationships among the key terms in Mises's framework for money and banking (see Figure 12.1 on the next page).

The newcomer to Mises's work may at first recoil from learning so many unfamiliar terms, but Mises had a definite purpose in mind when constructing the above classification system. As he explains, economists must choose their theoretical concepts and terminology "to facilitate the problems involved," which are "the determination of prices and interest rates."[8] Although other economists didn't distinguish between what Mises called money in the

---

6. To the extent that a merchant did discriminate against debit card use or personal checks, the reasons would probably be the fees and equipment associated with the former and the risk of a bounced check in the latter. The reason probably wouldn't be that the merchant didn't trust commercial banks in general and thought that immediate claims on them were less valuable than green pieces of paper.

7. Mises, *Theory of Money and Credit*, 483.

8. Mises, *Human Action*, 431.

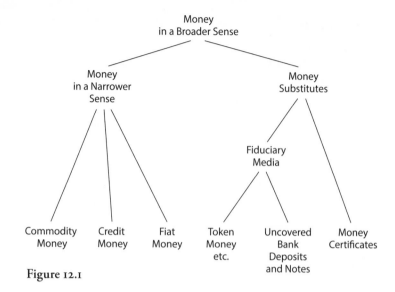

Figure 12.1

narrower sense and money substitutes, Mises thought such a distinction was crucial to correctly analyze important features of a mature market economy with a developed commercial banking sector.

The advantage of Mises's terminology will be clearer when we explain his theory of the business cycle in Chapter 14. For now, we will plant the seeds for that discussion by highlighting the significance of fiduciary media as they enter the economy from the commercial banking system. Under 100 percent reserve banking—where the banks are only allowed to issue money certificates—the banks cannot alter the quantity of money in the broader sense. For example, suppose we have an economy of 10 million people, based on a fiat dollar monetary system, but where the commercial banks do not issue fiduciary media. Further suppose that each person initially starts out with $1,000 in currency. The quantity of money in the narrower sense is thus $10 billion. Now each person deposits $800 in a checking account with a commercial bank because that is much safer and convenient than walking around with $1,000 in actual currency. So long as the commercial banks kept each customer's $800 deposit in the vaults as a reserve, the quantity of money in the broader sense will remain $10 billion. The average money holdings per person would be the same; it's just that people would hold their money in the form of 20 percent currency, 80 percent bank deposit. There would be little direct impact on the purchasing power of money or interest rates.

On the other hand, if there is only a 10 percent reserve requirement, then the $8 billion in currency serving as reserves in the vaults of the commercial banks can back up a total of $80 billion in checking account balances among the banks' customers. Thus the quantity of money in the broader sense would be the $2 billion in currency still held by the public, plus $80 billion in checking account balances, for a total of $82 billion. Because money substitutes, in this case, checking account deposits at the commercial banks, perform the same functions as money proper, there would probably be a sharp drop in the purchasing power of money—and a sharp rise in the prices of goods and services—from this effective creation of $72 billion of money in the broader sense, just as surely as if the government had printed up an additional $72 billion in paper currency.

The impact of the new fiduciary media wouldn't be limited to a general fall in the purchasing power of money. The entry point for the new money would be the loan market. Specifically, the banks would create new money every time they granted an additional loan that was not fully backed up by reserves in the vault. Compared to the original equilibrium position, then, the banks would need to lower the rate of interest they charged on loans in order to induce borrowers to acquire the new funds. When banks issue loans by granting fiduciary media, Mises calls it a granting of *circulation credit*. If this is done with newly created fiduciary media, Mises calls the entire process a *credit expansion*.

To sum up: When commercial banks engage in credit expansion, they issue new fiduciary media in the form of loans to their customers. Other things being equal, credit expansion decreases the purchasing power of money, raises prices in general, and reduces the rate of interest.

The opposite results hold as well: If banks engage in a *credit contraction*, they do not re-lend the fiduciary media that they receive as customers pay back their loans. This effectively destroys money in the broader sense, such that—other things being equal—the purchasing power of money increases, prices tend to fall, and the rate of interest increases.

In Chapter 14, we will see how credit expansion and credit contraction interact with the physical structure of capital goods to yield the familiar boom-bust cycle. This explanation is Mises's famous circulation credit theory of the trade cycle, or what is nowadays more popularly known as Austrian business cycle theory.

A Note on the Two Distinct Functions of Banks

When people first encounter the Misesian view that the severe booms and busts in modern history are related to excessive credit expansion, they are often puzzled. Doesn't banking by its very nature require the commercial banks to take in customer deposits and pay a certain rate of interest and then lend those very same deposits out at a higher rate of interest to earn a spread? If the bankers aren't allowed to take their customers' deposits and put them to work in outside investments, how are savers and borrowers linked up in the economy? Without the option of lending out deposits, how could banks make any money?

This confusion stems from growing up in a system based on fractional reserve banking, in which all customer deposits are fair game for making loans to borrowers at the bank. However, banks actually perform two distinct functions in a market economy, which—at least in principle—could be kept strictly segregated. Among modern Austrians, opinion is split on the issue of whether fractional reserve banking is inherently problematic.[9] Yet regardless of whether it would be good or bad, it's important to understand how 100 percent reserve banking is possible.

One of the functions of banks is to serve as warehouses for money. Consider: Even though people may decide to keep a certain fraction of their wealth in the form of money, they may not want to keep all of their money in the form of money in the narrower sense. Their money is less vulnerable to being lost or

---

9. An excellent introduction to the 100 percent reserve camp—in other words, those Austrians opposed to any issuance of fiduciary media—is Murray Rothbard, *What Has Government Done to Our Money?* (Auburn, AL: Ludwig von Mises Institute, 2005). In contrast, an excellent introduction to the fractional reserve camp—in other words, those Austrians who believe that genuinely free market banking would exhibit fiduciary media and that this would actually be preferable to 100 percent reserve banking—is George Selgin and Lawrence H. White, "In Defense of Fiduciary Media," *Review of Austrian Economics*, 9, no. 2 (1996): 83–107.

stolen if they place it in the care of a bank, with its strong vaults. Furthermore, large transactions are easier to accomplish with the writing of a check or the swipe of a debit card, rather than counting out the green pieces of paper or delivering a large weight of metal.

Under 100 percent reserve banking, banks can still provide such services to their customers. People give their money in the narrower sense to the bank, and they are credited with a demand deposit on the bank's books, meaning a deposit that is redeemable from the bank's branches upon demand. This is what people have in mind when they make a deposit to open a standard checking account. However, if the banks maintain a 100percent reserve policy, they must hold genuine money in their vaults to be sure they can satisfy any customers who exercise their contractual right to redeem their full checking account balance upon demand. Since the banks cannot lend these deposits out to others, they must explicitly charge the customers in some way for the service they are providing. After all, it is expensive to build a bank, maintain its vaults, hire security guards and tellers, process incoming checks, keep the ATMs filled with money, and so on. The fees might be a flat periodic charge, or they might be a small percentage of either the balance or of any transactions that involve the account. In any event, the important point is that banks could still perform the function of providing safekeeping and convenience to their customers who wanted to use money substitutes without using fiduciary media; it's just that the banks would have to find a way to be compensated for such services.

The second function of banks is to serve as a credit intermediary, a middleman between the ultimate lenders and borrowers in the economy. This, too, is possible in a system of 100 percent reserve banking. The savers lend their money to the bank, rather than deposit it in a checking account. One way to accomplish this is to buy a certificate of deposit (CD) from the bank, which has a specified maturity and interest rate. For example, a customer might buy a CD from the bank for $1,000, which will mature in one year, at which point the bank will return $1,035 to the customer, for a yield of 3.5 percent. In the meantime, the bank has taken the $1,000 and lent it out to, say, a small business owner in the community, on a loan that is to be repaid in one year with an interest rate of 6 percent. If all goes well, after the year has passed the bank receives $1,060 from the business owner, gives $1,035 of it to the original saver who bought the CD, and keeps $25 in bank earnings from the transactions. This scenario is consistent with 100 percent reserve banking, and the $1,000 loan to the small business owner is not made with fiduciary media. The reason is that the original saver bought a CD and relinquished control of his $1,000; his money holdings—even in the broader sense—shrank. Another way of accomplishing loan banking is for the original saver to make a *time deposit* in a true savings account, not a checking account, relinquishing the right to withdraw the money for a specified time. Whether through CDs or time deposits, the commercial bank can act as a credit intermediary, earning income from the spread in interest rates, and still be consistent with 100 percent reserve banking.

Thus we see that in principle, it would be possible for banks to fulfill their two main functions—acting as a warehouse for money and as a credit intermediary—even while keeping 100 percent reserves on their customers' demand deposits. In such an environment, bank runs would be impossible. Only with fractional reserve banking do the two functions seem to be merged into the same operation, where a customer who opens a checking account provides the opportunity for the bank to expand the amount it lends to other clients.

Modern Austrians are divided on the question of whether 100 percent reserve banking is a desirable feature in a banking system. The purpose of this section was merely to clarify the distinct functions performed by commercial banks in order to better isolate the effect of fiduciary media.

Mises's View of Free Banking

Not surprisingly, Mises—the champion of the market economy—argues that government intervention in monetary and banking affairs is ultimately the cause of the business cycle. Mises argues in favor of free banking, where the government applies the standard rules of contract enforcement but otherwise allows open entry into the banking sector, imposing no special regulations but also giving no special privileges. According to Mises, "There was no reason whatever to abandon the principle of free enterprise in the field of banking." He explains:

Free banking is the only method available for the prevention of the dangers inherent in credit expansion. It would, it is true, not hinder a slow credit expansion, kept within very narrow limits, on the part of cautious banks which provide the public with all information required about their financial status. But under free banking it would have been impossible for credit expansion with all its inevitable consequences to have developed into a regular—one is tempted to say normal—feature of the economic system. Only free banking would have rendered the market economy secure against crises and depressions.[10]

We are not yet ready—and neither is Mises at this point in *Human Action*—to explain the exact mechanism by which credit expansion causes the boom-bust cycle. Yet if the reader will accept that step in the argument for the moment, we can explain Mises's statements above. Under a regime of free banking, where the government does not set any particular regulations limiting commercial banks' issuance of fiduciary media but also offers no support if the banks run into trouble with their depositors, the ability of banks to engage in credit expansion would be severely curtailed. First, we will quote liberally from Mises's explanation of the market forces operating under a regime of free banking, and then we will elaborate on his description:

We assume that within a market system several independent banks have been established in the past. While previously only money was in use, these banks have introduced the use of money-substitutes a part of which are fiduciary media. Each bank has a clientele and has issued a certain quantity of fiduciary media which are kept as money-substitutes in the cash holdings of various clients . . .

But now, we assume further, one bank alone embarks upon an additional issue of fiduciary media while the other banks do not follow suit. The clients of the expanding bank—whether its old clients or new ones acquired on account of the expansion—receive additional credits, they expand their business activities, they appear on the market with an additional demand for goods and services, they bid up prices. Those people who are not clients of the expanding bank are not in a position

---

10. Mises, *Human Action*, 440.

to afford these higher prices; they are forced to restrict their purchases. Thus there prevails on the market a shifting of goods from the non-clients to the clients of the expanding bank. The clients buy more from the nonclients than they sell to them; they have more to pay to the nonclients than they receive from them. But money-substitutes issued by the expanding bank are not suitable for payments to nonclients, as these people do not assign to them the character of money-substitutes. In order to settle the payments due to nonclients, the clients must first exchange the money-substitutes issued by their own—viz., the expanding bank—against money. The expanding bank must redeem its banknotes and pay out its deposits. Its reserve . . . dwindles. The instant approaches in which the bank will—after the exhaustion of its money reserve—no longer be in a position to redeem the money-substitutes still current. In order to avoid insolvency it must as soon as possible return to a policy of strengthening its money reserve. It must abandon its expansionist methods. . . .

A bank can never issue more money-substitutes than its clients can keep in their cash holdings . . . . Thus a limit is drawn to the issue of fiduciary media. We may admit that everybody is ready to accept in his current transactions indiscriminately banknotes issued by any bank and checks drawn upon any bank. But he deposits without delay with his own bank not only the checks but also the banknotes of banks of which he is not himself a client. In the further course his bank settles its accounts with the bank engaged. Thus the process described above comes into motion.[11]

Through the above mechanism, Mises has shown that—contrary to popular belief—there would be stringent constraints on an individual bank's ability to inflate in a laissez-faire environment. Rather than limiting credit expansion, government intervention historically has had the opposite effect; government intervention in banking has made possible and promoted much more credit expansion than would otherwise have occurred.

---

11. Mises, *Human Action*, 434–35.

The process by which the market economy—if allowed to operate—would naturally hinder bank credit expansion is crucial to understanding Mises's position, so we will illustrate his description with a simple numerical example.

Suppose there is a society with twenty-six banks, named Bank A, B, C, D, and so on. Everyone in the economy chooses his or her bank on the basis of name: Andy, Aaron, Amanda, and so on, all open up checking accounts with Bank A, while Bob, Bill, Betty, and so on, open up checking accounts with Bank B. Of the 26 million people in this society—coincidentally enough—exactly one million people have names starting with A, one million have names starting with B, and so forth. Thus each bank has one million customers who have a checking account with that bank and only that bank.

The ultimate money in the narrower sense in this economy is the fiat dollar, which is provided by the government's Treasury. Throughout our description, the quantity of green pieces of paper is fixed at $26 billion, which works out to $1,000 in paper currency per person. However, this society is cashless in the sense that nobody walks around with green pieces of paper in his wallet or her purse. Rather, everyone keeps his or her money deposited in a checking account at the appropriately named bank. Individuals make all of their purchases by writing paper checks drawn on their checking accounts. Thus every green piece of paper money in existence is housed in the vault of a particular bank.

Initially, the society is in an equilibrium where all the banks keep 50 percent reserves on their customers' checking accounts. If we further assume that every person in society initially starts out with the same amount of money, we conclude that each bank holds $1 billion in reserves to back up the outstanding $2 billion in total customer checking account balances. Since each bank has one million customers, that means each customer has $2,000 in his or her checking account.

Let's stop at this point to be clear on the characteristics of our hypothetical economy, in this initial equilibrium state: Even though the government has physically printed only $26 billion in paper currency, there is a very legitimate sense in which the quantity of money in the broader sense is actually double that, namely $52 billion, because each of the 26 million people can check the ATM and see a checking account balance of $2,000. This is "really" money, in the sense that each person can go buy items from others with a price up to

$2,000. Furthermore, each person is legally permitted to convert his checking account balances into money in the narrower sense at any time. For example, Frank can walk into a branch of Bank F and withdraw $500 in cash. The bank teller will give $500 in green pieces of paper—perhaps three $100 bills and ten $20 bills—to Frank but will also reduce the balance in his checking account from $2,000 down to $1,500. Because of this unquestioned ability to instantly turn checking account balances into actual paper currency, everyone in the community treats the bank balances as money substitutes.

However, this is a precarious situation. Remember that the banks are holding only fractional reserves—in our example, half of the outstanding checking account balances are fiduciary media, not money certificates—which means that they are all vulnerable to a bank run. If Frank, Fred, Fiona, Francine, and all the other F-names tried to take out their money at the same time, then Bank F would run out of cash reserves and would go out of business. The bank run is the ultimate check on private credit expansion, but even normal withdrawals provide a limit to how low commercial banks can push their reserve ratios: The banks must maintain public confidence that they can turn their deposits into paper cash at any time.

In our scenario, we are purposely stacking the deck in favor of credit expansion by assuming that people are perfectly content to hold all of their money in the form of money substitutes rather than money proper. Furthermore, we assume no one has any problem accepting a check drawn on a different bank; the merchant Gary, for example, has no qualms accepting personal checks from people named Amy, Brian, Chad, Yolinda, or Zed. With the assumptions we've chosen, it seems as if there would be no limit emanating from the competitive marketplace to bank credit expansion. Why wouldn't Bank C, for example, make more loans simply by adding numbers to its customers' checking account balances? It's not as if the customers will ever ask to convert their balances into currency, and no one in the community will have any reluctance in accepting personal checks drawn on Bank C. So what's to stop Bank C from inflating the quantity of money with another round of credit expansion?

The answer is that the interbank check clearing process would ultimately hinder Bank C. To see why, we first must think through the conditions of the original equilibrium. In that situation, if each person is to remain hold-

Table 12.1. Sample Transactions In Initial Equilibrium
(All Banks Keep 50% Reserves)

Transaction	Reaction by Bank(s)
(1) Aaron writes a check to Amy for $10 to buy a book.	Bank A debits Aaron's account by $10 and credits Amy's account by $10.
(2) Amy writes a check to Alan for $10 to buy lunch.	Bank A debits Amy's account by $10 and credits Alan's account by $10.
(3) Alan writes a check to Aaron for $10 to buy a baseball.	Bank A debits Alan's account by $10 and credits Aaron's account by $10.
(4) Aaron writes a check to Bob for $15 to buy a book.	Bank A debits Aaron's account by $15, and sends $15 of its vault paper currency to Bank B. Bank B adds the $15 in paper currency to its vault cash, and credits Bob's account by $15.
(5) Bob writes a check to Chris for $15 to buy lunch.	Bank B debits Bob's account by $15, and sends $15 of its vault paper currency to Bank C. Bank C adds the $15 in paper currency to its vault cash, and credits Chris's account by $15.
(6) Chris writes a check to Aaron for $15 to buy a baseball.	Bank C debits Chris's account by $15, and sends $15 of its vault paper currency to Bank A. Bank A adds the $15 in paper currency to its vault cash, and credits Aaron's account by $15.

ing $2,000 in his or her checking account, then the checks drawn on various banks must cancel out in the aggregate. To see how this works, in Table 12.1, we'll lay out just a microcosm of the economy, focusing on a few transactions, to demonstrate the pattern.

In the table, the first three transactions all concern customers of Bank A, so there is no impact on the vault cash. Whenever Bank A's own customers write checks to each other, Bank A simply debits and credits their balances accordingly. Bank A is not affected by such operations. Notice that to maintain our equilibrium, we have chosen the numbers such that Aaron, Amy, and Alan do not accumulate or draw down their bank balances on net during these first three transactions; each person pays $10 to someone else with a name starting with A, while receiving a $10 payment from someone whose name starts with A.

However, the second half of the transactions—numbers (4) through (6)—involve customers of different banks. For example, in transaction (4) Aaron writes a personal check to Bob for $15. Clearly Bank A will subtract $15 from Aaron's checking account balance. When Bob takes the check from Aaron and deposits it at his own bank, then Bank B will add $15 to Bob's checking account balance. However, if matters stopped there, then the people running Bank B would clearly be at a disadvantage: They had to increase one of their customer's checking account balances, giving him the legal ability to show up at their branches and ask to withdraw $15 in paper currency. Thus, after Bob gives Bank B his endorsed check from Aaron, Bank B will stamp it with some identification and then send the check along to Bank A, asking Bank A to send it $15 in paper currency. If for some reason Bank A refused to do this whenever Bank B sent along personal checks written by Bank A's clients, then Bank B would tell all of its own customers, "Don't ever accept a personal check written by clients of Bank A, since those checks aren't good."[12] To maintain their reputations in the community, therefore, all banks must promptly respond to requests to send paper currency from their vaults whenever presented with a legitimate personal check written by one of their clients.

Because we want to maintain the original equilibrium, the table above shows everyone's cash position remaining the same, after all of the transactions have been reckoned. The description in the table above suggests that $15 in paper currency moves from Bank A to B, then again from B to C, and finally from C to A. However, in practice this would be a waste of resources. Rather than request paper currency after every check is processed from another bank, the banks would surely agree to let their respective claims and counterclaims accumulate against each other, to be settled by a movement of actual cash only periodically, such as every week or every month. The banks

---

12. Note that such an announcement by the other banks in the society would be devastating to Bank A. After all, the only reason Alice, Andy, Amy, and so on patronize Bank A is that it is more convenient to write personal checks drawn on their Bank A checking account than to walk around holding paper currency. This convenience largely vanishes if nobody is willing to accept their checks except other customers of Bank A.

would thus establish a clearinghouse mechanism to cancel out a large portion of their claims on each other, so that only the net amounts would have to be shipped from one bank's vault to another's. In our example depicted in the table above, no net cash would be owed by any bank to another, and so no paper currency would ever leave the vaults.

Now that we have spent some time setting up our hypothetical economy and its free banking system—we assume no government regulations concerning minimum reserve requirements—it will be easy to understand the natural check on credit expansion that Mises described earlier. Suppose in our initial equilibrium, the managers of Bank C look at the $1 billion in reserve sitting in their vault, apparently doing nothing for the bank. Bank C's own customers are content with their checking account balances serving their need for money holdings, and the claims emanating from other banks are offset by counterclaims emanating from Bank C.

Because of this relative tranquility, the managers of Bank C decide to make more loans to their own customers. They approach Cathy, Carl, Charles, and so on, and say, "Right now, you have $2,000 in your checking account with us. What if we increased that number to $4,000—granting you a $2,000 loan—on which you will pay us a small interest rate?" If the interest rate is low enough, the clients will all agree, and it apparently costs Bank C nothing to make such loans. After all, these are all clients of Bank C; it simply needs to change the numbers in its computer database to reflect the fact that everyone in their system now has $4,000 in his or her checking account. Immediately after this move, Bank C has a reserve ratio of only 25 percent—it has $4 billion in outstanding customer checking account balances with $1 billion in vault cash—but that seems to be an acceptable risk. No customer ever tries to withdraw large amounts of cash, and the activity with other banks rarely requires a net drain on the vault either. Note also that by its bookkeeping move, Bank C has instantly created $2 billion more money in the broader sense in the economy.

However, the managers of Bank C would soon realize they had made a foolish mistake. Even though they could still rely on their own clients to be content with the higher checking account balances rather than asking for paper currency, this will not be true of the other banks in the community. With twice as much money as others in the society, clients of Bank C will spend more than they did in the original equilibrium, perhaps on consumption goods, but also on investments. Because they are spending more, while the clients of the other banks stick to their original plans, suddenly the interbank clearinghouse mechanism will not be a wash. On net, the clients of Bank C will spend more buying things from the clients of Banks A, B, D, E and so on than vice versa. Thus, when the banks settle up with respect to the personal checks written by their respective customers, Bank C will, on net, owe more to the other banks than vice versa. Therefore, Bank C will have to ship paper currency from its vaults to the other banks.

To get a ballpark idea of just how much cash would be drained, consider the most symmetrical scenario in which everyone in the society ends up holding an equal amount of the new quantity of money in the broader sense, which is now $2 billion higher, thanks to Bank C's credit expansion. Although Bank C's customers were the original recipients of the $2 billion, they will end up retaining only $2 billion divided by 26 = $77 million of the new money. The other $1.9 billion will end up in the accounts of clients at the other twenty-five banks.[13] The immediate result of Bank C's credit expansion, therefore, is that it might have to ship out $1.9 billion of vault cash as soon as its customers have spent their new balances on consumer goods and investments.

Yet hold on: Bank C starts with only $1 billion in paper currency in its vault. Therefore, it would be driven out of business long before the full effects of its credit expansion could play out.

Although our numerical example used some very simplifying assumptions, its purpose was to walk us through the nuts and bolts of a private, free banking system, in which the government imposes no special regulations on commercial banks except the enforcement of contracts. So long as a given

---

13. More specifically, the so-called Cantillon effects occur, so that prices in the community rise as the new money is spent and then spent again by the new recipients. Eventually, equilibrium is restored when prices have risen enough so that people move down and to the right along the demand curve for money until the total quantity of money demanded to hold is $2 billion higher than it was originally. Note that we are ignoring the fact that Banks A, B, D, E and so on would possibly increase their own issuance of loans in response to an influx of cash.

bank has only a small fraction of the total population as its own clients, any attempt to expand credit will lead to a quick drain on its vault reserves.

In Mises's view, the purpose of government intervention in banking was not to protect the general public from unscrupulous "fly by night" bankers issuing bogus certificates. Rather, Mises argues that the purpose was to weaken the checks on credit expansion inherent in a genuinely free market in banking. The government wanted to encourage the commercial banks to inflate together, so that cash reserves wouldn't leave the inflationary banks and accumulate in the conservative banks. The establishment of central banks, as well as legal and regulatory hurdles on opening up new banks, also helped to form a cartel in the banking sector. These harmful developments led to price inflation and exacerbated the boom-bust cycle, as we will explain in Chapter 14.

13

Capital, Time Preference, and the Theory of Interest

Introduction

ONE OF THE distinguishing features of Mises's economics is the *pure time preference theory of interest*, in which positive interest rates are explained by reference to the fact that people prefer goods available in the present versus the same goods available only at a future date. This approach seems at sharp odds[1] with the orthodox explanation; most professional economists outside of the Austrian School would say that interest is a return to the marginal product of capital, in the same way that wages are a return to the marginal product of labor.

The great economic theorist Eugen von Böhm-Bawerk—who was a second-generation member of the Austrian School, following Menger but preceding Mises—wrote a masterful work in which he classified and critiqued all pre-existing explanations of interest. One of the explanations Böhm-Bawerk criticized was what he dubbed "the naïve productivity theory" of interest. It is a category mistake, he said, to try to explain a positive rate of return on invested financial capital by reference to the productivity of the physical capital goods in which the investments are made. In a subsequent work, Böhm-Bawerk then provided his own positive theory to explain interest, which he

---

1. Actually, there is not a literal contradiction, but rather the mainstream approach typically relies on simplifying conditions—for example, assuming that only one type of good serves as both consumer good and capital good—that obscure the more nuanced understanding provided by the Austrians. See the somewhat technical paper, Robert P. Murphy, "Interest and the Marginal Product of Capital: A Critique of Samuelson," *Journal of the History of Economic Thought*, 29, no. 4 (2007): 453–64.

claimed was impervious to the dozens of fallacies he had identified in his previous work regarding the prior attempts to solve the problem.[2]

Perhaps ironically, Böhm-Bawerk's explanation involved the technical productivity of what he called *roundabout production processes.* This move surprised American economist Frank Fetter, who thought Böhm-Bawerk had inexplicably relapsed back into the erroneous productivity approach to explaining interest. Instead, Fetter offered a pure time preference theory of interest, in which the economist explains interest by reference to the higher subjective valuation placed on present versus future goods—period.[3]

For his part, Mises endorsed everything that Fetter had done in his handling of Böhm-Bawerk's work on capital and interest. In particular, Mises agreed that Böhm-Bawerk had been a giant in the field, clearing away the tangled brush of confusion and fallacy, but who had fallen short with his own positive theory. Mises himself adopted the pure time preference theory of interest, but with a Misesian twist: Fetter had simply taken time preference to be an empirical, psychological fact that happened to be true of humans. Mises instead elevated time preference to a category of action, which must be true whenever action is present.

In this chapter, we will elaborate upon the outline of ideas presented above. Our quick lesson in the history of economic thought[4] is necessary because Mises's remarks in *Human Action* on this topic implicitly assume that the reader is familiar with the work of previous economists. After explaining the Austrian approach to interest—which has nothing to do with the productivity of capital goods per se—we will see how the accumulation of capital goods increases the productivity of labor and land resources, thereby increasing income.

---

2. See Eugen von Böhm-Bawerk, *Capital and Interest*, 3 vols. (South Holland, IL: Libertarian Press [1884, 1889, 1909] 1959).

3. For a collection of Fetter's writings on these topics, see Frank A. Fetter, *Capital, Interest and Rent: Essays in the Theory of Distribution*, ed. with intro. by Murray N. Rothbard (Kansas City: Sheed, Andrews and McMeel, 1977).

4. For a more detailed examination of the evolution of Austrian theory regarding capital and interest, see the first two essays in Robert P. Murphy, *Unanticipated Intertemporal Change in Theories of Interest*, PhD diss., New York University, 2003.

Böhm-Bawerk's Critique of the
So-Called Naïve Productivity Theory of Interest[5]

One of the most important contributions Böhm-Bawerk made in understanding interest was in his identification and framing of the phenomenon under scrutiny. Specifically, Böhm-Bawerk argued that the task of the economic theorist was to explain why owners of capital could regularly earn a net return on their assets, even though, unlike laborers, they apparently did nothing to earn this interest income. After this starting point, Böhm-Bawerk transformed the task by showing that it was equivalent to explaining why there was an apparent premium—what he called *agio*—in intertemporal exchanges, those that involve goods from different time periods.

We can illustrate Böhm-Bawerk's approach with the example of a tractor. Typically, a capitalist who invests in a tractor, either directly or by lending funds to a farmer, can earn an interest return on the investment; that is, he will have more wealth, measured in money terms,[6] after the tractor has been used to harvest crops. What Böhm-Bawerk realized was that this phenomenon— the growth in financial wealth through investment in the tractor—relies on an apparent undervaluation of the tractor.

To see this, suppose that the tractor is expected to yield an additional $1,000 worth of revenue every year, and that it will last ten years before being junked. Böhm-Bawerk argued that the only reason a capitalist could earn money through ownership of the tractor is that its initial purchase price is *less* than $10,000. Only in that case could an investor use an initial amount of financial wealth and turn it into a *greater* subsequent amount (ten years later). In other words, if the capitalist had to spend a full $10,000 upfront to buy the tractor, and then it increased the harvest on the farm to allow for an extra $1,000 in crops to be earned each year for a decade, the capitalist would only break even, recouping his initial $10,000 investment. To earn a positive rate of return, the initial purchase price had to be less than the $10,000.

---

5. This section of the text is based on the essay, Robert P. Murphy, "Why Do Capitalists Earn Interest Income?" *Mises.org Daily Article*, July 1, 2003, http://mises.org/daily/1263/.

6. In his writings, Böhm-Bawerk typically did not distinguish between what we nowadays call nominal and real variables.

If, for example, a new tractor had a purchase price of only $5,000, then the capitalist would effectively double his money over the course of 10 years for an annualized rate of return of about 7 percent.[7]

By this procedure, Böhm-Bawerk had transformed his original question. Rather than asking, "Why do capitalists earn an effortless flow of interest income?" he could instead wonder, "Why is it that the initial purchase prices of capital goods systematically fall short of the future income their use is expected to yield?" Against this metric, Böhm-Bawerk measured all of the explanations of interest that economic theorists had offered before his own writing.

One of those earlier explanations relied on the productivity of capital to explain the ability of capitalists to earn interest income. Surviving to this day, the orthodox treatment explains interest as the return to the marginal product of capital. Coming from this perspective, an economist would look at our example and claim that the capitalist earns a net return on his wealth for the simple reason that the tractor is productive: After all, a farmer can harvest more crops, year after year, with a tractor than without one, and so naturally someone who buys a tractor can earn an income over time.

This orthodox treatment seems analogous to the standard treatment of labor and wages. After all, Austrians and most other economists agree that if employers hire a worker then they must a pay a wage commensurate with the increase in output that the labor makes possible. By the same token, if capitalists provide a capital good such as a tractor to a farmer, then the farmer must pay them interest commensurate with the increase in output that the capital good makes possible.

Böhm-Bawerk brilliantly refuted this line of reasoning,[8] which he referred to as the naïve productivity theory of interest:

---

7. To keep the computations simple, we are not allowing the capitalist to reinvest the $1,000 annual earnings as they flow from his ownership of the tractor. He accumulates the money over the ten-year cycle and sees that by the end of the decade, he has doubled his initial investment.

8. To avoid confusion, we should stress that the orthodox treatment of interest is correct mathematically, but when trying to give intuitive explanations of what is happening in their simplistic models, mainstream economists often fall into the naïve productivity theory trap that Böhm-Bawerk exploded so long ago. This distinction is explained in Murphy, "Interest and the Marginal Product of Capital," 2007.

I grant without ado that capital actually possesses the physical productivity ascribed to it, that is to say, that more goods can actually be produced with its help than without. I will also grant . . . that the greater amount of goods produced with the help of capital has higher value than the smaller amount of goods produced without it. But there is not one single feature in the whole set of circumstances to indicate that this greater amount of goods must be worth more *than the capital consumed in its production*. And that is the feature of the phenomenon of excess value which has to be explained. [Emphasis in original.][9]

We can understand Böhm-Bawerk's argument in terms of our tractor example. The naïve productivity theorist claims that the owner of a tractor earns a net return on his investment because the tractor yields $1,000 in net income over and above its cost of operation each year of its life. So this explains the annual percentage return reaped by the capitalist on his invested funds (so thinks the naïve productivity theorist).

But Böhm-Bawerk points out that this is looking at only one side of the matter. Yes, the productivity of the tractor explains why its owner enjoys $1,000 per year in extra income; if he wished, the owner could rent out the tractor and charge up to $1,000 per year for its services.

However, this flow of income will represent a net return on the original investment only if the original purchase price is less than $10,000. If the purchase price is $10,000, the depreciation of the tractor over its ten-year lifespan would exactly offset the flow of dividends, so that the net rate of interest on the investment would be zero. Note that this is perfectly consistent with the fact that the tractor is productive, and so the tractor's productivity as such cannot be the explanation for a positive rate of interest.

Indeed, Böhm-Bawerk pointed out that if anything, the naïve productivity theory goes the opposite direction of where the answer must lie. Remember, we are trying to explain the apparent undervaluation of the tractor: Why is it that a capitalist can spend less than $10,000 today to buy a tractor that will—over the course of ten years—yield a cumulative sum of $10,000 in net income? Böhm-Bawerk observed that it makes little sense to say, "The

---

9. Eugen von Böhm-Bawerk, *Capital and Interest*, Vol. I, 93.

tractor is physically productive and allows the farmer to harvest more crops than he could without it," as a way of explaining this fact about the market. The productivity of the tractor explains why it throws off an annual net income—why the farmer can generate $1,000 more in crops with the tractor than without it—but Böhm-Bawerk's question didn't concern the figure of $1,000 per year. Rather, Böhm-Bawerk's question concerned the relationship of the initial purchase price to the subsequent flow of $1,000 annual payments over the course of a decade.

In *Human Action*, Mises alludes to Böhm-Bawerk's great insight when he writes:

> A lengthening of the period of production can increase the quantity of output per unit of input or produce goods which cannot be produced at all within a shorter period of production. But it is not true that the imputation of the value of this additional wealth to the capital goods required for the lengthening of the period of production generates interest. If one were to assume this, one would relapse into the crassest errors of the productivity approach, irrefutably exploded by Böhm-Bawerk. The contribution of the complementary factors of production to the result of the process is the reason for their being considered as valuable; it explains the prices paid for them and is fully taken into account in the determination of these prices. No residuum is left that is not accounted for and could explain interest.[10]

In this passage, Mises considers it the "crassest errors of the productivity approach" to explain interest by reference to the increased output made possible by the contribution of inputs to a production process. If a particular input—whether an hour of labor, an acre of farmland, or a machine—generates more output for its owner when incorporated into an operation, then the

---

10. Mises, *Human Action*, 526–27. In the context of Mises's discussion, he is ironically taking aim not only at orthodox economists but also at Böhm-Bawerk himself, since the latter's own positive explanation of interest involved the technical productivity of more roundabout production processes. (See Murphy, *Unanticipated Intertemporal Change*, for a full discussion.) Confused readers should be reassured that we are here touching on what is truly one of the most difficult subjects in all of economic theory; we bring up the subtlety here only to make the newcomer aware that Mises did not fully endorse Böhm-Bawerk's work on capital and interest.

owner will be willing to pay money for it. Yet, as first Böhm-Bawerk and then Mises pointed out, the brute fact that resources are productive does not explain interest. The phenomenon of interest has to do with an apparent undervaluation in the original purchase price of various inputs, so that the capitalist can buy them for less money upfront that they are expected to yield in the form of net income over their lifespans. In a sense, interest is about the relationship between two prices rather than one particular price. The fact that interest is expressed as a percentage—rather than as a dollar figure—should have been a clue in this respect.

Explaining Interest with Subjective Time Preference

If the naïve productivity theory doesn't fit the bill, how *can* we explain interest? Böhm-Bawerk argued that the "nub and kernel" of his solution was the fact that present goods are preferred to future goods. Generally speaking, people value present apples, houses, and so on more than they value *claims* to such goods that cannot be redeemed until the future. In the case of our hypothetical tractor, its purchase price is denominated in present dollars, while it offers only the hope of a stream of future dividends of $1,000 each year for ten years. Since no one would be willing to give $10,000 now in exchange for a promise of $1,000 payments for each of the next ten years, it naturally follows that no one would pay $10,000 for our hypothetical tractor. Because of this fact—that present goods are worth more than future goods—the tractor can be purchased for less than $10,000, and capitalists can increase the market value of their wealth by investing in tractors.

We should be clear that Böhm-Bawerk was *not* arguing in a circle; he wasn't merely saying, "People value a dollar today more than a dollar in the future because they value a dollar today more than a dollar in the future." Rather, Böhm-Bawerk was arguing that people value present money more than future money because present money allows us to buy present goods while money delivered in the future only allows us to buy goods available in the future.

One way of understanding Böhm-Bawerk's contribution is to view him as applying the Mengerian subjectivist value theory to prices of goods that were available in different times. For example, to explain why diamonds today had a higher market price than water today, Menger referred to the subjective marginal utilities of present diamonds versus present water. Böhm-Bawerk, for his part, explained why diamonds today had a higher price than diamonds not available until next year by referring to the subjective marginal utilities of present diamonds versus future diamonds.

The phenomenon of a general subjective preference for present versus future goods is called *time preference*. We can use a specific numerical illustration to show how time preference solves Böhm-Bawerk's formulation of the interest problem. Suppose it is November 2014 and a woman is in the market for a Christmas tree. She can buy a Christmas tree available immediately, or she can buy an ironclad claim ticket that entitles her to a Christmas tree delivered to her house in November 2015. No one would be surprised to learn that the woman will pay, say, $100 for the Christmas tree available immediately but will pay only a smaller sum—perhaps $85—to guarantee herself a comparable tree delivered in exactly one year's time. Just as she would pay more for a steak than a burger, here too the woman pays more for the good she prefers, namely the present Christmas tree as opposed to the Christmas tree available in one year. The woman's preference for the earlier delivery of the Christmas tree is a specific manifestation of the general phenomenon of time preference.

Note that this is all we need to explain the emergence of interest in the market. Most obvious, a capitalist in 2014 who had $85 could use his money to buy a claim ticket to a 2015 Christmas tree. After a year had passed, the ticket would mature, and he would receive the fully grown tree. Holding other factors constant,[11] he would then be able to sell the tree for $100 since—at that time, in 2015—it would now be a present Christmas tree. Thus, the capitalist would have converted his $85 of financial capital in 2014 into $100 in 2015, for a return of about 18 percent.

Once we see how this procedure works with paper claims, we can expand it to include investments of capital into physical goods. For example, suppose our capitalist in 2014 used $85 to buy a sapling that would—if left alone for a year—grow into an adult Christmas tree by 2015. This would be equivalent

---

11. The analysis becomes more complicated if we allow for the spot price of the Christmas tree to change over time, which may happen in the real world. However, such complexities lie outside the scope of the present book; the interested reader should consult Murphy, *Unanticipated Intertemporal Change*, 2003.

to our first scenario; the capitalist would hold on to his investment for a year, then sell it for $100 and earn an 18 percent return.

The driving force in both of our scenarios is that capitalists can earn interest by buying a future Christmas tree, then holding the asset until it matures or ripens into a present Christmas tree. The crucial feature is not the physical transformation of a young into a mature tree (in the second scenario), because the paper claim obviously doesn't physically turn into a Christmas tree (in the first scenario). The common element in the two scenarios is possession of an asset in 2014 that will eventually yield the owner a present Christmas tree in 2015. The market value of this asset rises as time passes because consumers subjectively prefer a present Christmas tree versus a future Christmas tree.

The point holds more generally. For example, suppose a capitalist can invest $85,000 in lumber, glass, shingles, nails, a parcel of land, and the skilled labor to build a house. The construction takes nine months, and then it takes an additional three months to put the house on the market and finally sell it for $100,000. So long as this procedure were predictable, the roughly 18 percent return on the capitalist's investment would be interest. As with the Christmas tree, the ultimate explanation of the source of this interest income is time preference: Home buyers subjectively prefer a present house versus a future house; they would pay $85,000 now for a house that they are not allowed to use for a year, whereas they would pay $100,000 for a house that would be immediately available. The technological facts related to the transformation of lumber, shingles, and so on into a finished house would be utterly irrelevant to the question of the rate of return to the capitalist.

At this point, we should step back and state an important fact about the market economy: Even if there were no changes in the underlying fundamentals and the economy moved into a stationary, long-run equilibrium—what Mises called the evenly rotating economy—the prices of the inputs into a production process would not fully absorb the price of the finished output. Workers would be paid their wages in accordance with marginal productivity, and the owners of other resources would be paid in similar fashion, so long as the time element were correctly taken into account. For example, if a worker in January 2015 provided an hour of labor that would increase revenues in January 2016 by $50 when the product was eventually sold, then even getting paid the full value of his labor would entitle the worker to less than $50 paid in January 2015 for that hour of work. For example, if the interest rate were 5 percent, the worker would receive roughly $47.62 for his hourly wage.

Thus, even in an unrealistic world of perfect certainty, where there would be no entrepreneurial profit or loss, there would still always be a gap or markup between the total monetary outlays and the monetary revenues, allowing the capitalists to earn interest on their investment. Even after everything in the system settled down and there were no more adjustments, competition would not have bid up the prices of the inputs to the full price of the output. Mises explained the persistence of this gap as due to the fact of time preference, which exists even in a world of certainty where the entrepreneurs make no mistakes in anticipating future market conditions.

Now that we have seen the correct handling of the interest problem, we can circle back and revisit Böhm-Bawerk's critique of the naïve productivity theory of interest; his criticism will make more sense now that we have discussed time preference. Historically, part of the appeal of the naïve productivity theory were misleading analogies with natural resources that offer a flow of services to their owners. Mises explains the problem:

> Naive reasoning does not see any problem in the current revenue derived from hunting, fishing, cattle breeding, forestry, and agriculture. Nature generates deer, fish, and cattle and makes them grow, causes the cows to give milk and the chickens to lay eggs, the trees to put on wood and to bear fruit, and the seeds to shoot into ears. He who has a title to appropriate for himself this recurring wealth enjoys a steady income. Like a stream which continually carries new water, the "stream of income" flows continually and conveys again and again new wealth. The whole process is plainly a natural phenomenon. But for the economist a problem is presented in the determination of prices for land, cattle, and all the rest. If future goods were not bought and sold at a discount as against present goods, the buyer of land would have to pay a price which equals the sum of all future net revenues and which would leave nothing for a current reiterated income.[12]

---

12. Mises, *Human Action*, 521–22.

It was understandable that people at first thought the perpetual yield of interest income from an initial sum of financial capital had to do with the physical flow of output goods made possible by the productivity of physical capital goods. As Mises points out in the passage above, this seemed to be analogous to the owner of a forest being able to reap a perpetual flow of lumber. Yet this doesn't explain the phenomenon of interest because interest involves a flow of revenue that is greater than the drop in the market value of the asset.

It's difficult to grasp the Böhm-Bawerkian critique of the naïve productivity theory in the case of inexhaustible natural resources because without time preference the purchase price of the resource would be infinite, and consequently it seems as if some rhetorical trick is involved rather than a deep point. Böhm-Bawerk's insight is much easier to see with exhaustible resources, such as our example of the tractor. Mises himself uses the example of a building that has a lifespan of ten years. Mises explains that in a world without time preference—where people valued the present services of a superstructure the same as they valued the prospect of future services flowing from the building—then,

> [A] superstructure that can yield during a period of ten years an annual revenue of one hundred dollars would be priced (apart from the soil on which it is built) at the beginning of this period at one thousand dollars, at the beginning of the second year at nine hundred dollars, and so on.[13]

Mises's example shows what is wrong with those who look at, say, a stream providing a constant flow of fish and believe that this is an example of what generates interest income in the market economy. In the case of a superstructure with a lifespan of ten years, each year's rent ($100) is exactly counterbalanced by the drop in market value of the capital good (also $100). Thus the capitalist who invests in such a building will merely tread water, earning a zero rate of return each year. In the beginning, she starts with $1,000 in money and buys the building worth $1,000. By the second year, she has reaped $100 in rental income, but her building is now worth only $900, meaning her

---

13. Mises, *Human Action*, 523.

total wealth is still $1,000. By the third year, the capitalist is holding $200 in cash, but the building has fallen in market value to $800, meaning her total wealth once again is constant at $1,000. Mises's simple example illustrates that a flow of services accruing from an asset—whether the shelter provided by a superstructure or the trout provided by a stream—cannot by itself explain the steady increase in financial wealth of the person who buys it. If future services had the same market value as services available immediately, then the market price of capital goods would already fully account for the services at the moment of initial purchase, and the buyer would not grow wealthier with the passage of time.

The important takeaway message from our discussion is that subjective time preference—the preference for present versus future goods—can explain interest. In contrast, physical facts of the productivity of natural resources or capital goods cannot explain interest if time preference is absent. Such natural resources and capital goods would still yield a flow of services and hence periodic revenue to their owners, but to calculate the rate of return on the financial capital invested, we need to know the market value of the resources. Thus, interest is not about physical productivity per se, but about the subjective evaluation of present versus future goods and services. The approach we have just described is the pure time preference theory of interest.

Mises Elevates Time Preference to a Necessary Feature of All Action

The pure time preference theory of interest was crystallized by the economist Frank Fetter, who viewed himself as taking the brilliant foundation laid by Böhm-Bawerk and pruning it of the unfortunate vestiges of considerations of productivity. He called the result the capitalization theory. Fetter viewed time preference as simply an empirical regularity in human affairs; it just so happened that people generally preferred present to future goods, he thought, and that was why it just so happened that investors could earn interest in the market economy.

Mises adopted the pure time preference theory himself but conceived of time preference as a necessary feature of action. In other words, Mises didn't try to explain time preference by appeal to psychological or physiological facts about human beings. Rather, Mises believed that if we think through the logical implications of the concept of action—using reason to select means to achieve goals—then it must be the case that the acting being wants to achieve those goals sooner rather than later:

> Time preference is a categorial requisite of human action. No mode of action can be thought of in which satisfaction within a nearer period of the future is not—other things being equal—preferred to that in a later period. The very act of gratifying a desire implies that gratification at the present instant is preferred to that at a later instant. He who consumes a nonperishable good instead of postponing consumption for an indefinite later moment thereby reveals a higher valuation of present satisfaction as compared with later satisfaction. If he were not to prefer satisfaction in a nearer period of the future to that in a remoter period, he would never consume and so satisfy wants. He would always accumulate, he would never consume and enjoy. He would not consume today, but he would not consume tomorrow either, as the morrow would confront him with the same alternative.[14]

How can Mises claim that present goods are always preferred to future goods? Aren't there obvious scenarios in which a person would rather a particular good be delivered in the future, rather than right now? For example, wouldn't people in January prefer to receive tickets to their favorite amusement park in the summer, rather than tomorrow, when it might be snowing?

The answer is that the principle of time preference says a present good is preferred to a future good if other things are equal. In our example, other things—especially the weather—are not equal. In subjective value theory, it is not the physical characteristics of a good that ultimately matter, but rather the ability of the good to satisfy an individual's goals. People value admission tickets to an amusement park not really because they want to physically step onto the property, but because of the enjoyments they get from trying the different rides on a warm day surrounded by other people. An admission ticket to the amusement park in January is a different good from an admission ticket in June, even apart from the time delay. It clearly wouldn't be a violation of time

---

14. Mises, *Human Action*, 481.

preference for someone to choose a steak dinner next month, rather than applesauce today; a steak dinner is a different good from applesauce. In the same way, it is not a violation of time preference for someone to choose to go to an amusement park in the summer rather than today (in January) because those are different goods.[15]

Originary Interest and the Loan Market

Another possible objection to Mises's treatment of interest is that it focuses on real goods rather than money. After all, isn't interest related to how much the lender charges on a loan of money? Why isn't the interest rate simply the price that balances the supply and demand for loanable funds?

Here the answer is that Mises, following Böhm-Bawerk, views interest as a general phenomenon that pervades all sectors of the market. From this perspective, it's not the case that the rate of interest is "set" in the loan market, and then ripples out to other markets where people adjust their behavior based on the interest rate. On the contrary, in a market free from outside interference, individuals' subjective time preferences manifest themselves in every market. Time preference influences the supply and demand in the loanable funds market, but time preference also regulates how much a home builder will pay today for the lumber, shingles, nails, and so on that will yield a house to be sold in a year's time. The implied rate of return on a production project—in other words, the percentage excess of the total revenues compared to the total monetary expenses—is called *originary interest*. Originary interest is ultimately determined by subjective time preference because it reflects the fundamental difference in valuation between present and future goods. In our example, the lumber, shingles, nails, and so on are the means—a technological claim ticket, as it were—to achieve a future house. That is why they do not currently command the same price in the market as a present house. This discrepancy in both subjective and market value between present and future goods allows entrepreneurs to earn originary interest by investing their funds in the production of a house.

---

15. For a comprehensive discussion of the standard Austrian defense of the pure time preference theory from such objections, see Walter Block, "The Negative Interest Rate: Toward a Taxonomic Critique," *Journal of Libertarian Studies*, 2, no. 2 (1978): 121–24.

To be sure, money plays the same vital, coordinating role when it comes to interest, as in every other feature of the market. Just as money prices for inputs and outputs make it possible to compute the rate of return on a given project, having a market where present money effectively trades for future money—otherwise known as the loan market—makes it easy to assess the going rate of interest. If homebuilders reckon that they can earn 17 percent on their project, they don't need to survey the entire market economy to see how this number compares with other projects; they can merely look at the relevant market for loans of money of the same duration.

Discrepancies in the rate of originary interest across various sectors will soon be eliminated through competition and arbitrage.[16] For example, if homebuilders are earning 17 percent on one-year projects, while contractors who build apartment complexes earn only 10 percent, then builders will switch away from apartment complexes and expand homebuilding. The restriction in apartment construction and increase in house construction will tend to increase the price of an apartment complex and decrease the price for houses. Also, specific inputs are needed for homebuilding but not for apartment complexes, these inputs will become more expensive. These forces will lower the rate of originary interest for homebuilders and increase it for apartment builders. The shift in production will continue until the rate of originary interest is the same in both lines, proper adjustment being made for the perceived uncertainty of the enterprises.

Financial Capital versus Capital Goods

Armed with the pure time preference theory, we understand that interest is not a special type of income earned by capital, if that term is taken to mean

---

16. Throughout this discussion, we are assuming investors evaluate projects solely on the criterion of the implied originary rate of interest—the markup between factor prices and the expected revenues from the sale of the finished product—and do not worry that the return on some projects is more certain than for other projects. In the real world, of course, this assumption is false. Investors and entrepreneurs would need a higher expected return (or yield) on a project, the less certain they perceive its success. Mises refers to this as the "entrepreneurial component" in the gross market rate of interest (*Human Action*, 536). Therefore, even in equilibrium, we expect to see implicit rates of return on various projects that are higher than the interest rate charged in the loan market for a safe bond, such as U.S. Treasury securities.

capital goods. Rather, interest accrues to anyone who owns resources that will yield their services over a period of time; owners reap an interest income as the future service matures or ripens into a present service. Mises writes:

> Interest is not merely interest on capital. Interest is not the specific income derived from the utilization of capital goods. The correspondence between three factors of production—labor, capital, and land— and three classes of income—wages, profit, and rent—as taught by the classical economists is untenable. Rent is not the specific revenue from land. Rent is a general catallactic phenomenon; it plays in the yield of labor and capital goods the same role it plays in the yield of land.[17]

We can explain Mises's claims with three examples: First, suppose there is a plot of land that the owner can rent to tenants for $10,000 per year. In principle, this land will entitle the owner to a perpetual stream of agricultural services. Yet the market price will be finite because those infinite future services are discounted; they are not as valuable as present services. If the land has a market price of, say, $200,000, then the buyer of the land will earn a perpetual 5 percent interest return on his investment. This is true, even though there is no question of physical capital goods; this example deals exclusively with land.

Second, suppose someone buys a brand new limousine, which she then allows students to use for prom night. The money she charges the students for the temporary use of the limousine is clearly rent; after all, even the vernacular says the students "rent the limo" for the night. Therefore rental income is clearly not something exclusively flowing to land owners; in this example, it flows to the owner of a capital good.[18]

Third, imagine a slave economy. One plantation owner allows his neighbor to use his mules and some of his slaves for a week, as the neighbor has a particularly bountiful harvest. The owner clearly charges rent for the use of the services provided by the animals and the human beings. In a modern market economy, where human bondage has been abolished, workers own their own bodies. They effectively rent themselves out to entrepreneurs in order to earn wages. This is what Mises means in the passage above, when he

17. Mises, *Human Action*, 521.

18. In this example, although the services of the limousine are consumed by the students, the limousine is a capital good from the perspective of its owner.

says that rent is a general phenomenon applicable to land, labor, and capital goods. (This analysis also sheds light on the Marxist description of the plight of the proletariat as "wage slavery.")

As our discussion has made clear, there is a fundamental distinction between physical capital goods and capital as a broader financial concept indicating wealth in an accounting sense. As we have emphasized throughout this book, a key theme in Mises's work is the importance of economic calculation. The broader notion of capital is intricately tied to economic calculation; one way of describing the purpose of calculation is to determine whether a course of action has increased or decreased the capital associated with it. In other words, economic calculation—as epitomized in modern accounting techniques—shows entrepreneurs whether their actions have maintained, accumulated, or consumed capital. Yet, capital in this respect is not capital goods, which are by their very nature fleeting. Mises explains the subtle way in which capital is embodied in particular capital goods, which themselves constantly turn over:

> Capital goods are intermediary products which in the further course of production activities are transformed into consumers' goods. All capital goods, including those not called perishable, perish either in wearing out their serviceableness in the performance of production processes or in losing their serviceableness, even before this happens, through a change in the market data. There is no question of keeping a stock of capital goods intact. They are transient. The notion of wealth constancy is an outgrowth of deliberate planning and acting. It refers to the concept of capital as applied in capital accounting, not to the capital goods as such. The idea of capital has no counterpart in the physical universe of tangible things. It is nowhere but in the minds of planning men. It is an element in economic calculation. Capital accounting serves one purpose only. It is designed to make us know how our arrangement of production and consumption acts upon our power to satisfy future wants. The question it answers is whether a certain course of conduct increases or decreases the productivity of our future exertion.[19]

19. Mises, *Human Action*, 511.

As usual, we will illustrate Mises's remarks with a specific numerical example. Consider Table 13.1, outlining the assets and income statement of a hypothetical bakery owned by Mary:

Table 13.1. Assets and Income Statement for Mary's Bakery as of January 31, 2014

Assets		Income Statement (February 2013 through January 2014)	
Cash	$5,000	Revenues	$128,500
Inventory (Cakes and Pastries)	$1,000	Wages (including $50,000 owner's implicit salary for time in bakery)	($85,000)
		Building Rent (includes utilities)	($24,000)
Flour, eggs, sugar, milk, etc.	$800	Cost of Ingredients	($12,000)
Spatulas, bowls, mixers, spoons, etc.	$3,200	Cost to Maintain Implements	($1,000)
Oven and Refrigerator (both brand new)	$20,000	Depreciation on Oven/Refrigerator	($2,000)
Total Assets	**$30,000**	**Net Income**	**$4,500**

The categories given in Table 13.1 are not the approach an actual accountant would take, but we are segregating the assets and cost entries to illustrate Mises's statements about capital flowing through particular capital goods of varying durations. At any given moment, our hypothetical bakery owner Mary has $30,000 tied up in the business. This represents the capital Mary has invested in the operation; in principle, she could unwind the business and devote that money elsewhere. Since Mary is not taking on debt, her total assets indicate whether the capital in her business is growing, shrinking, or staying the same.

As her income statement reveals, Mary's business generated net income of $4,500 in the previous year. This is the amount she can safely withdraw from the operation as the return on her invested capital, which works out to

15 percent. This interest income[20] is not due to Mary's labor as a baker; she has already paid herself a $50,000 salary because she could earn that much working for someone else's bakery. Rather, the $4,500 is income accruing from Mary's decision to deploy her $30,000 of capital in her bakery. If she withdraws the $4,500 from the operation, its capital remains intact. If she draws out less, she will accumulate more capital in the business. If she draws out more than $4,500, she will be *consuming* the capital in the business.

Suppose Mary wants to maintain the capital intact in her operation and therefore aims to keep its assets (since she doesn't want to incur any debt) at $30,000. Even so, the embodiment of that capital in the form of specific capital goods is hardly static. The inventory of finished cakes, croissants, and muffins sitting in her glass cases experiences constant turnover; at any given time, Mary has about $1,000 worth of ready-to-eat goods on display, but obviously any particular muffin needs to be sold very quickly or it will become stale. Even though a customer will view a pastry on display as a consumer good, from Mary's perspective it is a capital good, a means for acquiring revenue.

Just as obvious, the $800 worth of eggs, flour, milk, and other ingredients that Mary keeps on hand is also relatively perishable. Mary and her assistant must apply their labor to transform these ingredients into inventory within a short period of time after she acquires them.

Thus the edible products in the bakery are, from Mary's perspective, capital goods, even though many people would not normally conjure up such examples when thinking about the concept. Mary also has items that fit the more familiar template: large bowls, spatulas, muffin pans, electric mixers, measuring cups, and other implements used in a bakery. Finally, she has large fixed pieces of equipment—namely the commercial oven and refrigerator—that are specific physical embodiments of the $30,000 in capital tied up in the bakery.

As we have said, if Mary wants to keep her business capital intact, she must continually replenish her depleting stockpile of inventory, as well as the flour,

---

20. The 15 percent return on Mary's $30,000 invested in the business is a gross interest return. In the evenly rotating economy, it would simply reflect time preference and would be net interest income. In the real world, the $4,500 could reflect other factors, such as Mary's anticipation of changes in the purchasing power of money, as well as the fact that a bakery offers a less certain return than, say, a AAA-rated corporate bond.

eggs, and other ingredients. In other words, Mary can't treat the entire flow of revenue from customers as her money to spend on her own enjoyments. During the course of the year, she had to spend $12,000 on the ingredients; had she failed to reinvest in this way, the operation would have soon screeched to a halt. Not as obvious, but just as important, Mary needs to account for the fact that her more durable capital goods wear away (or depreciate) as well. Mary reckons that she needs to set aside $3,000 out of the prior year's revenues into a fund that will allow her to replace the utensils, oven, and refrigerator when needed.

Now, what would it mean for Mary to consume her capital? She could literally do so because the bakery involves capital goods that are edible. For example, suppose Mary volunteers to bring the dessert for a family reunion, and she grabs a quarter of her store's inventory. Unless she takes steps to replenish the cases, Mary will now permanently carry only $750 in inventory. She effectively consumed $250 worth of the bakery's capital by allowing her relatives to literally eat the associated capital goods.

However, capital consumption is a more general phenomenon. For example, suppose Mary falls on hard times and cannot afford to put $2,000 into the sinking fund dedicated to replacing the oven and refrigerator. Mary still reinvests in flour, eggs, and even utensils as needed, which gives the illusion that her business is fine. Her customers would come and go, always seeing cases full of baked goods, and would have no idea that Mary was siphoning $2,000 per year out of the business. Yet, the next year's balance sheet would list the oven and refrigerator as worth only $18,000, and there would be no fund to offset the depreciation. Thus, the capital would have fallen; Mary consumed it. Unless she reverses course, Mary will eventually put herself in an impossible situation where her oven or refrigerator breaks down, and she has no money set aside to replace it.

Finally, we can use our bakery example to illustrate what Mises meant when he said, "All capital goods, including those not called perishable, perish either in wearing out their serviceableness . . . or in losing their serviceableness, even before this happens, through a change in the market data." Consider the extreme example where the community in which Mary lives suddenly embraces the low-carb diet and virtually everyone renounces the very types of goods that Mary sells. Mary finds that even if she slashes the price by 90 percent, she can't sell the items in her cases. Thus, the supposed $1,000 of capital associated with her inventory suddenly drops to $0. The market value of the eggs, flour, and other ingredients collapses as well: Unless she knows the owner of a local diner who can use the eggs to make omelets, Mary may end up throwing out much of this inventory. She may be able to sell the utensils on the Internet and recover some of her capital that way, but she will take a huge loss with the oven and refrigerator, as their book value was associated with their ongoing use in the bakery operation.

In the final analysis, suppose that our hypothetical change in the market data—when Mary's former customers suddenly renounce foods rich in carbohydrates—leaves Mary with only the $5,000 in her business checking account and an additional $5,000 that she raises by selling off her other assets. Her total capital would thus be $10,000, implying a $20,000 loss or consumption of capital. Specifically, this loss would be due not to Mary's conscious decision to live above her means, but rather due to her poor foresight. The $20,000 loss would reflect her entrepreneurial error. Had Mary correctly anticipated the desires of the consumers, she would not have continually reinvested funds into the business. Such foresight would have been desirable not just for Mary but for the consumers as well, because then scarce resources would not have gone into the production of items that were not the best use of those resources: cakes destined to be thrown out, eggs that will sit in Mary's refrigerator until they spoil, spatulas that will be used a few times at the bakery and then sold on the Internet, and an oven installed at Mary's bakery that cannot easily be moved.

Capital Accumulation and Rising Living Standards

Although Mises and other proponents of the pure time preference theory do not credit the productivity of capital for generating interest, the Austrian economists nonetheless do consider capital accumulation of the utmost importance. When members of society consume less than their income—living below their means—this constitutes saving. People then channel these savings by investing them in particular outlets. Physically, in a progressing economy with net capital accumulation due to saving, resources that could have been devoted to the production of consumer goods are instead devoted to the production of tools, equipment, and other capital goods. Future workers will be more productive per hour of their labor, and natural resources will also yield more, when they work in conjunction with a greater stock of capital goods.

Although the benefits of capital accumulation are obvious enough, the downside is that it requires a postponement of consumption. It takes foresight and willpower to refrain from a present enjoyment to augment the quantity of capital goods and thereby increase future enjoyments. This partially explains why we see large gaps in standards of living among different regions, even though the engineers and doctors in, say, Nigeria and India can train at the best schools in the world. Their countries cannot instantly advance to Western living standards because they lack the necessary capital goods. Mises explains the situation:

> Shortage of capital means that one is further away from the attainment of a goal sought than if one had started to aim at it at an earlier date. Because one neglected to do this in the past, the intermediary products are wanting, although the nature-given factors from which they are to be produced are available. Capital shortage is dearth of time. It is the effect of the fact that one was late in beginning the march toward the aim concerned . . .
>
> To have capital goods at one's disposal is tantamount to being nearer to a goal aimed at. An increment in capital goods available makes it possible to attain temporally remoter ends without being forced to restrict consumption . . . . As against those who lack capital goods, the capitalist, under the given state of technological knowledge, is in a position to reach a definite goal sooner without restricting consumption and without increasing the input of labor and nature-given material factors of production. His head start is in time. A rival endowed with a smaller supply of capital goods can catch up only by restricting his consumption.
>
> The start which the peoples of the West have gained over the other peoples consists in the fact that they have long since created the political and institutional conditions required for a smooth and by and large

uninterrupted progress of the process of larger-scale saving, capital accumulation, and investment.[21]

It is important to realize that the reason people in the twenty-first century have a higher standard of living than those in the nineteenth century is not merely technological discoveries. Even if we held scientific knowledge and engineering know-how constant, it would still be possible to experience ever-rising living standards so long as we maintained continual saving and capital accumulation. Consider: At any given moment, most of the equipment and plants in operation are not state of the art. Whenever an entrepreneur discovers a new way to refine a production process, or whenever a scientist makes a new breakthrough, the efficient response is not for the whole world to revamp operations accordingly. While any new factory or other relevant operation will fully reflect the new understanding, it will usually be efficient to keep the old operations in place, as they wear down their existing capital equipment, allowing for a gradual phasing in of the new ideas.

A succinct illustration of the distinction between technological know-how versus capital accumulation is to imagine a cruise ship carrying the world's experts in various fields, becoming lost at sea and running aground on a deserted tropical island. As thousands of people flocked onto the island, their standard of living would plummet. Even though they would have world-renowned heart and brain surgeons in their ranks, people would eventually begin dying from routine injuries and illnesses because once the supplies originally on the cruise ship had run out, the doctors wouldn't be able to work with the resources at their disposal. Furthermore, people would be forced to explore the island on foot; even though automotive engineers were on the cruise, they could hardly be expected to manufacture cars.

If we came back and surveyed our hypothetical stranded cruise passengers in twenty-five years, they would be nowhere near the standard of living they had enjoyed back home.[22] Before they could build the tools they took for

---

21. Mises, *Human Action*, 494.

22. We are ignoring the complication that even with modern capital goods, the population of a cruise ship could not mimic modern living standards because they would be isolated

granted at their old jobs, they first would need to build the tools to build the tools, and so on, perhaps for several layers depending on the discipline. It's true that our expert passengers would avoid many of the mistakes that their ancestors made historically in the accumulation of capital that made modern living standards possible, but even so, it would be a laborious and painful process to start from virtually scratch and begin again.

---

from international trade; the division of labor could not progress effectively among so few people, and they would have no access to vast deposits of natural resources around the globe.

14

Austrian Business Cycle Theory

Introduction

WE HAVE SLOWLY walked through Mises's understanding of money, banking, economic calculation, capital, and interest theory because they all come together in what he called the *circulation credit theory of the trade cycle*. Nowadays, Mises's explanation of the familiar boom-bust pattern in market economies is often called *Austrian business cycle theory*.

From Mises's discussion of money, we know that it is not neutral; injections of new money into the economy can affect sectors in different order, rather than causing a uniform increase in all prices simultaneously. From his discussion of banking, we know that if they do not maintain 100 percent reserves on their demand deposits, banks can issue fiduciary media and thereby increase the quantity of money (in the broader sense). From his discussion of economic calculation, we know that entrepreneurs are guided by market prices and the profit-and-loss test to steer resources in the direction that consumers want. From his discussion of interest, we know that it reflects time preference, the underlying subjective preference for present versus future goods. Finally, from Mises's discussion of capital, we know that it is embodied in specific capital goods that must be well-suited to meet consumer desires and that the accumulation of capital goods over time leads to rising living standards but is onerous since it involves renunciation of present consumption.

Each of these insights plays a role in Mises's theory of the business cycle. In a nutshell: Because of government restrictions on the normal operation of a competitive industry, commercial banks are able to expand their issue of fiduciary media by extending more loans to the community, even though there has been no increase in genuine saving. Because this increase in the quantity of money hits the loan market first, it temporarily depresses the market rate of interest, while other prices in the economy have not yet fully adjusted to the infusion of new money. Guided by the false and artificially low interest rate, entrepreneurs see apparently profitable business ventures and invest accordingly. However, the actual time preference in the community is unchanged. This means that the entrepreneurs are making bad investments—what Mises calls *malinvestments*—in devoting their capital into a specific configuration of capital goods that is not calibrated to the consumers' desired timing of consumption goods. By effectively trying to employ longer production processes than the consumers are willing to endure, the entrepreneurs end up squandering resources and impoverishing the community, at least relative to the baseline with no interference from the commercial banks.

In this chapter will we quote from Mises's treatment to elaborate on this outline, in particular to see how the familiar feel of a typical boom and then bust correspond to the description we have given.[1] Although the boom is euphoric and the bust is painful, Mises argues that the boom is actually pernicious while the bust is curative. Needless to say, this is the opposite of what most economists say, particularly those from the Keynesian school. Precisely because it differs so radically in both its diagnosis of, and prescription for, the business cycle, all educated citizens should learn the basics of Austrian business cycle theory.

As a final introductory remark, we should explain why Mises places his discussion of the business cycle in Part Four, which deals with the economics of the pure market economy, rather than in Part Six, which deals with "The Hampered Market Economy." Mises argues that it would be possible for a business cycle of the type he describes to develop on the purely free market.[2] For example, even with a 100 percent reserve gold standard, it would still be possible for a massive gold discovery to enter the economy primarily through the loan market. Mises argues that this too would temporarily reduce interest

---

1. Although the general pattern of a boom-bust cycle can be deduced as a matter of economic theory, similar to other conclusions in economic science as Mises understood it, in practice economists must rely on their judgment to decide whether Mises's theory of the business cycle played a large role in any particular historical disturbance in the economy.

2. Mises, *Human Action*, 571.

rates below the level consistent with time preference, thereby setting in motion an unsustainable credit boom.

However, even though Mises believes a boom-bust cycle occurring on the free market is possible, in practice he argues it is due to government interference with the banks, and in particular political efforts to foster credit expansion. Just as Mises acknowledged the theoretical possibility of free-market monopoly price, in the realm of business cycles too Mises concludes that the threat in the real world comes entirely from activist government.

The Problem to Be Explained

Just as Böhm-Bawerk's framing of the interest problem shed light on his solution to it, Mises's discussion of the business cycle will be clearer if we understand the way he conceived the problem that had to be explained. First, he points out the false signal given by interest rates that have been suppressed by a credit expansion:

> [Entrepreneurs and promoters] base their calculations upon the prices, wage rates, and interest rates as determined on the market. They discover discrepancies between the present prices of the complementary factors of production and the anticipated prices of the products minus the market rate of interest, and are eager to profit from them. *The role which the rate of interest plays in these deliberations of the planning businessman is obvious.* It shows him how far he can go in withholding factors of production from employment for want-satisfaction in nearer periods of the future and in dedicating them to want satisfaction in remoter periods. It shows him what period of production conforms in every concrete case to the difference which the public makes in the ratio of valuation between present goods and future goods. *It prevents him from embarking upon projects the execution of which would not agree with the limited amount of capital goods provided by the saving of the public.*
>
> *It is in influencing this primordial function of the rate of interest that the driving force of money can become operative in a particular way.* Cash-induced changes in the money relation can under certain circumstances affect the loan market before they affect the prices of commodities and

of labor. The increase or decrease in the supply of money (in the broader sense) can increase or decrease the supply of money offered on the loan market and thereby lower or raise the gross market rate of interest although no change in the rate of [originary] interest has taken place. If this happens, the market rate deviates from the height which the state of originary interest and the supply of capital goods available for production would require. *Then the market rate of interest fails to fulfill the function it plays in guiding entrepreneurial decisions.* It frustrates the entrepreneur's calculation and diverts his actions from those lines in which they would in the best possible way satisfy the most urgent needs of the consumers. (italics added)[3]

Yet to understand the business cycle, it is not enough to pinpoint the cause. Mises later goes on to describe the task of the economic theorist:

The phenomenon to be dealt with is this: The rate of originary interest is determined by the discount of future goods as against present goods. It is essentially independent of the supply of money and money-substitutes...But the gross market rate of interest can be affected by changes in the money relation. A readjustment must take place. What is the nature of the process which brings it about?[4]

Through his answer to this question—namely, how does the underlying "real" rate of originary interest due to time preference reassert itself in the marketplace in light of a disturbance in the loan market?—Mises ends up explaining the business cycle. Mises focuses on what he identifies as the core theoretical problem, and as a bonus, he ends up solving one of the most pressing policy questions economists face. Ironically, those economists who—unlike Mises—consciously set out to "cure the business cycle" often end up focusing on incidental features, such as high unemployment, cutbacks in consumer spending and business investment, an increased demand for cash balances, and so on. In the hands of a Keynesian economist, policy recommendations that merely fight these symptoms become the very cause of the business cycle, as identified in Mises's analysis.

---

3. Mises, *Human Action*, 544–45.
4. Mises, *Human Action*, 548.

The Onset of the Unsustainable Boom

Mises explains exactly why the boom begins and why it is associated with prosperity:

> *The drop in interest rates falsifies the businessman's calculation.* Although the amount of capital goods available did not increase, the calculation employs figures which would be utilizable only if such an increase had taken place. The result of such calculations is therefore misleading. They make some projects appear profitable and realizable which a correct calculation, based on an interest rate not manipulated by credit expansion, would have shown as unrealizable. Entrepreneurs embark upon the execution of such projects. *Business activities are stimulated. A boom begins.*
>
> The additional demand on the part of the expanding entrepreneurs tends to raise the prices of producers' goods and wage rates. With the rise in wage rates the prices of consumers' goods rise too. Besides, the entrepreneurs are contributing a share to the rise in the prices of consumers' goods as they too, deluded by the illusory gains which their business accounts show, are ready to consume more. *The general upswing in prices spreads optimism.* (italics added)[5]

Because it plays such a crucial role in Mises's explanation, we should emphasize the connection between artificially low interest rates and an expansion of business projects. Recall from our example of the stranded passengers from the cruise ship: Even though they possess the knowledge to execute advanced production processes, they cannot afford to postpone consumption long enough to reap their fruits.

The same is true in general in the market economy, where more physically productive but longer production techniques are always on the shelf waiting to be deployed, as soon as sufficient savings are made available. The function of the market rate of interest is to signal to entrepreneurs which projects are short enough and productive enough to justify absorbing scarce resources and to rule out of bounds those projects that are too long and not productive

---

5. Mises, *Human Action*, 550.

enough to receive funding, in light of consumer preferences of the tradeoff between present goods and future goods.

When the interest rate is artificially lowered by credit expansion, it suddenly renders projects profitable that previously were not. Perhaps more insidious, the sensitivity of a project's profitability to the interest rate is directly related to its duration. For example, suppose a concert promoter is considering bringing a major band to an arena. All told, the promoter expects to pay out $500,000 mostly upfront, three months before the event, getting ready for the big day. Then the question is whether the promoter thinks she can sell enough tickets to bring in enough revenue to turn a profit. It's true, the interest rate factors into the decision because technically she could have invested the $500,000 for three months in a corporate bond. But the interest expense here is relatively minor, since the capital in this project is tied up for at most three months. At a 5 percent interest rate, the opportunity cost of investing in the concert project is a little more than $6,000. At a 10 percent interest rate, the opportunity cost is about $12,000. Thus, doubling the interest rate from 5 to 10 percent increases the expense of the project by $6,000, which is hardly a significant factor for such a large undertaking.

On the other hand, suppose a wine bottler spends $500,000 in 2015 to create several thousand bottles of wine that he intends to sell in 2025—of course selling 10-year-old wine at that point. If we disregard the expense of physically storing the wine bottles as they mature, the implicit interest expense of the project is $314,000 using a 5 percent interest rate, but $797,000 at a 10 percent rate. Doubling the interest rate much more than doubles the interest expense because of compounding, and at either rate, the interest expense is very large relative to the size of the project.

As these two examples illustrate, different projects have different sensitivities to interest rates. Projects with expenses concentrated upfront, while their revenues are spread out far into the future, can often flip from being unprofitable to profitable by lowering the interest rate. Austrian economists often explain this situation intuitively by saying that the lower interest rate is a signal to entrepreneurs that the consumers are more patient, and so it is now economically efficient to tie up resources in longer processes. Of course, the problem is that if credit expansion is the source of the lower interest rates, then this signal is incorrect—the public hasn't become more willing to defer gratification for a greater output.

Why the Boom Cannot Last

When we understand the relationships among time preference, interest rates, saving, and capital accumulation in a healthy economy, we see why Austrians describe a boom induced by credit expansion as unsustainable. As Mises explains:

> It is certain that no manipulations of the banks can provide the economic system with capital goods. What is needed for a sound expansion of production is additional capital goods, not money or fiduciary media. The boom is built on the sands of banknotes and deposits. It must collapse.[6]

Now the specific timing of the collapse is related to the actions of the banks. In the typical scenario, they eventually abandon their inflationary policy, perhaps because they fear a drain on their reserves under a commodity standard or because the central bank becomes alarmed at the rapid price increases under a fiat standard. This leads to a slowdown or even fall in the quantity of money and a rise in interest rates. At the higher interest rates, many entrepreneurs realize that their projects are now unprofitable; the boom collapses, and the bust ensues.

Yet Mises is quite clear that even if the banks continued with their inflationary policy, eventually the boom would end when the price inflation had grown so severe that the public abandoned the currency altogether. Mises called this horrendous outcome the *crack-up boom.*[7] In this scenario, once the public has switched currencies, their underlying real time preferences would assert themselves in the market rate of interest, showing many of the entrepreneurs that they had greatly erred during the false prosperity of the boom.

---

6. Mises, *Human Action*, 559.
7. Mises, *Human Action*, 559.

The Nature of the Boom:
Malinvestment, Not Overinvestment

Mainstream economists often have difficulty even understanding Austrian business cycle theory. This is not surprising since it is literally impossible to have a Misesian boom-bust cycle in the standard macro models. Such models depict the entire economy as a single production function, which takes aggregate labor mixed with the aggregate capital stock to produce total output, which is then divided between consumption and investment.[8] In such a simplistic setting, the only problem from investing too much is that total consumption will be lower than the optimal amount in the near term; it is as if people are being forced to put more in their savings accounts than they really want to.

Things are qualitatively different in the Austrian account. The artificially low interest rates cause entrepreneurs to make irrevocable investments in specific types of capital goods that transform the complex structure of production into a form that is physically unsustainable because it does not conform to the actual subjective preferences of the consumers regarding the timing of consumption. In other words, the entrepreneurs are receiving signals that tell them to divert resources away from producing present consumption goods and into the production of future consumption goods. Yet the consumers desired no such change. Because monetary inflation in the form of credit expansion doesn't actually produce more producer or consumer goods, eventually the mismatch between the structure of production and the consumers' preferences will manifest itself.

Only within the rich capital framework of the Austrian School can we even present Mises's explanation of the boom-bust cycle. The concept of malinvestment is not even possible within a cruder, more orthodox framework. Yet the distinction between mere overinvestment, on the one hand, and *malinvestment*, on the other, is crucial. As Mises explains:

---

8. For example, the famous mid-twentieth-century Solow growth model, as well as its descendants, match our description. (See Romer, *Advanced Macroeconomics*, 1996.) But economics Ph.D. programs to this day employ simplistic models of this form to explain the basics of economic growth and the business cycle.

The essence of the credit-expansion boom is not overinvestment, but investment in wrong lines, i.e., malinvestment. The entrepreneurs . . . embark upon an expansion of investment on a scale for which the capital goods available do not suffice. Their projects are unrealizable on account of the insufficient supply of capital goods. They must fail sooner or later. The unavoidable end of the credit expansion makes the faults committed visible. There are plants which cannot be utilized because the plants needed for the production of the complementary factors of production are lacking; plants the products of which cannot be sold because the consumers are more intent upon purchasing other goods.[9]

Only the Austrian heterogeneous view of the capital structure makes sense of Mises's explanation. A simple example will clarify. Suppose one economist has a model in which the workers and natural resources are mixed with the existing stockpile of tools in order to create more units of output, which can either consist of food or more tools. If the workers decide to create more food, then they get immediate enjoyment, but if they instead add to the stockpile of tools, then next period their output will be higher. The tradeoff then is between food now versus food later, and the stockpile of tools is the means by which less food today translates into more food down the road. In such a world, overinvestment would be conceivable; if the workers made only a small amount of food and large amount of tools, they might suffer greatly, even though next period they would be much more productive. Perhaps, given their time preferences, the workers would rather not engage in such privation in the present.

However, if we enrich the model so that instead of the capital stock merely being tools, we subdivide it into canned food, hammers, and nails, now malinvestment is possible. The economy could be cranking along for several periods with a high level of output, but if that output were devoted exclusively to making more hammers, eventually the workers would find themselves in an awful fix: They could wake up one day to find themselves with no canned food, no nails, and a mountain of hammers that were completely useless.

Generalizing from our simple example to the real world, we can see that mere capital accumulation is not enough to guarantee rising living standards.

---

9. Mises, *Human Action*, 556.

On the contrary, investment in various types of capital goods must be balanced so as to allow for the proper flow over time of finished consumption goods. It does little good to have more commercial jets without the additional pilots, jet fuel, and runway space to use them in expanding the number of flights available to consumers.

During the unsustainable boom, credit expansion and its artificially low interest rates stimulate investment, especially in those sectors that are connected with long-lived projects. Yet in order for these new batches of capital goods to emerge—perhaps years later—as an increased flow of consumer goods,[10] the entrepreneurs would need to make additional and complementary investments all along the way. Yet because individuals have not increased their genuine saving in real terms—if anything, they have reduced it because the illusory prosperity of the boom leads them to increase consumption—it is physically impossible for the entrepreneurs to carry all of their new projects to the finish line.

The Nature of the Bust: Mises's "Master Builder" Analogy

The best way to grasp the Austrian understanding of the business cycle —and to make sense of their typical disdain for Keynesian solutions to recessions—is to elaborate on the analogy Mises himself used, that of the "masterbuilder":

> In order to expand the production of shoes, clothes, motorcars, furniture, houses, one must begin with increasing the production of iron, steel, copper, and other such goods . . . . The whole entrepreneurial class [during the boom] is, as it were, in the position of a master-builder whose task it is to erect a building out of a limited supply of building materials. If this man overestimates the quantity of the available supply, he drafts a plan for the execution of which the means at his disposal are not sufficient. He oversizes the groundwork and the foun-

---

10. A famous pedagogical device to illustrate these ideas is the so-called Hayekian triangle. This is discussed in accessible language in Roger Garrison, *Time and Money: The Macroeconomics of Capital Structure* (New York: Routledge, 2001).

dations and only discovers later in the progress of the construction that he lacks the material needed for the completion of the structure. It is obvious that our master-builder's fault was not overinvestment, but an inappropriate employment of the means at his disposal.[11]

Let's flesh out Mises's analogy. Suppose a builder has a fixed quantity of various items at a work site, including workers of various skill types and fixed quantities of lumber, nails, shingles, panes of glass, bricks, and so forth. On the basis of these supplies, the builder draws up a plan for a house. The problem is that the builder erroneously believes he has 20,000 bricks at his disposal, when in reality he only has 19,000. Since the blueprints call for using all 20,000 bricks, it is obvious that eventually there will be a crisis: It is physically impossible for the house to be completed in a way to satisfy the mental plans of the builder.

Given that there is a mismatch between the plans of the builder and the available physical supplies, when is the best time for him to discover his mistake? Suppose some of the workers realize what has happened. Should they tell the boss immediately? After all, it would be very bad news, and he would be sorely disappointed. Isn't it better to keep the illusion going, perhaps by using tarps to cover up the dwindling supply of bricks and prevent the builder from realizing his mistake?

Obviously, these workers would be doing a grave disservice to the builder and to the project. The sooner the builder realizes the mismatch, the better he can adjust. No matter what, the finished house will not be as impressive as the house depicted in the original blueprints—with only 19,000 bricks, such an outcome is physically impossible. But the finished house will still be better, the earlier the builder learns of the true brick supply. For example, if he learns it before any work has been done, then he can simply redraw the blueprints from scratch; the only harm was the time he wasted on the first blueprint.

Yet the longer the builder persists in his error, the worse the eventual crisis will be. In the extreme case, if his workers manage to deceive him right until the end, he will eventually lay the 19,000th brick, having no idea it is the last one available. His workers will be unable to deceive him any longer at that

---

11. Mises, *Human Action*, 556–57.

point; they can't turn tarps into bricks. Because so many of the raw materials would have already been transformed into specific components of the semi-finished house, the builder will have painted himself into a corner and will have great difficulty finishing the house. It may be so disfigured that it looks ugly from the street because the builder learned at such a late date that he lacked 1,000 bricks needed to complete the original blueprint.

Let's pause at this point in the analogy to draw the obvious lesson for economic policy: Contrary to most other economists, the Austrians claim that artificially low interest rates are not an example of stimulus but in fact actively harm the economy. The point of government and central bank policy should not be to prolong the boom because that only allows the entrepreneurs to persist longer in their erroneous projects. As capital goods are transformed into more specific forms—such as turning iron ore into machine parts—it is more difficult for entrepreneurs to readjust their plans in light of the true fundamentals. Thus, it is completely misguided to argue that Federal Reserve Chairman Ben Bernanke was doing what he could by slashing interest rates to nearly 0 percent following the financial crisis of 2008. The actions of the Bernanke-led Federal Reserve merely postponed the ultimate reckoning, allowing American businesses to continue in unsustainable projects.

Reverting back to our builder analogy, we can see what happens when the error is discovered and a crisis occurs. When the builder realizes the mismatch between his blueprints and the actual quantity of bricks, what will be his immediate reaction? A moment of reflection yields the obvious answer: He will yell at the top of his lungs, "Everybody stop working!" Once he realizes that the original blueprints are impossible to achieve, he needs to reassess the situation in light of (a) the existing state of the house and (b) the remaining raw materials at his disposal. Because he may end up drastically altering his plans, the builder can't have the carpenters continue working on the gazebo in the backyard because it's possible that the lumber they are using is now more urgently needed to ensure that the main house has a roof to keep out the rain. That is why it's critical for everybody on the site to stop working while the builder alters his blueprints.

Even after the builder has fixed the plans, there are interesting possibilities regarding the workers on the site. Some of them will go back to work right away. Yet others may have to wait for some preliminary work to be performed, before they are once again able to contribute to the construction of the house. For example, if the original blueprints called for a three-story house, but the revised blueprints call for a two-story house, the carpenters may have to wait for other laborers to rip up some of the pre-existing work before they can resume their own work. Furthermore, other workers on the site—especially the bricklayers—may not play a large role at all in finishing the revised house. Had the builder known the true brick supply all along, he would have made a more uniform use of the available workers, as their activities complemented each other in a coordinated fashion. But as it is—and depending on how deeply into the original blueprints the project proceeded, before the builder realized his error—there is a boom and then bust in certain occupations on the work site.

This boom-bust pattern would apply to the physical structures or sectors of the property as well. Some projects, such as the gazebo and child's tree house, might be abandoned midstream because the materials necessary for their completion were more urgently needed to finish the main house. Other projects, such as the separate garage made largely out of bricks, might be completed, even though the builder would never have designed the garage with bricks, had he known the situation in the beginning.

In our hypothetical scenario of building a house, it is obvious that external efforts to stimulate construction activity would be utterly harmful. For example, suppose the builder discovered his mistake when only 500 bricks remained. He revised the blueprints, devoting those 500 bricks to finishing the main house, in a way to minimize the awkward appearance of the building. In the new arrangement, half of the bricklayers are now unnecessary; they sit on the grass, watching everyone else bustling about. A newcomer then strolls onto the scene, spies the 50 percent unemployment in the bricklaying occupation and also sees the idle gazebo. The newcomer sees this as pure waste on the builder's part and encourages the bricklayers to grab some of the remaining bricks from the pile and resume work on the gazebo. The newcomer is pleased that he has stimulated construction activity, putting the unemployed back to work and producing a beautiful new gazebo that would never have existed, had the builder's orders been heeded.

The relevance of our above musings to real-world economic policy should be obvious: Once the crisis sets in, the activity in the economy slows. Prices readjust—perhaps radically—as the market process gives new guidance to the entrepreneurs. Some projects are so wasteful that they must be discontinued; these firms go out of business, lay off their workers, and sell off their equipment and materials to other firms. Other projects are worth continuing, even though they should never have been started in their current form. (Specifically, the project is unprofitable when considering fixed costs, but—now that those costs are "sunk"—the marginal revenue from operations exceeds marginal costs, so it is better to stay in business.) There may be a lag in which unemployed workers and other resources only gradually return to productive activity, as they wait for workers in other sectors to take the necessary steps in addressing the mistakes of the boom. Government budget deficits on shovel-ready projects—designed to put idle resources back to work—simply aggravate the problems of the boom and make it that much harder for the private sector to make the best of a bad situation.

The large and persistent unemployment during a recession is the chief concern among the public, and virtually all government remedies are couched in terms of their ability to restore full employment. Yet Mises argues that in the unhampered market economy, unemployment is voluntary in the sense that able-bodied workers are always able to find a job, so long as they are willing to lower their wage demands. This voluntary unemployment is called *catallactic unemployment* and must not be confused with the large-scale involuntary unemployment associated with recessions.[12] Even after the collapse of an unsustainable boom, workers would eventually return to work—albeit at lower wages and perhaps in entirely different industries. The permanence of unemployment is due to institutional barriers erected by government, perhaps in conjunction with labor unions, which prevent wage rates from adjusting in light of the new realities.[13]

---

12. Mises, *Human Action*, 595–96.

13. We will return to these issues in Part Six of the book, which covers the hampered market economy.

Conclusion

Now that we have seen the Austrian perspective of the boom and bust, we understand why—in contrast to most other economists—Austrians claim that the boom is bad while the bust is, ironically, good. As Mises explains:

> The popularity of inflation and credit expansion . . . manifests itself clearly in the customary terminology. The boom is called good business, prosperity, and upswing. Its unavoidable aftermath, the readjustment of conditions to the real data of the market, is called crisis, slump, bad business, depression. People rebel against the insight that the disturbing element is to be seen in the malinvestment and the overconsumption of the boom period and that such an artificially induced boom is doomed. They are looking for the philosophers' stone to make it last.
>
> It has been pointed out already in what respect we are free to call an improvement in the quality and an increase in the quantity of products economic progress. If we apply this yardstick to the various phases of the cyclical fluctuations of business, we must call the boom retrogression and the depression progress. The boom squanders through malinvestment scarce factors of production and reduces the stock available through overconsumption; its alleged blessings are paid for by impoverishment. The depression, on the other hand, is the way back to a state of affairs in which all factors of production are employed for the best possible satisfaction of the most urgent needs of the consumers.[14]

The Austrian School of economics, and Ludwig von Mises in particular, offer a wide array of insights into the workings of the market economy. Yet especially during the so-called Great Recession—and what is in reality the Second Great Depression—their most important contribution is the explanation of the business cycle. If Mises and the other Austrians are right, then governments and central banks not only have been counterproductive in their efforts at fiscal and monetary stimulus but have sown the seeds for yet another crisis, worse than the original.

---

14. Mises, *Human Action*, 573.

PART V

Social Cooperation without a Market

15

The Impossibility of Economic Calculation under Socialism

Introduction

IN PART FOUR of *Human Action*, Mises analyzes the pure market economy. Now in Part Five, he turns his attention to socialism, a system in which people attempt to allocate resources without the institution of private property. In light of the extensive treatment we have already given to Mises's discussion of economic calculation—which is utterly dependent on the prices emerging from markets in which privately held property is exchanged against money—it should not be surprising to learn that Mises thought socialism would not work as a viable alternative to capitalism. Specifically, Mises argued that economic calculation was literally impossible in a socialist system, because of its very nature.

In the history of economic thought, the dispute between Mises and his followers, on one side, and the proponents of socialism is referred to as the socialist calculation debate. Mises's original article appeared in 1920, soon followed by his book-length treatment in 1922. One of Mises's chief allies in the debate was Friedrich Hayek.[1] On the socialist side, two key contributions came from H. D. Dickinson and Oskar Lange in the 1930s.[2] Taken together, their articles argued that the equations of mathematical economics showed how in principle the socialist planners could evade Mises's critique and that

---

1. Mises's article appeared in German in 1920. An English translation, "Economic Calculation in the Socialist Commonwealth," appeared in Hayek's ([1935] 1990) collection *Collectivist Economic Planning*. Mises's own book, *Socialism*, appeared in 1922.

2. See H. D. Dickinson, "Price Formation in a Socialist Commonwealth," *The Economic Journal*, 43, no. 170 (June 1933): 237–50; and Oskar Lange, "On the Economic Theory of Socialism: Part One," *The Review of Economic Studies*, 4, no. 1 (October 1936): 53–71.

a trial-and-error approach to market socialism could allow a socialist system in practice to outperform capitalism.

For decades, the official verdict of professional economists was that Mises and Hayek had lost the calculation debate. After all, Mises had initially launched a bold salvo, claiming that by its very nature a socialist system could not engage in economic calculation even in principle. Yet it seemed that Dickinson et al. had forced Hayek and other antisocialists to retreat to a second line of defense, claiming merely that it would be practically impossible for a board of planners to match the performance of a market economy in real time. With the fall of the Soviet Union, this standard view softened, with more intellectuals admitting Mises was right.[3]

In the present chapter, we will clarify what Mises's actual argument was, as he presented it in *Human Action*. Mises did not think he had surrendered one iota to the socialist theorists, nor did he concede that their proposal for market socialism challenged his thesis in any way. Furthermore, we will show that Mises's argument was about the rational allocation of resources; it was not an empirical claim about the viability of a government committed to socialism. In other words, Mises was either right or wrong when he made the argument, based on its internal logic. It is not that his claims remained an open question until the fall of the Soviet Union confirmed them. Here as elsewhere in his treatise, Mises was not making a falsifiable claim about the longevity of certain political regimes. Rather, he was making an apodictic claim about the institutional prerequisites for economic calculation—prerequisites that were lacking when the government owned all important resources.

Setting Up the Misesian Position

In terms of the economic or praxeological analysis of socialism, Mises thought, its "essential mark" is that *"one will* alone acts."[4] This single will can be embodied in the mind of an actual individual—the socialist dictator—or it can be the result of a team of experts or rulers, perhaps chosen by democratic

---

3. See the discussion of Robert Heilbroner in David Boaz's article, "The Man Who Told the Truth," *Reason Magazine*, January 21, 2005, http://reason.com/archives/2005/01/21/the-man-who-told-the-truth.

4. Mises, *Human Action*, 691, italics in original.

vote. "The main thing is that the employment of all factors of production is directed by one agency only."[5] In practical terms, the essence of socialism is the effective abolition of private property in the so-called means of production; the socialist planners have the authority to direct the uses to which farmland, factories, copper mines, and other resources are devoted. The very term *planner* in this context implies that the socialists have a plan, in contrast to the alleged aimlessness, from a social point of view, in the market economy.

Historically, opponents of socialism warned of the corruption it would invite among the rulers, also arguing that the incentives to work and produce would be far weaker than under capitalism. Yet these are merely empirical claims. Mises desired an a priori claim, based not on human psychology or the wisdom of experience, but on the nature of the market process itself. To this end, he conceded—for the sake of argument—that the single will of a hypothetical socialist system was completely benevolent and well-informed and furthermore that his subjects obeyed him unconditionally. In Mises's words:

> In a praxeological analysis of the problems of socialism, we are not concerned with the moral and ethical character of the director. Neither do we discuss his value judgments and his choice of ultimate ends. What we are dealing with is merely the question of whether any mortal man, equipped with the logical structure of the human mind, can be equal to the tasks incumbent upon a director of a socialist society.
>
> We assume that the director has at his disposal all the technological knowledge of his age. Moreover, he has a complete inventory of all the material factors of production available and a roster enumerating all manpower employable. In these respects the crowd of experts and specialists which he assembles in his offices provide him with perfect information and answer correctly all questions he may ask them. Their voluminous reports accumulate in huge piles on his desk. But now he must act. He must choose among an infinite variety of projects in such a way that no want which he himself considers more urgent remains unsatisfied because the factors of production required for its satisfaction are employed for the satisfaction of wants which he considers less urgent.

---

5. Mises, *Human Action*, 691–92.

It is important to realize that this problem has nothing at all to do with the valuation of the ultimate ends. It refers only to the means by the employment of which the ultimate ends chosen are to be attained. We assume that the director has made up his mind with regard to the valuation of ultimate ends. We do not question his decision. Neither do we raise the question of whether the people, the wards, approve or disapprove of their director's decisions. We may assume, for the sake of argument, that a mysterious power makes everyone agree with one another and with the director in the valuation of ultimate ends.

Our problem, the crucial and only problem of socialism, is a purely economic problem, and as such refers merely to means and not to ultimate ends.[6]

As this excerpt makes clear, Mises's claim was quite strong: He wanted to show that economic calculation was impossible for any socialist arrangement, not just for the ones that would be likely to occur in practice. His extreme position led many economists to conclude that Mises had lost the socialist calculation debate because Lange and others had demonstrated that a socialist director who enjoyed the above conditions could in fact rationally allocate resources to satisfy his uncontested value scales.

In the remainder of this chapter, we will state Mises's argument and then his reaction to critics.

The Impossibility of Economic Calculation under Socialism

Mises goes on to argue that such a planner (or group of planners drafting a single plan) cannot rationally allocate resources. Because he lacks market prices, the planner will not be able to calculate the costs of various projects and will thus be unable to determine if they represent a wise use of scarce resources.

To see the problems involved, imagine a socialist planner who proposes to build an apartment building with large amounts of gold. The socialist planner could know that her subjects would enjoy living in such an apartment complex. If she were to order the construction workers, gold mine operators,

---

6. Mises, *Human Action*, 692–93.

and other relevant individuals to erect such a building, and then assigned a few hundred people to live in it, they would be overjoyed at their good fortune and would no doubt praise her generosity.

Yet in reality, building an apartment complex with large amounts of gold would be incredibly wasteful because it would necessarily reduce the quantity of gold jewelry and other goods using gold. Taking the opportunity cost into account, the production of the gold apartment complex would represent mal-investment; the socialist planner would be sacrificing more important goals in her achievement of the benefit of a luxurious living space.

We have chosen the extreme example of a gold-coated apartment complex to illustrate the general principle. In reality, millions of decisions—some major, some minor—are involved in the construction of an apartment complex. Should the floors be hardwood, tile, or carpet? Should the walls be painted or covered with wallpaper? Should the apartment units have individual washer and dryer units, or should there be a community arrangement? Should the building have central air conditioning, individual window units, or merely fans? Should the apartment units have microwaves? Although it might seem obvious to most readers that large amounts of gold should not be used in apartment design, it is not at all obvious how to answer the more realistic questions raised in this paragraph.

In the market economy, entrepreneurs resolve such questions by resorting to economic calculation. A builder will pick the assortment of features in light of anticipated profitability. Although prospective tenants would be willing to pay more for an apartment unit with central air conditioning—rather than relying on fans during the summer—the builder would need to compare the boost in rental revenues with the increased cost of installing and maintaining central air conditioning. Similar analyses would hold for every other decision.

However, it is precisely such calculations of profitability that a socialist planner cannot perform. Because the state is the only genuine owner of the factors of production, there are no true markets for the tractors, farmland, crude oil, and other resources in the socialist system. Consequently, no genuine market prices can be attached to each tractor, acre of farmland, barrel of oil, and so on. When a socialist planner evaluates a project, he will see—with the aid of his technical advisers—the list of inputs and the associated list of outputs. For example, he will know that so many tons of steel, worker-hours, kilowatt-hours of electricity, and so forth can be used in a particular factory to generate so many new automobiles of a particular quality. Even so, there will be nothing analogous to the entrepreneur's estimate of profit or loss because there will be no way for the socialist planner to reduce his inputs and outputs to a common denominator. He will have no way of determining whether the benefits of the new automobiles outweigh the costs of their production.

Mises's Response to Critics

Writing from his vantage point in the 1940s, Mises in *Human Action* was able to respond to the socialist writers who had rejected his initial 1920 critique. Mises classifies their responses into six separate categories and responds to each:

First, some writers argued that calculation under socialism could be performed in kind, rather than in money. Yet this entirely ignores the original critique: Without resort to a single commodity against which all others can trade, no common denominator is possible, and hence calculations would be made in terms of disparate units. The planner has no way of knowing how to compare, say, seven automobiles with fourteen tons of steel, five gallons of paint, and seven panes of glass. Physicists, chemists, and engineers can tell the planner the technological recipes for converting inputs into outputs in various ratios, but these raw facts do not in any way indicate the economic efficiency of such projects.

Second, some writers relied upon the labor theory of value to solve the calculation problem. Yet this is not right because the economic significance of natural resources has nothing to do with labor power. In addition, even looking at labor, there are different qualities among workers; an hour of a surgeon's labor is more valuable than an hour of a busboy's labor.

Third, some writers recommended that the socialist planner calculate in terms of units of utility. Yet this also is a nonsensical proposal because utility, in the sense associated with human action, is an ordinal concept and is not comparable across individuals. To say that the planner should distribute resources so as to maximize utility is akin to saying that a teacher should assign seats in her class so as to maximize total friendship units.

Fourth, some writers, such as Dickinson and Lange, suggested that the socialist planner resort to quasi-markets; this solution has been dubbed market socialism. In this approach, the socialist planner would announce a vector of prices for the various factors of production, would appoint certain individuals to be the managers of the various firms, and then would instruct the managers to act as if they were profit-maximizing entrepreneurs in a capitalist society, who faced the market prices that were announced by the socialist planner. Mises remarks that the proposal of market socialism is "nothing short of a full acknowledgement of the correctness and irrefutability of the economists' analysis and devastating critique" of socialism.[7] Historically, the appeal of socialism was the entire abolition of the crass marketplace with its haggling and commodification of workers; yet now, Mises points out, the leading socialist intellectuals acknowledge that under socialism, too, it will be necessary to have prices and competition. Yet even these concessions do not save the socialist project. Such proposals "look at the economic problem from the perspective of the subaltern clerk."[8] It is not enough to ask a socialist factory manager to take the announced vector of prices and produce the amount of output that will maximize profit according to these numbers. The much more fundamental questions are: Should this factory remain in operation at all? Should new factories be built—and if so, where, and what size? To answer such questions, the socialist planner cannot resort to a simulated market. She cannot, as some theorists suggested, act as a bank and administer funds to various competing promoters because some of the potential borrowers will exaggerate the viability of their projects. Ultimately, the planner must make the final decision on how to allocate all of society's funds. "Then we are back again where we started: the director . . . is not aided by the division of intellectual labor which under capitalism provides a practicable method for economic calculation."[9]

Fifth, some writers suggested that the socialist planner could resort to differential equations to determine the efficient allocation of resources. (This proposal was related to the suggestion of quasi-markets.) Here Mises heaps particular scorn, as he believed the approach of mathematical economics had

---

7. Mises, *Human Action*, 702.
8. Mises, *Human Action*, 703.
9. Mises, *Human Action*, 705.

bolstered the untenable idea of socialist calculation in the first place. Typically, the mathematical economist studies the conditions of equilibrium in a static setting. There is no role for the entrepreneur or what Mises dubbed the market process in such sterile models.

Sixth and finally, some writers suggested that the socialist planner could resort to trial and error. In other words, these writers could have agreed with Mises that the planner would have no surefire way beforehand of knowing the proper allocation of resources among different industries and projects, but after the fact the planner could evaluate the results and tweak the plan, improving it incrementally as time passed. Here, too, the response entirely misses the problem. Trial and error works only when there is a definitive way to evaluate the outcome. A woman can search for her car keys through trial and error in the sense of looking under various pieces of furniture in her house. This method can work because if she happens to stumble upon the keys, she will recognize success. Yet when it comes to the allocation of resources, there is no such mark of success for the socialist planner. Even after the fact, she will have no way of ascertaining whether a particular project represented an efficient use of society's resources. Under capitalism, trial and error does work, because "the correct solution is easily recognizable as such; it is the emergence of a surplus of proceeds over costs."[10] But, in a socialist system lacking genuine market prices, accountants cannot tell their boss—even after the fact—whether a given project turned a profit or a loss. Such a calculation requires money prices for the inputs and outputs, but these are lacking under socialism.

Conclusion

Ludwig von Mises's critique of socialist calculation is one of his most celebrated contributions to economic science. Precisely because he understood—more than most of his peers in the profession—the tremendous importance of economic calculation in a market economy, Mises was able to pinpoint the fundamental flaw of socialism as an economic system. Even putting aside questions of competence, morality, and incentives, Mises demon-

---

10. Mises, *Human Action*, 700–01.

strated that by its very nature, a socialist system could not efficiently allocate resources. Specifically, Mises was not claiming that a socialist government would eventually collapse. Rather, he was claiming that from Day One, a socialist planner would have no means of determining whether his use of resources was the best possible, even with respect to the planner's own value scale. In practice, the actual socialist governments, such as those in Soviet Russia and Nazi Germany, relied on market prices established abroad,[11] but a world-embracing socialist state would be utterly in the dark.

---

11. Mises, *Human Action*, 698.

PART VI

The Hampered Market Economy

16

Government Intervention in the Market Economy

Introduction

IN PART FOUR of *Human Action*, Mises analyzes the pure market economy. In Part Five, he analyzes the idea of social cooperation without a market—in other words, socialism—and concludes that it is not a viable substitute for capitalism. Putting aside the concerns about the intentions of the rulers and the incentives for the workers, socialism cannot work because the central planner(s) would lack market prices and hence would have no way of determining, even after the fact, if their "rational" plan for production made an efficient use of resources.

Now in Part Six, Mises addresses the idea of a third way, a middle ground between pure capitalism and pure socialism. Mises brands this *interventionism*. It is still within the realm of the market economy because even government-owned enterprises are subject to the law of the market and government officials can still rely on market prices.[1] Yet when the government runs certain enterprises, and especially when it enacts regulations and prohibitions on business, we are no longer in the realm of the pure market economy as analyzed in Part Four. Instead we are studying the hampered market economy, the subject of Part Six.

---

1. Murray Rothbard reports that he once asked Mises what the dividing line was between a capitalist system (albeit hampered with interventions), on the one hand, and a socialist system (though perhaps with pockets of private ownership, such as workers owning their tools), on the other. Mises apparently responded that the existence of a stock market was the crucial criterion: If private individuals were allowed to buy and sell shares of corporations and thereby own the means of production, then the system could not be described as true socialism. See Rothbard, *Making Economic Sense*, Chapter 103.

We can anticipate Mises's ultimate conclusion: There is no viable third system. People must choose between capitalism and socialism. The reason is that interventionism breeds results that are undesirable, not from the point of view of the observing economist, but rather according to the value judgments of the public who support the intervention. Frustrated with the failure of the initial intervention to fix a supposed problem, the public is then led to either renounce the intervention and move back toward pure capitalism or to embrace further interventions on the path to outright socialism.

In the present volume, we will not spend as much space detailing Mises's specific analyses of various types of intervention as we have devoted to other topics. This is because Mises's critique of various forms of taxation and business regulations are relatively standard, compared to the relatively unorthodox Austrian position on interest theory and the business cycle.

The Nature of Government Intervention

In Mises's framework, interventionism is distinct from outright socialism because in the former the government "does not want to eliminate the market altogether." Rather, under interventionism the government

> wants production and consumption to develop along lines different from those prescribed by an unhampered market, and it wants to achieve its aim by injecting into the working of the market orders, commands, and prohibitions for whose enforcement the police power and its apparatus of violent compulsion and coercion stand ready. But these are *isolated* acts of intervention. It is not the aim of the government to combine them into an integrated system which determines all prices, wages and interest rates and thus places full control of production and consumption into the hands of the authorities.

> The system of the hampered market economy or interventionism aims at preserving the dualism of the distinct spheres of government activities on the one hand and economic freedom under the market system on the other hand. What characterizes it as such is the fact that the government does not limit its activities to the preservation

of private ownership of the means of production and its protection against violent encroachments. The government interferes with the operation of business by means of orders and prohibitions.[2]

In the context of his broader discussion, Mises in the above quotation makes two distinct clarifications: First, it is a mistake to believe that the fascist system of Nazi Germany represented a form of capitalism and thus was the opposite of the communist system of Soviet Russia. In reality, both Soviet Russia and Nazi Germany were examples of outright socialism,[3] in which the government implemented total control of all aspects of the system of production, including the explicit setting of prices, interest rates, and wages. In Mises's view, then, the opposite of Nazi Germany was not Soviet Russia but rather the classical liberal idea of a limited state concerned only with the protection of property rights and the enforcement of the rule of law.

These observations lead into the second clarification: Although many of Mises's most ardent followers, especially Murray Rothbard, would be anarcho-capitalists,[4] favoring the complete privatization of legitimate government services and the total abolition of the state, Mises himself was not an anarchist. Thus, when he speaks of government intervention in the economy, Mises has in mind measures that specifically aim at diverting the market away from its laissez-faire outcome. If the government levies a modest tax to fund the police force necessary to protect homeowners from burglars, Mises would not classify this as government intervention in the economy. Mises believed a limited government was necessary, not because of natural law, but rather for pragmatic reasons: Civilization depended on the police and military to ensure the smooth operation of the market economy, and in Mises's view, these operations could be performed only by the government.

It is worth quoting Mises's views on the nature of government policy to shed light on his strategy for critiquing interventionism and to show why it meshes so smoothly with his conception of praxeology:

---

2. Mises, *Human Action*, 714, italics in original.

3. Recall that the very term *Nazi* is shorthand for "national socialist."

4. A classic introduction to the anarcho-capitalist perspective is Murray Rothbard, *For a New Liberty*, rev. ed. (San Francisco, CA: Fox & Wilkes, [1973] 1994).

The only purpose of the laws and the social apparatus of coercion and compulsion is to safeguard the smooth functioning of social cooperation. It is obvious that the government has the power to decree maximum prices and to imprison or to execute those selling or buying at a higher price. But the question is whether such a policy can or cannot attain the ends which the government wants to attain by resorting to it. This is a purely praxeological and economic problem. Neither the philosophy of law nor political science can contribute anything to its solution.

The problem of interventionism is not a problem of the correct delimitation of the "natural," "just," and "adequate" tasks of state and government. The issue is: How does a system of interventionism work? Can it realize those ends which people, in resorting to it, want to attain?[5]

Thus, Mises is not arguing against interventionism on the grounds that it violates the proper role of government or that it interferes with the natural rights of the people. Rather, Mises is trying to give his critique of interventionism the same value-free objectivity as the praxeological enterprise itself. The economist qua economist does not himself judge a person's preference rankings, but instead takes them as given and then deduces certain implications about action as such.

In a similar vein, Mises is not questioning the specific value judgments implicit in the popular calls for government intervention, in which the public demands outcomes such as more leisure for workers, higher pay, and elimination of the business cycle. Rather, Mises acts as a disinterested social scientist and inquires whether the proposed interventionist measures will in fact achieve the desired ends. If they will not, then this is the sense in which Mises will reject them as suitable policy. His case does not rest on his personal views of what is good or just government policy. Instead, he will objectively demonstrate to the supporters of the interventionist measures that they are mistaken in their understanding of cause and effect.

---

5. Mises, *Human Action*, 718.

Taxation

If the purpose of a tax is the complete expropriation of the rich in order to reduce everyone to the same standard of living and to transfer any surplus to the state, this is tantamount to the abolition of private enterprise and the institution of outright socialism, according to Mises. If that is indeed the goal, then we cannot object to it on technical grounds; the government can in fact confiscate wealth and abolish the market economy.

In addition, in some cases the purpose of a tax is not primarily to raise revenue but instead to discourage consumption. For example, so-called "sin taxes" on alcohol and tobacco products are explicitly billed as paternalistic devices to wean citizens from drinking and smoking. In the context of climate change, taxes on gasoline, driving, or carbon content are also justified not because of their ability to raise revenue but because they discourage individuals from engaging in the activity being taxed—and this discouragement is taken as a desirable end in itself.

However, insofar as the authorities wish to retain a capitalist framework and resort to taxation merely as a method of financing government expenditures, then they face an objective limit to their power: At some point, a tax becomes so onerous that further increases in the official rate will actually reduce the revenue paid to the government. In the extreme, confiscatory levels of taxation lead to the collapse of the market economy, with outright socialism being the only logical replacement.

Restriction of Production

A government can employ various measures to restrict production, which can include differential taxation (a prime example being a tariff on foreign goods), prohibitions (such as a ban on child labor), or regulations (such as a requirement that doctors receive medical licenses).

Especially when it comes to restrictions on foreign production, the advocates of interventionism will often claim that their measures boost national output. Yet this is fallacious because the free market tends to allocate resources in a manner that best satisfies the desires of the consumers. If the government interferes with this process, it necessarily impairs entrepreneurs' efforts: In a meaningful and objective sense, society becomes poorer, if not in an absolute sense, at least relative to what it otherwise would have achieved. The government cannot improve on the market outcome; any advantage or stimulus it gives to one industry must be counterbalanced by a disadvantage or penalty elsewhere. "A government can spend or invest only what it takes away from its citizens,"[6] Mises says.

When it comes to so-called progressive restrictions in Western countries—with measures such as bans or heavy barriers placed on child labor, various safety regulations in the workplace, and limits on the workweek of adult laborers—these often merely codified what would have occurred naturally, as capitalism raised the standard of living, Mises asserts. In other words, parents in Great Britain and the United States would have naturally and on their own kept their children out of the factories, as these countries grew richer during the twentieth century. The transition from Dickensian conditions in nineteenth-century England to the modern day, therefore, is a credit to capitalism, not to progressive legislation. To make the point clearer: In countries with very low standards of living, where children currently do work in factories and in the fields, government bans on child labor would harm the very families they allegedly want to help. According to Mises, "If the parents are too poor to feed their children adequately, prohibition of child labor condemns the children to starvation."[7]

The classical economists, particularly David Ricardo, destroyed the intellectual foundation of mercantilism. Restrictions on foreign imports can indeed raise employment and wages in a particular industry, but only by reducing employment and wages elsewhere. In the long run, a country pays for its imports by exports. If the U.S. government makes it harder for Americans to buy Japanese cars, this will boost employment and production in Detroit. But if Americans spend less on Japanese cars, then the Japanese have fewer dollars with which to buy American exports, such as wheat. Thus, the U.S. government tariff doesn't boost industry or create jobs on net but merely *rearranges* production and employment patterns. What's worse, the rearrangement leaves

---

6. Mises, *Human Action*, 737.
7. Mises, *Human Action*, 740.

Americans and Japanese poorer, on average, because labor has been diverted in both countries into lines where it is less productive, all things considered.

The standard case for free trade is not an Austrian contribution. However, Mises does offer a relatively unique insight when he explains:

> The main function of tariffs and other protectionist devices today is to disguise the real effects of interventionist policies designed to raise the standard of living of the masses. Economic nationalism is the necessary complement of these popular policies which pretend to improve the wage earners' material well-being while they are in fact impairing it.[8]

Here, what Mises has in mind is that against a backdrop of free trade, an interventionist measure that restricts the workplace would have immediately undesirable consequences. For example, if the U.S. government suddenly imposed a requirement that employers grant all workers a minimum of two hours each day for lunch, then labor-intensive industries would suffer. Foreign manufacturers—who would be exempt from U.S. labor laws—could easily undercut U.S. manufacturers in products where the United States had originally employed a large number of workers. Rather than enjoying a longer lunch break, many of these workers would be thrown out of work immediately. There would be no question, even in the short run, that the pro-labor legislation had actually hurt many of the people it was designed to help.

However, the obvious and immediate negative effects of the labor regulation can be masked if the government simultaneously imposes a tariff on the goods that otherwise would have flooded the American market. In a sense, the negative effect on employment from the labor law is counterbalanced by the positive effect from the tariff.

The reader should not conclude from Mises's analysis that two wrongs make a right. Each of the interventionist measures in our example—namely, the mandate setting a minimum two-hour lunch break and the tariff on certain foreign products—interferes with the market economy and makes Americans poorer. Going the other way, removing even just one of the measures would make Americans better off, considered as a whole.

---

8. Mises, *Human Action*, 248–49.

Yet the critical point is that the average citizen won't recognize the harm of the labor regulation if the labor-intensive industries are protected by a tariff barrier. Rather than being focused on the specific recipients of the benefit, instead the harm will be spread more uniformly across the entire population, who must pay higher prices as consumers because of the tariff. Thus, the array of interventions in domestic business, coupled with a battery of tariffs shielding them from foreign imports, interacts in a way to make the whole system politically viable. Once it is established, the suggestion to remove any particular plank in the interventionist scheme will be opposed because people can point out—quite correctly—that free trade works nice in theory, but in the real world our companies face environmental, labor, and safety regulations that don't apply to foreign companies. They couldn't compete if we removed tariffs and other import restrictions.

Price Controls

Price controls are specific forms of intervention in which the government uses a punishment, such as a fine, imprisonment, or even death, to enact a minimum floor or maximum ceiling on the acceptable movement of a price. Here Mises's analysis is quite conventional, familiar to all economists: A price floor, such as a minimum wage law, creates a surplus of the good in question. In the case of the minimum wage, more low-skilled workers try to sell labor than employers want to hire at the artificially high wage rate. This creates institutional unemployment among those whose productivity is below the threshold set by the minimum wage legislation. Since the ostensible purpose of a minimum wage is to help poor workers with little training and experience, throwing many of them out of work is hardly a sensible policy.

On the other hand, a price ceiling, such as rent controls on apartment units, creates a shortage of the good in question. Landlords do not want to offer as many apartment units for rent as tenants wish to occupy. The result is a permanent situation in which it is extremely difficult for people to find housing. Since the ostensible purpose of rent control is to make it easier for poor tenants to find affordable housing, the removal of apartments from the rental market is hardly a sensible policy.

Mises sees more in the analysis of price control than these standard demonstrations, however. Indeed, Mises claims that the political controversies over price controls revolve around the status of economic science itself: "The interventionist, in advocating price control, cannot help nullifying the very existence of economics. Nothing is left of economics if one denies the law of the market."[9]

Mises also uses price controls as the specific illustration of his broader argument showing the futility of interventionism as a third system in between capitalism and socialism. He supposes that the government enacts a price ceiling on certain consumer goods to keep them affordable for the poor and then walks through the inevitable consequences. First, the production of the goods in question will drop, because

> the marginal producers will discontinue producing them lest they suffer losses. The not absolutely specific factors of production will be employed to a greater extent for the production of other goods not subject to price ceilings . . . . There emerges a tendency to shift production activities from the production of the goods affected by the maximum prices into the production of other goods. This outcome is, however, manifestly contrary to the intentions of the government . . .
>
> It would be vain for the government to try to remove these undesired consequences by decreeing maximum prices likewise for the factors of production needed for the production of the consumers' goods the prices of which it has fixed. Such a measure would be successful only if all factors of production required were absolutely specific. As this can never be the case, the government must add to its first measure, fixing the price of only one consumers' good below the potential market price, more and more price ceilings, not only for all other consumers' goods and for all material factors of production, but no less for labor. It must compel every entrepreneur, capitalist, and employee to continue producing at the prices, wage rates, and interest rates which the government has fixed, to produce those quantities which the government orders them to produce, and to sell the products

---

9. Mises, *Human Action*, 755.

to those people . . . whom the government determines. If one branch of production were to be exempt from this regimentation, capital and labor would flow into it; production would be restricted precisely in those other—regimented—branches which the government considered so important that it interfered with the conduct of their affairs.

Economics does not say that isolated government interference with the prices of only one commodity or a few commodities is unfair, bad, or unfeasible. It says that such interference produces results contrary to its purpose, that it makes conditions worse, not better, *from the point of view of the government and those backing its interference.* Before the government interfered, the goods concerned were, in the eyes of the government, too dear. As a result of the maximum price their supply dwindles or disappears altogether. The government interfered because it considered these commodities especially vital, necessary, indispensable. But its action curtailed the supply available. It is therefore, from the point of view of the government, absurd and nonsensical. [italics in original][10]

The above quotation crystallizes Mises's main themes concerning interventionism. First, limited interventions are a failure, not according to the outside economist's personal value judgment, but according to the very criterion by which the intervention was originally justified. Second, the government can attempt to remedy the initial failing with further rounds of intervention, but these too will lead to unintended consequences that frustrate the supporters of the scheme. In the end, the government will either resort to full-blown socialism, or it must return to laissez-faire capitalism.

Before leaving our discussion of price controls, we should note that the government can effectively delegate their administration to outside groups, by selective enforcement of the police power. The most obvious example concerns labor unions. If the government turns a blind eye to striking union members who use violence against employers or "scabs" (strike breakers), while at the same time the government stands ready to use its police power to prevent management from hiring armed personnel to disperse the picketing union members, then the union is implicitly allowed to set its own minimum wage

---

10. Mises, *Human Action*, 757–58.

rate for the firm being targeted. The economic effects are the same as with an explicit government-imposed minimum wage: institutional unemployment, which in such cases falls disproportionately on lower-skilled workers outside of the union.

Currency and Credit Manipulation

Even if a government were to adhere to classical liberal notions of its proper sphere of action, it would be necessary for the courts to have working legal definitions of money, if the judges are to understand what particular terms in contracts mean. Such legal definitions would not define money in the sense of conferring special status on objects but instead would merely codify prevailing market choices of the media of exchange and would standardize terminology. By the same token, the government might establish standard definitions for units of length and weight, which would also be necessary to ensure the smooth functioning of commercial transactions.

Historically, private mints existed, in which the precious metals were stamped into particular coins of recognizable shape and design, which allowed members of the public to more easily conduct business. Eventually, governments took over such operations. Yet even here, it would be possible for the government to act responsibly, serving only to provide a "seal of authenticity" certifying, for example, that a particular yellow disc contains an ounce of gold.

Of course, governments throughout the ages have not acted responsibly in their handling of currency. The "simplest and oldest variety of monetary interventionism is debasement of coins or diminution of their weight or size for the sake of debt abatement," Mises points out. "The authority assigns to the cheaper currency full legal tender power."[11]

To see how such a scheme works, suppose that a country uses gold as its money. The government has an outstanding debt of, say, two billion ounces of gold. Rather than pay it off by running an honest budget surplus of two billion ounces, instead the government runs a surplus of only half that size. Then it takes the coins—let us suppose there are one billion one-ounce gold

---

11. Mises, *Human Action*, 777.

coins in its treasury—melts them down, adds the same weight in the form of a baser metal, and then strikes twice as many coins, each with only one-half the gold content of the originals. It then declares that these coins must be accepted by creditors as fully equivalent to the full-body one-ounce gold coins in the cancellation of debts. Thus, the government can pay off a debt of two billion ounces of gold with only one billion ounces of actual gold.

It is obvious that such a policy of literal currency debasement can work only if it is a surprise. Going forward, if lenders expect such a debasement, they will build a price premium component into the gross rate of interest they charge on loans. Therefore, if the aim of currency debasement is to benefit debtors at the expense of creditors, this intervention too is doomed to failure. The market responds in a way to offset the alleged benefit.

Besides the effective repudiation of debts, governments have other objectives with the intentional debasement of their currencies. For example, if other interventions have artificially raised wage rates and the other, implicit costs of employment, institutional unemployment results. Rather than admitting the folly of these original interventions, another possible remedy is to inflate the currency, thereby raising prices in general and effectively reducing the real wage rate. In other words, rather than asking unions to go along with lower nominal wages in order to restore full employment, the government can simply create more price inflation to make workers effectively poorer without it being as obvious.

The problem with such schemes is that they rely on money illusion, in other words they can work only if labor leaders do not understand the difference between nominal and real wages. But once the workers catch on to the situation, they begin to demand cost of living adjustments or other devices to ensure that their hard-won gains are concrete. In this case, the monetary inflation no longer masks the harmful effects of the other interventions, and the result is the worst of both worlds: institutional unemployment with accelerating price inflation. This phenomenon was dubbed "stagflation" when it occurred in the United States in the 1970s. Such stagflation was instrumental in convincing many economists that the orthodox Keynesian analysis of the postwar era was badly mistaken.

Another possible aim of currency debasement is to weaken a country's currency against a foreign one, thereby promoting exports. Yet again, the benefits of such intervention are at best short-lived. For one thing, the monetary inflation necessary to debase the currency will lead to rising prices in the domestic market, thereby offsetting the currency depreciation in the foreign exchange markets. For example, if the Federal Reserve causes the dollar to fall 50 percent against the euro, this would—other things equal—promote a huge boost in net exports from the United States to Europe because Americans would find European goods suddenly expensive, while Europeans would suddenly find American goods cheap. Yet the Fed's actions would also cause U.S. prices, quoted in dollars, to rise. If they rose in general by 100 percent, then the entire operation would be a wash: Europeans could fetch twice as many dollars per euro, but American goods would cost twice as many dollars as before. Thus the boost to net exports would be fleeting.

Beyond this effect, currency debasement can boost exports only if a single country engages in it. If other countries reciprocate and debase their respective currencies as well, then there is no boost to the first country's exports, even in the short run. The only sure effect is that citizens in all countries will find it more difficult to plan for the future, as they can no longer trust the purchasing power of their respective currencies.

Another major arena of government intervention is the deliberate effort to lower the rate of interest through credit expansion. We have already studied this issue extensively in Chapter 14. Here, too, the interventionists do not achieve the publicly stated goal of their policy. It is hardly desirable to lower the cost of capital and stimulate business expansion if the result is an unsustainable boom followed by an inevitable bust.

The Economics of War

For some reason, many writers who are normally sympathetic to the market suddenly praise the powers of intervention when it comes to war. Specifically, many who recognize the problems of peacetime government interference with business nonetheless argue that government is justified in nationalizing entire industries in order to ensure the appropriate production of tanks, bombers, and other materiel for the war effort.

Here, once again, the interventionists err, according to Mises. If the goal is to transform the nation's productive apparatus away from civilian output and toward military output, the most efficient mechanism is still via the market. Specifically, the government must either tax or borrow the necessary funds and then enter the market to purchase the desired equipment and supplies. The public will naturally curtail their consumption of civilian goods because they will be that much poorer after paying the higher taxes or buying the war bonds. Private firms will find it profitable to retool for military production because the government will be a much bigger buyer on the market.

Mises turns on its head the standard argument that hard-nosed realism requires government controls during wartime, citing the actual lessons of the World Wars:

> Not government decrees and the paper work of hosts of people on the government's payroll, but the efforts of private enterprise produced those goods which enabled the American armed forces to win the war and to provide all the material equipment its allies needed for their co-operation .... The interventionists would have us believe that a decree prohibiting the employment of steel for the construction of apartment houses automatically produces airplanes and battleships . . .
>
> It was not socialist Russia that aided capitalist America with lend-lease; the Russians were lamentably defeated before American-made bombs fell on Germany and before they got the arms manufactured by American big business. The most important thing in war is not to avoid the emergence of high profits, but to give the best equipment to one's own country's soldiers and sailors. The worst enemies of a nation are those malicious demagogues who would give their envy precedence over the vital interests of their nation's cause.
>
> Of course, in the long run war and the preservation of the market economy are incompatible. Capitalism is essentially a scheme for peaceful nations. But this does not mean that a nation which is forced to repel foreign aggressors must substitute government control for private enterprise. If it were to do this, it would deprive itself of the most efficient means of defense. There is no record of a socialist nation which defeated a capitalist nation. In spite of their much glorified war socialism, the Germans were defeated in both World Wars.[12]

---

12. Mises, *Human Action*, 823–24.

To be clear, Mises was by no means glorifying war, in the way that many militarist writers claimed that warfare brought out the most admirable features of humanity. On the contrary, Mises preached the blessings of peace as the necessary foundation of civilization. One of the most pernicious aspects of interventionism and outright socialism was that they gave strong governments the incentive to dominate their weaker neighbors. Under free trade and domestic laissez-faire, there is no point to international conquest. Yet this harmony of interests was dashed in a global struggle among rival socialist blocs.

Even so, despite the overall incompatibility of war and capitalism, Mises also made clear that even during wartime, the superiority of the market over planning was manifest: Decentralized entrepreneurs, seeking to earn profits, were essential in eliciting the strongest possible war machine for a limited period of hostility. A commitment to laissez-faire wouldn't ensure that a small nation could repel the invasion of a large, statist neighbor such as Nazi Germany, but such a policy would nonetheless give the small nation the best possible chance in the struggle.

Social Security

Another common form of intervention is the government provision of retirement, disability, and survivor benefits to citizens, what is often referred to as social security programs. In this realm, as in others, the government at best can confer benefits only on a select group, Mises thought, while harming the rest; the government makes the nation collectively poorer through such schemes.

One of the chief problems with the typical administration of a government pension plan is that it is effectively a Ponzi scheme, in which the government taxes current workers to fund the benefit checks for current retirees (and widows, disabled workers, etc.). Then, when today's workers eventually retire, they in turn will have their Social Security contributions returned to them via taxes levied on the new crop of younger people working at that time. One problem with this scheme—currently revealing its effects in the United States and other Western nations—is that the aging population has implanted a demographic time bomb. The ratio of retirees to active workers has grown since the baby boom postwar era, meaning that taxes on workers will have to rise, benefits to retirees will have to be cut, or both.

Another, related problem is that workers earn a far lower average rate of return on their retirement contributions than they would in a private system, based on genuine saving and investment. With the typical government "pay-go" scheme, society as a whole doesn't actually live below its means and divert resources into the accumulation of capital goods. Instead, the workers' savings are siphoned off by the government to fund the extra consumption of the beneficiaries. This is why the internal rate of return in such a system is far below what the workers would earn if their Social Security contributions were invested in private-sector assets over their working careers, growing exponentially until the beginning of drawdown after retirement.

In his discussion of such schemes, Mises explodes a common fallacy that survives to this day: the claim that government debt isn't really a burden because "we owe it to ourselves."[13] Mises points out the flaw in such reasoning:

> In the process of government interference with saving and investment, Paul in the year 1940 saves by paying one hundred dollars to the national social security institution. He receives in exchange a claim which is virtually an unconditional government IOU. If the government spends the hundred dollars for current expenditure, no additional capital comes into existence, and no increase in the productivity of labor results. The government's IOU is a check drawn upon the future taxpayers. In 1970 a certain Peter may have to fulfill the government's promise although he himself does not derive any benefit from the fact that Paul in 1940 saved one hundred dollars.
>
> . . . . The trumpery argument that the public debt is no burden because "we owe it to ourselves" is delusive. The Pauls of 1940 do not owe it to themselves. It is the Peters of 1970 who owe it to the Pauls of 1940. The whole system is the acme of the short-run principle. The statesmen of 1940 solve their problems by shifting them to the statesmen of 1970. On that date the statesmen of 1940 will be either dead

---

13. For a discussion of economists who recently espoused this doctrine, see Robert P. Murphy, "Debt Can't Burden Future Generations? It Just Ain't So," *The Freeman*, March 28, 2012, http://www.fee.org/the_freeman/detail/debt-cant-burden-future-generations#axzz2k OlsKp5F.

or elder statesmen glorying in their wonderful achievement, social security.[14]

A system of social security has the power to enrich certain individuals—for example, the first retirees, who received beneficiary checks far in excess of what they had contributed—while impoverishing others. But as the government cannot create resources out of thin air, its administration of such a system will not make society richer. In fact, by weakening the incentive for individuals to save through private channels since they expect social security checks upon retirement, the government reduces total investment and hence capital accumulation. Other government interventions, such as the debasement of the money and the lack of respect for private property rights, also reduce the individual's incentive to save. The longer the social security system and related interventions remain in operation, the poorer society becomes, relative to what otherwise would have occurred.

Conclusion

The specific examples above illustrate Mises's general theme: Interventionism does not provide a stable middle ground because its effects are undesirable even from the point of view of the interventionists. Consequently, "[m]en must choose between the market economy and socialism."[15] Since Mises has already demonstrated that socialism has no means of allocating resources in an efficient manner, he thinks the conclusion is inescapable: Study of the objective, value-free laws of economics shows that modern civilization is possible only if the public embraces and supports the institutions of the market economy.

---

14. Mises, *Human Action*, 843–44.
15. Mises, *Human Action*, 857

PART VII

The Place of Economics in Society

17

Economics and Public Opinion

The Unusual Nature of Economic Science

TWO FEATURES OF economics set it apart from other sciences. First, the laws or principles of economics cannot be established through laboratory experiment or empirical data, in the same way that a fact of the natural sciences can be demonstrated. Economic principles are a priori knowledge, which must be deduced theoretically and then deployed by the economist to interpret historical observations.

In practice, episodes in economic history are complex phenomena, involving multiple factors. As there are no truly controlled experiments in economics—especially in macroeconomics—it is impossible to isolate and test rival theories. This is why, for example, Austrians and Keynesians still argue about the Great Depression or more recently about the success or failure of the so-called Obama stimulus package of early 2009. In economics, rival theories cannot be judged the way they can be in the natural sciences. As Mises puts it, "The economist can never refute the economic cranks and quacks in the way in which the doctor refutes the medicine man and charlatan."[1]

In light of this first feature of economics—that it is a field from which faulty doctrines are difficult to expunge—the second feature is ironic and indeed tragic: Its doctrines can benefit mankind only if a sufficiently large number of people endorse them.

Notice that this feature too makes economics differ from other sciences. For example, it is not necessary for the public to understand quantum physics; it is enough that a few physicists understand it. Likewise, humanity still

---

1. Mises, *Human Action*, 859.

benefits from specially trained heart surgeons, even if most people can't even list the various blood types.

In economics, things are different. Even though economic science decisively made the case for free trade more than two centuries ago, destructive trade barriers still permeate the globe because people still support age-old mercantilist superstitions. "In the long run, there cannot be any such thing as an unpopular system of government,"[2] Mises notes. If people believe that tariffs create jobs for domestic workers and hurt only foreign producers—not domestic consumers—then government officials will curry favor with the public by implementing tariffs.

The Duty of the Citizen

In light of these considerations, economists have a responsibility to make their ideas intelligible to the layperson, and other writers must do their part to spread these crucial ideas to the wider public. Citizens, in turn, must do their part by learning at least the basics of economics so they can appreciate the blessings of the market economy and see through the fallacies of government promises to deliver a superior outcome via interventionism. Near the end of his grand treatise, Mises writes:

> There is no means by which anyone can evade his personal responsibility. Whoever neglects to examine to the best of his abilities all the problems involved voluntarily surrenders his birthright to a self-appointed elite of supermen. In such vital matters blind reliance upon "experts" and uncritical acceptance of popular catchwords and prejudices is tantamount to the abandonment of self-determination and to yielding to other people's domination. As conditions are today, nothing can be more important to every intelligent man than economics. His own fate and that of his progeny is at stake.
>
> Very few are capable of contributing any consequential idea to the body of economic thought. But all reasonable men are called upon to

---

2. Mises, *Human Action*, 859.

familiarize themselves with the teachings of economics. This is, in our age, the primary civic duty.

Whether we like it or not, it is a fact that economics cannot remain an esoteric branch of knowledge accessible only to small groups of scholars and specialists. Economics deals with society's fundamental problems; it concerns everyone and belongs to all. It is the main and proper study of every citizen.[3]

By providing a condensed translation of Ludwig von Mises's *magnum opus* in a more accessible form for the modern reader, the present volume is itself a contribution in the battle of ideas. We hope to have relayed Mises's major findings: Economic calculation underpins modern civilization and is possible only within the framework of a market economy. Deviations from laissez-faire capitalism are self-defeating, and pushed to their logical extreme—outright socialism—only invite total war and economic chaos.

If the reader has been convinced of these Misesian insights, it is his or her duty to relay this precious knowledge to others. There is nothing to guarantee that good ideas will trump bad ideas. Yet what is certain is that the prevalence of faulty ideas in the realm of economics threatens civilization itself.

---

3. Mises, *Human Action*, 874–75.

Bibliography

Ayer, A. J. [1936] 1971. *Language, Truth, and Logic.* London, UK: Penguin Books.

Block, Walter. 1978. "The Negative Interest Rate: Toward a Taxonomic Critique," *Journal of Libertarian Studies*, 2, no. 2: 121–24.

Boaz, David. 2005. "The Man Who Told the Truth," *Reason Magazine,* January 21, 2005, http://reason.com/archives/2005/01/21/the-man-who-told-the-truth.

Boettke, Peter J. 2012. *Living Economics: Yesterday, Today, and Tomorrow.* Oakland, CA: The Independent Institute.

Böhm-Bawerk, Eugen von. [1884, 1889, 1909] 1959. *Capital and Interest,* 3 vols. South Holland, IL: Libertarian Press.

———. [1886] 2005. *Basic Principles of Economic Value.* Grove City, PA: Libertarian Press.

Buchanan, James. 1964. "What Should Economists Do?" *Southern Economic Journal,* 30, no. 3 (January).

Cantillon, Richard. [1755] 2010. *Essai sur la Nature du Commerce en Général,* translated as *An Essay on Economic Theory,* edited by Mark Thornton. Auburn, AL: Ludwig von Mises Institute.

Cowen, Tyler, and Alex Tabarrok. 2010. *Modern Principles: Macroeconomics.* United States: Worth Publishers.

Dickinson, H. D. 1933. "Price Formation in a Socialist Commonwealth," *The Economic Journal*, 43, no. 170 (June): 237–50.

Eastman, Max (ed.). 1932. *Capital, The Communist Manifesto, and Other Writings by Karl Marx.* New York: The Modern Library.

Ebeling, Richard, ed. [1978] 1996. *The Austrian Theory of the Trade Cycle and Other Essays.* Auburn, AL: Ludwig von Mises Institute.

Fetter, Frank A. 1977. *Capital, Interest and Rent: Essays in the Theory of Distribution.* Edited with an introduction by Murray N. Rothbard. Kansas City, MO: Sheed Andrews and McMeel.

Friedman, David. 1996. *Hidden Order: The Economics of Everyday Life,* New York: HarperCollins.

Friedman, Milton. 1953. *Essays in Positive Economics.* Chicago: University of Chicago Press.

———. 1962. *Capitalism and Freedom.* Chicago: University of Chicago Press.

Garrison, Roger. 2001. *Time and Money: The Macroeconomics of Capital Structure.* New York: Routledge.

Gordon, David. 1996. "The Philosophical Origins of Austrian Economics," monograph. Auburn, AL: Ludwig von Mises Institute.

Graeber, David. 2012. *Debt: The First 5,000 Years.* Brooklyn, NY: Melville House.

Haberler, Gottfried. 1961. "Mises's Private Seminar," *The Mont Pelerin Quarterly,* 3, no. 3 (October): 20f.

Hayek, Friedrich A., ed. [1935] 1990. *Collectivist Economic Planning.* Clifton, NJ: Augustus M. Kelley.

Hayek, Friedrich A. [1935] 1990. "The Present State of the Debate," In *Collectivist Economic Planning.* Edited by Friedrich A. Hayek. Clifton, NJ: Augustus M. Kelley.

———. 1952. *The Counter-Revolution of Science: Studies on the Abuse of Reason.* New York: Glencoe.

Hicks, John R. [1939] 1961. *Value and Capital: An Inquiry into Some Fundamental Principles of Economic Theory,* 2nd ed. Oxford, UK: Oxford University Press.

Higgs, Robert. [1987] 2012. *Crisis and Leviathan: Critical Episodes in the Growth of American Government.* New York: Oxford University Press. Oakland, Calif.: Independent Institute. 25th Anniversary Edition.

———. [2006] 2009. *Depression, War, and Cold War: Challenging the Myths of Conflict and Prosperity.* New York: Oxford University Press. Oakland, Calif.: Independent Institute.

_____. 2007. *Neither Liberty Nor Safety: Fear, Ideology, and the Growth of Government*. Oakland, Calif.: Independent Institute.

Hoppe, Hans-Hermann. 1995. *Economic Science and the Austrian Method*. Auburn, AL: Ludwig von Mises Institute. http://mises.o rg/pdf/esam.pdf.

Hülsmann, Jörg Guido. 2007. *Mises: The Last Knight of Liberalism*. Auburn, AL: Ludwig von Mises Institute.

Keynes, John Maynard. [1936] 1965. *The General Theory of Employment, Interest and Money*. New York: Harcourt, Brace.

Knapp, Georg. [1905] 2003. *The State Theory of Money*. Simon Publications.

Landsburg, Steven E. [1993] 1995. *The Armchair Economist: Economics & Everyday Life*. New York: The Free Press.

Lange, Oskar. 1936. "On the Economic Theory of Socialism: Part One," *The Review of Economic Studies*, 4, no. 1 (October): 53–71.

Levitt, Steven, and Stephen Dubner. 2005. *Freakonomics: A Rogue Economist Explores the Hidden Side of Everything*. New York: William Morrow.

Mankiw, Greg. [2007] 2009. *Principles of Microeconomics*, 5th ed. United States: South-Western Cengage Learning.

Menger, Carl. [1871] 1994. *Principles of Economics*, Translated by James Dingwall and Bert F. Hoselitz. United States: Libertarian Press.

_____. 1892. "On the Origins of Money," *Economic Journal*, 2 (June): 239–55, http://mises.org/Books/originsmoney.pdf.

Mises, Ludwig von. [1912] 2009. *The Theory of Money and Credit*. Auburn, AL: Ludwig von Mises Institute.

_____. [1922] 1981. *Socialism*. Indianapolis, IN: Liberty Classics.

_____. [1927] 1985. *Liberalism*. Translated by Ralph Raico. Irvington-on-Hudson, NY: Foundation for Economic Education.

_____. [1935] 1990. "Economic Calculation in the Socialist Commonwealth." An English translation of a 1920 German-language article, appearing in F. A. Hayek, ed. *Collectivist Economic Planning*. Clifton, NJ: Augustus M. Kelley.

_____. [1940] 1998. *Interventionism: An Economic Analysis*. Edited by Bettina Bien Greaves. Irvington on Hudson, NY: The Foundation for Economic Education.

———. [1949] 1998. *Human Action*. Scholar's edition. Auburn, AL: Ludwig von Mises Institute.

———. [1957] 2000. *Theory and History*. Auburn, AL: Ludwig von Mises Institute.

———. [1969] 2003. *The Historical Setting of the Austrian School of Economics*. Auburn, AL: Ludwig von Mises Institute.

———. [1978] 2009. *Memoirs*. Auburn, AL: Ludwig von Mises Institute.

Murphy, Robert P. 2003. "Unanticipated Intertemporal Change in Theories of Interest." PhD diss., New York University.

———. 2003. "Why Do Capitalists Earn Interest Income?" Mises.org Daily Article (blog), July 1. http://mises.org/daily/1263/.

———. 2006. "The Labor Theory of Value: A Critique of Carson's *Studies in Mutualist Political Economy*," *Journal of Libertarian Studies*, 20, no. 1 (Winter): 17–33. http://mises.org/journals/jls/20_1/20_1_3.pdf.

———. 2007. "Interest and the Marginal Product of Capital: A Critique of Samuelson," *Journal of the History of Economic Thought*, 29, no. 4: 453–64.

———. 2009. *The Politically Incorrect Guide to the Great Depression and the New Deal*. Washington, DC: Regnery.

———. 2010. *Lessons for the Young Economist*. Auburn, AL: Ludwig von Mises Institute.

———. 2012. "Debt Can't Burden Future Generations? It Just Ain't So," *The Freeman*, March 28, 2012. http://www.fee.org/the_freeman/detail/debt-cant-burden -future-generations#axzz2kOlsKp5F.

O'Driscoll, Gerald, and Mario Rizzo. 1985. *The Economics of Time and Ignorance*. New York: Basil Blackwell.

Romer, David. 1996. *Advanced Macroeconomics*. New York: McGraw-Hill.

Rothbard, Murray N. 1957. "In Defense of Extreme Apriorism," *Southern Economic Journal*, 23, no. 3.

———. 1962. *The Panic of 1819: Reactions and Policies*. New York: Columbia University Press.

———. [1962] 2009. *Man, Economy, and State*. Scholars edition, 2nd ed. Auburn, AL: Ludwig von Mises Institute.

_____. [1963] 2000. *America's Great Depression.* 5th ed. Auburn, AL: Ludwig von Mises Institute.

_____. [1973] 1994. *For a New Liberty: The Libertarian Manifesto.* Rev. ed. San Francisco, CA: Fox & Wilkes.

_____. 1988. *Ludwig von Mises: Scholar, Creator, Hero.* Auburn, AL: Ludwig von Mises Institute.

_____. 1995. *Making Economic Sense.* Auburn, AL: Ludwig von Mises Institute.

_____. 2005. *What Has Government Done to Our Money?* Auburn, AL: Ludwig von Mises Institute.

Schmoller, Gustav von. 1902. *The Mercantile System and Its Historical Significance.* London, UK: Macmillan.

Selgin, George. 2008. *Good Money: Birmingham Button Makers, the Royal Mint, and the Beginnings of Modern Coinage, 1775–1821.* Oakland, CA: The Independent Institute.

Selgin, George, and Lawrence H. White. 1996. "In Defense of Fiduciary Media," *Review of Austrian Economics,* 9, no. 2: 83–107.

Sen, Amartya K. 1977. "Rational Fools: A Critique of the Behavioral Foundations of Economic Theory," *Philosophy & Public Affairs,* 6, no. 4 (Summer): 317–44.

Smiley, Gene. 2002. *Rethinking the Great Depression.* Chicago: Ivan R. Dee.

Smith, Adam. 1776 (1778, 1784, 1786, 1789, 1904). *An Inquiry Into the Nature and Causes of the Wealth of Nations.* London: Penguin Classics.

Varian, Hal. [1978] 1992. *Microeconomic Analysis.* 3rd ed. New York: W. W. Norton.

Index

About the Author

ROBERT P. MURPHY received his Ph.D. in economics from New York University and is currently a Research Fellow with the Independent Institute, as well as senior economist for the Institute for Energy Research. Previously, Dr. Murphy has been visiting assistant professor of economics at Hillsdale College, visiting scholar at New York University, research analyst at Laffer Associates, and senior fellow in business and economic studies at the Pacific Research Institute.

Dr. Murphy is author of the books *Lessons for the Young Economist, The Politically Incorrect Guide to the Great Depression and the New Deal, The Politically Incorrect Guide to Capitalism, How Privatized Banking Really Works, Study Guide for Ludwig von Mises's Human Action, Study Guide for Murray Rothbard's Man, Economy, and State with Power and Market,* and *Study Guide to The Theory of Money & Credit by Ludwig von Mises.*

His articles and reviews have appeared in such scholarly journals as *The Independent Review, Review of Austrian Economics, Journal of the History of Economic Thought, Quarterly Journal of Austrian Economics, Economic Affairs, American Journal of Economics and Sociology, Journal of Libertarian Studies,* and *Homo Oeconomicus.* Murphy's popular articles have appeared in the *Los Angeles Times, Detroit News, Washington Times, Orange County Register, Atlanta Journal-Constitution, MarketWatch, The Freeman, Buffalo News, San Jose Mercury News, Barron's, Forbes,* and *Investor's Business Daily.* In addition, he has appeared on CNBC, Fox Business Network, C-SPAN, and other TV and radio networks and programs.

Independent Studies in Political Economy